PROGRESS IN
THE BALANCE

PROGRESS IN THE BALANCE

Mythologies of Development
in Santos, Brazil

Daniel R. Reichman

CORNELL UNIVERSITY PRESS **ITHACA AND LONDON**

First published 2023 by Cornell University Press

Library of Congress Cataloging-in-Publication Data

Names: Reichman, Daniel R. (Daniel Ross), 1976– author.
Title: Progress in the balance: mythologies of development in Santos, Brazil / Daniel R. Reichman.
Description: Ithaca: Cornell University Press, 2023. | Includes bibliographical references and index.
Identifiers: LCCN 2022047853 (print) | LCCN 2022047854 (ebook) | ISBN 9781501770425 (hardcover) | ISBN 9781501770432 (paperback) | ISBN 9781501770449 (pdf) | ISBN 9781501770456 (epub)
Subjects: LCSH: Progress. | Santos (São Paulo, Brazil)—Civilization— 20th century. | Santos (São Paulo, Brazil)—Civilization—21st century. | Santos (São Paulo, Brazil)—Social conditions—20th century. | Santos (São Paulo, Brazil)—Social conditions—21st century.
Classification: LCC HM891 .R45 2023 (print) | LCC HM891 (ebook) | DDC 303.440981/61—dc23/eng/20221223
LC record available at https://lccn.loc.gov/2022047853
LC ebook record available at https://lccn.loc.gov/2022047854

Portions of chapter 2 previously appeared in Daniel R. Reichman, "Big Coffee in Brazil: Historical Origins and Implications for Anthropological Political Economy," *Journal of Latin American and Caribbean Anthropology* 23 (2018): 241–61, https://doi.org/10.1111/jlca.12293. Used with permission.

"The Beach of São Vicente" by Benedicto Calixto is used with the permission of the Pinacoteca Benedicto Calixto in Santos, Brazil.

Contents

Preface

Several years ago, I was having a conversation with a staffer at a well-known non-governmental organization (NGO) about so-called development indicators, the statistics that policymakers commonly use to measure a country's well-being. The staffer, whom I will call Kelly, was speaking quite negatively about social conditions in Honduras, a country where I was doing research at the time. I was trying to look for positive things to talk about, signs that the situation there was not as bad as what had been reported in the US media, where Honduras was (and still is) frequently depicted as a generic Third World dystopia. I mentioned that Honduras had one of the lowest per-capita carbon emission rates in the world, and the staffer replied, "Well of course, the country is too poor for people to consume a lot of fossil fuel, so they don't pollute." Kelly was right. Poor countries have low levels of consumption and industrial output per capita, and therefore they consume relatively small amounts of fossil fuels, therefore emitting low amounts of carbon. Fewer cars and factories give you a very low rate of carbon emissions—less money, less carbon. "But," I asked, "if we care about the environment, isn't that a positive sign? Aren't the developing nations trying to reduce their carbon emissions? If we really care about climate change, then isn't Honduras a leader according to that measurement?" In this one measure, I argued, Honduras was ahead of, not behind, the rest of the world if we rearranged the variables that define progress.

"No, no," Kelly responded. "Your argument is conflating poverty with progress, and that's not development." From her point of view, low carbon emissions were only positive when they were accompanied by high levels of material wealth, measured by GDP per capita. Of course, she had a valid point, and she knew I was trying to be provocative. If low carbon emissions were indeed markers of development, then the poorest countries in the world would be at the top of those annual rankings of world development that various experts publish each year. But there was a deeper point here about the meaning of terms such as "progress" and "development": these terms are completely dependent on context. Low carbon emissions could be a sign—an indicator, to use the favored term—of progress or of poverty, depending on the context and the value judgments inherent in any definition of "development."

In a roundabout way, this book unpacks the argument I was trying to make in that brief conversation: the criteria that any group uses to define "progress" are entirely dependent on context, and people can signify any aspect of life as progress to suit their worldview. When we are talking about what is or is not progress in any society, positive signs can turn negative, and negatives can turn positive, shifting back and forth over time. Returning to the conversation above, gas guzzling cars could be signs of progress or of impending disaster, depending on what matters to the person who is speaking.

In 2013, I started the research for this book as a way to understand what twenty-first-century progress looked like in Latin America and specifically in Brazil, a country that was, in some ways, the polar opposite of Honduras. At that time, Brazil was a country very much on the upswing. It was in the midst of a frenzied run of economic growth and social progress that made it the darling of policy experts around the world. My work began in an atmosphere of breathless optimism, a sense that Brazil was on the cusp of a hopeful new political paradigm for Latin America. On a personal note, I wanted to study a place where life seemed to be getting better for people or at least was not in a state of crisis. My first major research project in anthropology was a study of a rural community in Honduras (Reichman 2011) that was beset by a seemingly unending series of crises: a disastrous hurricane in 1998 was followed by a sharp drop in the price of coffee, the town's economic lifeblood, which was followed by a boom in undocumented migration, followed by a coup d'état in 2009, followed by a spike in gang violence that made Honduras into the most violent country in the world by 2013. After decades of reading dispiriting ethnographies on suffering, violence, and poverty in Latin America—a perfect location for the "dark anthropology" that defined my field (Ortner 2016)—I wanted to tell a different story, to embark on a study that might push against the dominant image of Latin American countries as violent, corrupt, and in need of benevolent repair from enlightened Northern experts. I particularly wanted to disrupt the sense of smug superiority often found in North American writings on Latin America, in which "they" have something to learn from "us" politically, socially, and economically, but not vice versa.

The other major connecting thread between this book and my earlier research was coffee. I chose to base my Brazilian work in Santos, the world's most important port for the coffee trade, a place where people can "study up" (Nader 2018; Gusterson 1997) on the world of agriculture by looking at the big, powerful players in the coffee trade, as opposed to the relatively small-scale producers that I came to know in Honduras. Most, if not all, of the existing anthropological work on Latin American coffee was premised on a simplistic equation: Global North equals rich equals coffee consumer, while Global South equals poor equals coffee producer. I hoped to destabilize this equation by looking at coffee in Brazil, which was an international leader in both production and consumption of coffee.

The irony is that I first visited the city of Santos in June 2013, at the exact time that Brazil was rocked by its largest-ever political protests, during which people called for the impeachment of President Dilma Rousseff. An intense atmosphere of political and social upheaval persisted throughout my research. I recall a colleague introducing me to a class at a Brazilian university (the Federal University of São Carlos) in 2016 by saying, "Professor Daniel shifted his research from Honduras to Brazil because he wanted to work in a more stable country." The class broke out in mocking laughter.

Ultimately, I found myself immersed in a situation in Santos where the meanings of "progress" in Brazil were being transformed and contested as never before—a period that a group of ethnographers recently termed "the Brazilian unraveling" (Junge et al. 2021). As is often the case in anthropology, my initial ideas about what I would be studying changed as well. I used the upheaval in Brazil as an ethnographic opportunity to reflect on how anthropologists think, write, and speak about progress. While the coffee industry remains the centerpiece of my analysis, I place the story of Santos alongside other major changes in the city to make a broader argument. This book is my attempt to think about progress in a way that bridges the gap between a relativist perspective, in which the meaning of progress is completely dependent on social, historical, and cultural context, and a universalist perspective, in which progress is defined by specific desirable outcomes, such as material well-being, social inclusion, equity, and democracy. Readers will probably notice that my own commitments veer toward relativism. I am far more interested in attempting to understand what progress means to specific groups of people in different places and times than I am in laying down my own judgments about what ought to be. I therefore am hesitant to make strong pronouncements about what is or is not progress, and I am relatively restrained in my criticism of any one political or philosophical viewpoint. Readers looking for a strong declaration on how to fix Brazil's problems will need to look elsewhere.

Nevertheless, I do think that a completely relativist definition of progress inhibits our ability to imagine positive social change across a variety of national and cultural contexts. I am certainly no fan of monolithic standards such as GDP and Gini coefficient. Indeed, I think it is not much of an overstatement to call the fetishization of these statistics crimes against humanity. If humanity is defined by complex webs of intersecting interests, emotions, passions, and dreams, then reducing social betterment to a single statistical measurement is indeed inhumane. However, as I will make clear throughout this book, I believe that societies need symbols and narratives of progress to serve as guide stars, helping to chart a course to a better future. (I don't think any society, even the most development obsessed, has ever built a monument to GDP growth, by the way.)

Progress doesn't need to be utopian or monolithic, but without such a concept, politics would seem meaningless—an endless struggle without a purpose. As an anthropologist, I set out to understand what the symbols and narratives of progress were in twenty-first-century Brazil, and how they were being contested and redefined at every turn. The end goal of my work is therefore not a defense of relativism when it comes to progress; it is to broaden our vision of progress by understanding the diversity of possible visions that exist, or might exist, across the globe.

Acknowledgments

I thank the colleagues who generously helped me find my footing in Brazil during trying times: Jane Fajans, Marcos Lanna, Anna Catarina Morawska Vianna, Renzo Taddei, Flávia Maria de Mello Bliska, and Patricia Turco. I am also grateful for the support of the US Fulbright Program, which allowed me to spend a semester as an affiliate of the social anthropology program at the Federal University of São Carlos, Brazil.

At the University of Rochester, I thank Kristin Doughty, Robert Foster, Tom Gibson, Eleana Kim, John Osburg, Kate Mariner, and Llerena Searle for many helpful hallway conversations about the ideas presented herein, and I thank Donna Mero for steadfast administrative support. I had the privilege of directing the Lewis Henry Morgan lectures with Robert Foster during the years I worked on this book, and it will be apparent to readers that my ideas have been influenced by the work of all the lecturers who came to Rochester, particularly Stefan Helmreich, Peter van der Veer, and Michael Herzfeld.

Two wonderful mentors, Michael Billig and Terence Turner, passed away while I worked on this book. I wish they were here to argue with me about it.

Thanks also to Frances Benson, Jim Lance, Clare Jones, and their team at Cornell University Press, who were supportive of my work from the earliest stages. Gregory Foster and Carla Huelsenbeck vastly improved the book with their editing expertise.

Finally, I thank my family, especially Amy, who held the fort down while I was away in Brazil and who provided patience, love, and good cheer when I needed it most.

Note on Terminology

Throughout this book, I use the terms "indigenous," "Amerindian," and "native populations" whenever possible to describe Brazil's native peoples. While the term "Indian" (*indio*) is still widely used in Brazil and was used by many anthropologists until quite recently, there is a strong contemporary movement to use the term *indígena* instead. I include many direct quotations of anthropologists who use the disfavored term, and I leave their words as written for historical accuracy. While I use "indigenous" when appropriate, there are some cases, such as when describing the Brazilian holiday "Day of the Indian," where I use the obsolete term. Also, I use "Indian" when describing the persons who are depicted in the historical reenactments included in chapter 1. In that case, I am referring to fictional characters who are depicted as caricatures rather than real historical individuals. The term "Indian" connotes this fiction and therefore seems truer to the meaning of the events than the term "indigenous person."

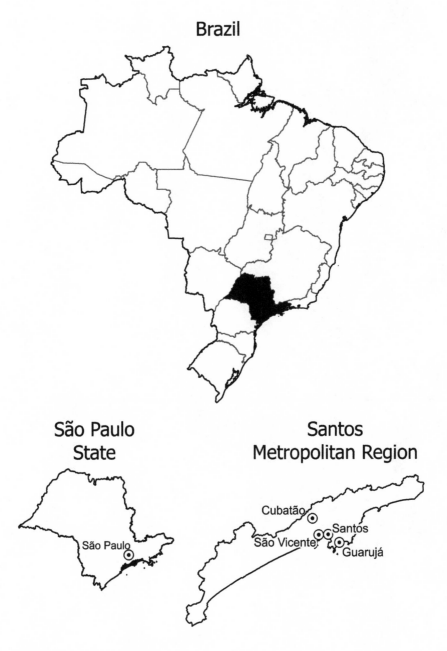

MAP 1. The Santos region

CRACKS IN THE FOUNDATION

"Progress demands respect, or it will fall apart the first time it hits rough surf, like one of our bike paths."

—The Brazilian anthropologist Roberto Da Matta (2016) after a seaside bike path collapsed when hit by a wave, killing two people

The shoreline of the port city of Santos is what much of the world thinks of when it imagines Brazil: a beautiful horseshoe-shaped bay, ringed by a three-mile-long stretch of wide sandy beach dotted with swaying palms and surrounded by dramatic green mountains. The waterfront is packed with bars, restaurants, and volleyball courts that pulse with life at all hours of the day, while along the shore runs the world's largest beachfront garden, bordered by the swirling mosaic sidewalks that have become a symbol of Brazil's aesthetic beauty. The beach is filled with enviable options for public recreation: playgrounds for kids; a bike path (with a bike-sharing program); a public surfing school (the Escola Radical); a skate park; a public art-house movie theater; even a helicopter pad. Giant stadium lights, erected by the military government in the 1980s, illuminate the beach at night. There is an amphitheater for plays, an aquarium, an art gallery, and dozens of statues, monuments, and sculptures, including a dramatic cliffside work by Tomie Ohtake, one of Brazil's most renowned modern artists. It's a vibrant, bustling place, with people of all ages and social classes riding bikes, strolling, or hanging out on the beach, which Roberto Da Matta has called one of the few truly democratic public spaces in Brazil.[1]

But look a little closer, and you will see something unusual, something out of place that casts a shadow on the idyllic postcard image. Among the scores of apartment buildings that line the beachfront avenue, about one in five is falling over. These mid-twentieth-century apartment towers, which are between eight and twenty stories in height, are lilting dangerously to one side or another, threatening to topple onto neighboring buildings like a line of dominoes about to be

FIGURE 1.   The leaning towers of Santos (Photo by author, 2016)

knocked over by a mischievous kid (fig. 1). Locals call them the *prédios tortos*, or "crooked buildings," and they have become one of the iconic images of Santos for locals and visitors alike. There is even a rock club called the Bar Torto (Crooked Bar) on the ground floor of one of the buildings.

Most of these buildings were constructed between 1950 and 1980, during Brazil's "high modernist" period, most of which took place under a military dictatorship (Holston 1989; Scott 1998). During that period, the more affluent residents of Santos left what they perceived to be crowded, old downtown neighborhoods to relocate to the clean, modern order of the beachfront high-rises. It was part of a building boom that defined the first "Brazilian Miracle." Around the same time the first towers went up (1955–1962), the Brazilian state built the country's monumental, planned capital, Brasília, from scratch, and President Juscelino Kubitschek promised the nation "fifty years of progress in five years," instituting a plan of thirty targets that would launch the nation into modernity. This was an ideology of progress with planners, blueprints, concrete, dams, power plants, high-rises, and engineers at its core. In Brazil, the future was a national project to be built—engineered, really—with the help of the guiding hand of the modernist military government. As Teresa Caldeira (2000) puts it, "during the 'miracle years,' the military announced that it was necessary to grow first and 'divide the cake' later" (42). It was a policy of progress at all costs: out with the old and in with the new.

Yet in Santos, the modern Brazilian Miracle was literally built on shifting sands. The apartment towers were constructed atop a muddy mangrove with such poor standards that they have barely lasted though the lifetimes of some of their residents. The buildings' concrete footings were buried to a depth of only a few meters, and the muddy, sandy soil has moved beneath them over time. Television news reports show the improvisational fixes that residents have had to use to make their apartments livable—modifying furniture so that it will stand up straight, cutting doors to fit into frames that are askew, propping up the legs of tables so that dinner will not roll onto the floor. While these off-kilter buildings might look like fanciful works of postmodern architecture, they are in fact monuments to the instability of the high modernist project.

And then there is the water. The nearby Santos Estuary—lined with a ten-mile-long forest canopy of shipping cranes and an undergrowth of steel containers and aging warehouses—pours pollutants from Brazil's petrochemical hub (Cubatão) and Latin America's largest industrial port (Santos) directly into the sea. Container ships and oil tankers ply the shipping lanes just offshore all day and night, carrying about 25 percent of Brazil's imports and exports to and from the Port of Santos, including 85 percent of Brazil's coffee exports. The estuary, as well as a river on the other side of the bay, is polluted even further by the *favelas*, informal urban settlements that line the banks and dump raw sewage and household garbage into the water. In Santos, there are more than twenty-five thousand people living in these impoverished neighborhoods in *palafitas*, makeshift shacks on stilts.

Back on the beach, only a small number of people are swimming, and a series of canals drains urban runoff from storm drains and clandestine sewage hookups right into the surf. In fact, the landmark Tomie Ohtake sculpture is built atop a large, treated sewage outflow pipe evocatively named the Emissário Submarino (undersea emissary). A parade of strolling beachgoers and joggers skips over puddles of dirty runoff that pours across the sandy shore. It is not unusual to see children swimming amid garbage in the stormwater drainage canals (fig. 2). The São Paulo state government's environmental service, CETESB, tests the ocean water for safety at the beach each day, puts up cautionary flags, and posts the results online—but that is a cold comfort. Most people do not swim

FIGURE 2.   Drainage canal with swimmers (Photo by author, 2016)

(even the locals told me not to), and the "dirty beaches of Santos" are a national inside joke. But there is a way to solve the problem: the city has built a series of public showers along the shore so that beachgoers can cool off in the heat. It is quite a sight: even on crowded days, the Atlantic is nearly devoid of swimmers, yet lines of people wait to cool off in public showers that are clogged with sand by the end of each day. Fortunately, the city regularly sends a squad of uniformed workers to clean up the showers with an elaborate pumping truck.

In many ways, the Santos beach epitomizes a central theme in the Brazilian experience of progress. From one point of view, Brazil has been a twenty-first-century success story—a rapidly modernizing economic powerhouse blessed with incredible natural resources, top-notch infrastructure in certain sectors, and an exceptional quality of life for a wealthy minority. By Latin American standards, the Brazilian state has made a great deal of progress in the promotion of public welfare, and, despite Brazil's notoriously high income inequality, there is no question that the Brazilian population as a whole has benefited from rapid modernization over the past few decades. Since 1960, infant mortality has dropped from 129 to 14 per 1,000 live births. Average life expectancy has risen by twenty years. Real GDP per capita has grown from $3,000 to $11,000, which is roughly the same rate of growth experienced by the United States over the same period. Yet rapid modernization has created what many Brazilians see as a facade of progress that hides an unstable foundation. There is a clear sense among Brazilians that the state has squandered an opportunity to achieve dreams of national greatness by investing in symbolic and sometimes spectacular projects that hide deep, structural problems in Brazilian society—the social and environmental costs of progress that constantly seem to disrupt the ideology of a linear advance toward modernity. There is pollution amid the beauty, poverty behind the prosperity, and chaos lurking beneath the veneer of social order.

This book is based on a study of Santos that I carried out in 2016, in the midst of an unprecedented period of economic and political turmoil.[2] I use a historical ethnography of Santos to explain the contested meanings of progress in Brazil, and to make a more general argument about how anthropologists and others can define progress today. Using Brazil as an ethnographic example, the central theoretical question that I explore in each chapter of the book is this: How does any society separate something called "progress" from plain old change? If change is happening constantly all around us, how and why do certain events get lifted out of a normal time frame and into a mythic narrative of progress? Each chapter follows the same basic structure: I describe a particular theme or episode in the history of Santos as it is represented in public culture (mainly through museums, monuments, art, and public events). I then describe an ongoing conflict or social process in which the public representation is called into question or challenged, developing a model that I refer to as a "clash of timescapes." The clash of timescapes model, which runs throughout the book, illustrates how the concept of progress requires a different temporal structure to separate sacralized social change from mundane historical events. To draw an analogy with a landscape, a *timescape* is a way to give a fixed form to an ever-unfolding process of social change.

The Paradox of Progress

Anthropology has always had an ambivalent relationship with the concept of progress. On the one hand, we anthropologists take pride in belonging to a progressive discipline, which in the twenty-first century tends to mean adherence to left-liberal political values accompanied by a vaguely defined desire to shake up the status quo.[3] This vision of progress almost always has a utopian aspect to it, which is based on our own particular imaginations of what a better, brighter, and more just future would look like. On the other hand, anthropologists have not been fans of mainstream visions of progress as they actually exist in the world. We tend to be relentlessly critical of the dominant blueprints for progress that have shaped world affairs since anthropology was founded in the nineteenth century: from Victorian concepts of civilization and the colonial mission they spawned, to twentieth-century modernization and Third World development, to twenty-first-century neoliberalism—a world of open markets and free flows of people and things.[4] In almost every case, anthropologists have utilized the experiences of peoples on the margins of the modern industrial world to critique and reconfigure mainstream definitions of progress. This has often meant that anthropologists view the encroachment of modern industrial capitalism with a sense of "sentimental pessimism" (Sahlins 1999), a feeling that much of the richness and diversity of humanity is being destroyed in the cause of so-called progress.

This is the anthropological paradox: we are a now progressive discipline with a pessimistic attitude toward progress.[5] While I do not claim to have resolved this paradox, this book does attempt to chip away at it by presenting a series of conflicts in and around Santos that illustrate the contested meanings of "progress." Each chapter presents an ethnographic case that exemplifies key tensions in the contemporary anthropology of global capitalism: indigenous people versus colonists (chapter 1); industry versus agriculture (chapter 2); labor versus capital (chapter 3); modernization versus environmentalism (chapter 4); and nationalism versus globalization (chapter 5). I argue that much of the political conflict that has engulfed Brazil over the past few years can be understood as a conflict between different visions of progress. While the promise of the Workers' Party was to unite Brazil's rich and poor under the banner of national prosperity, it produced a divide between the miracle and mirage of progress that seemed unbridgeable.[6] Yet, as visions of progress, both the miracle and mirage contain some important formal similarities, which I describe over the course of the book. If we think of progress as a mythology, it is a narrative with particular temporality, rhythm, and structure. We can therefore identify common patterns in what might otherwise be thought of as diametrically opposed political visions. Variants of the progress myth share similar structural traits.

Miracle or Mirage?

The word "miracle" is used time and again to describe periods of rapid economic development in Brazilian history, most notably between 1968 and 1980, when the economy grew at a rate of almost 10 percent per year. In fact, one of the first works of anthropology to expose the mistreatment of Brazilian Indians by the military government was titled *Victims of the Miracle* (Davis 1977). Whereas "miracle" suggests meaningful progress that is achieved through rapid—almost magical—transformations of economy and society, "mirage" suggests an illusory form of progress that hides underlying social problems and is always on the brink of collapse.

In Latin America, as well as many other countries on the periphery of the so-called developed world, there is a well-established pattern in which governments play the role of "magician" (Coronil 1997; Taussig 1997). Fernando Coronil argues that the Venezuelan state historically took on the role of magician due to its power to extract oil from the ground and turn that oil into wealth. He contends that the state's magic is not just about tricking the public but also about presenting a historical narrative that silences or occludes certain processes to produce a stable narrative of progress. He writes:

> The persuasiveness of a historical account, like that of a magical performance, depends on rendering invisible the artifice of its production. Just as history refers ambiguously to the past in its completeness and to the selective remembering of stories about the past, magic alludes to an extraordinary reality as well as to the selective elements that create the illusion of its existence through invisible tricks that exploit distraction and diversion. Like history, magic hangs suspended between fiction and fact, trick and truth. (3)

Magic, in anthropological terms, is an ability to produce an effect on the world through a specific mechanism or action that hides the relationship between cause and effect, like casting a spell to cure the sick or pulling a rabbit out of a hat. The results of the magical process are real, but the way they were brought about remains a secret, created through "tricks that exploit distraction and diversion." A miracle is also a form of magic, but it is one that is imbued with sacred meaning, seemingly proving the existence of a higher power. When magicians turn water into wine, they are still magicians; when Jesus does it, he is a messiah. The difference is that a magic trick is not imbued with sacred meaning that transcends a particular time and place. When people speak of the Brazilian Miracle, they are putting the government in the position of a sacred power that was able to transform the country from rural to urban, agricultural to industrial, and, implicitly, "backward" to "advanced." In this version of history, the miracle was not the result of the hard, steady labor of Brazilian citizens over time; nor was it the result of a revolution by "the people" or an amazing breakthrough by some lone genius. The government is put in the place of the miracle worker, the agent who brings about the change. However, I argue that progress requires both time and space to be marked as sacred. Progress is change, sacralized. Ultimately, the key ethnographic questions are these: Who defines progress? In turn, who defines the sacred? Whose narratives become sacralized and how?

A mirage (or an illusion), on the other hand, is failed magic. It is an act where the artifice of the magic trick becomes apparent, and the result of the trick is proven to be unreal. The rabbit did not really come out of the hat—it was just sleight of hand. When talking about economic, political, or social progress as a miracle or mirage, the key distinction is whether the end results of the process of transformation are what they appear to be: Did the government really curtail crime? Did it cut down on poverty? Did it improve the quality of life? In Brazil, the ambiguity between miracle and mirage, reality or fantasy, often centers on whether Brazil has achieved the level of progress that its leaders have claimed. The tendency for the government to put itself in the role of magician or miracle worker has become something of a joke, especially for the critics of the Workers' Party governments of Luiz "Lula" Da Silva and Dilma Rousseff, who frequently were accused of viewing themselves as miracle workers capable of single-handedly transforming Brazil and bringing about a second Brazilian Miracle or a *milagrinho* (little miracle) (Carvalho 2018). See, for example, figure 3, where President Lula laughs atop a mirage-like image of bullet trains, suburban homes, highways, and full plates of food. Lula, "the wizard" or "the

FIGURE 3. Lula the magician, *Veja* magazine January 4, 2017

magician," was a mocking nickname given to the president by his critics, mainly those on the right.

Illusions and Double Personalities?

The chapters that follow describe a Brazil that teetered between a mythology of progress and messy historical realities that constantly seemed to undermine the mythology. The leaning modernist towers served as an apt illustration of a mythology of progress that hung in the balance. Each chapter describes a disjuncture between mythology and an unfolding reality in different aspects of social life. This pattern—a gap between surface appearances and underlying essences—has been a longstanding motif in the anthropology of Brazil. In his earliest descriptions of the city of São Paulo, Claude Lévi-Strauss, the most famous anthropologist of the twentieth century, noticed something similar. He wrote that the rapid urbanization of São Paulo gave "a feeling of unreality, as if one were not dealing with a town but with a *trompe l'oeil* hastily erected to serve as a background for a film or a stage play" (1971, 96). This motif of a tension between miracle and mirage has continued for over a century. In their anthropological "biography" of Brazil, Lilia Schwarcz and Heloisa Starling (2015) identify *bovarismo* as a key element in national culture, defining it as

> The altered sense of reality when a person thinks of himself or herself as someone else. . . . This psychological state generates chronic dissatisfaction, produced by the contrast between illusions and aspirations, and, above all, by the continuous disparity between these illusions and reality. Now imagine this same phenomenon transferred from an individual to an entire community that conceives itself as something that it is not and is waiting for some unexpected event that will transform its dismal reality. (xxi)

J. Lorand Matory (2005) describes another common Brazilianism, the Portuguese saying *para ingles ver* (for the English to see), in reference to "acts of subterfuge or self-camouflage—presenting a facade to outsiders and dominant parties who might respond with contempt or punishment if they knew the truth" (188). In her study of residents of São Paulo in the 1990s, Teresa Caldeira argues that "the gap between the ideal of development and the Brazilian reality offered a background for discussions about the future" (59). She writes that "the ambiguity produced by simultaneously affirming and doubting the possibility of progress is common in Brazil" and that people commonly described progress as "illusory and impermanent" (59). Figuratively echoing the Santos experience, one of her interviewees even described Brazil's progress as "a castle built on the top of drifting sand, soft sand, and water" (58).

Schwartz and Starling extended their description of *bovarismo* to encapsulate a variety of Brazilian cultural traits:

> At football matches, an iconic metaphor for Brazilian nationality, everyone waits for 'something to happen' that will save the game. People cross their fingers in the hope that some magical intervention will fall from the skies (alleviating malaise and solving all problems). Immediatism takes the place of planning substantive, long-term changes. The current fashion is for Brazilians to identify themselves as members of BRICS, and to cling to the belief that the country has joined the ranks of Russia, India, China, and South Africa because of the extraordinary economic growth of recent years, and with a great deal of autonomy. If Brazil has truly achieved such remarkable economic growth—and is really the seventh largest economy in the world, not to mention the country's enormous, and little exploited, natural resources—it should not be ignoring serious social problems in the areas of transport, health, education, and housing which, although there has been considerable progress, are still woefully inadequate. (xxi)

Similar themes can be found in *River of Tears*, Alexander Dent's (2009) study of rural nostalgia and Brazilian modernization, which focuses on the appeal of country music (*sertanejo*) in the context of urbanization. He argues that the appeal of country music indexes popular anxieties over rapid modernization, and offers an alternative to hegemonic narratives of Brazil's linear march toward progress through industrialization and urbanization. In this case, rural nostalgia helps to smooth out the anxieties of rapid and unstable modernization. Jacob Blanc's (2019) *Before the Flood* describes a "double reality" in which rural people experience a gap between an official version of democracy thought to be experienced elsewhere "and the version they experienced as their own reality and their own hope for the future" (231). John Collins's (2015) *Revolt of the Saints* also explores contradictions in the myth of progress. He presents a kaleidoscopic analysis of clashing temporalities in the city of Salvador, in which the everyday lives of residents of the historic district of the Pelourinho became objectified as part of Brazil's national heritage. In an attempt to simultaneously "preserve" and "develop" the Pelourinho as a heritage site, the state ended up violently dispossessing the very people whose experiences it sought to valorize. People became "living archives," simultaneously serving as tokens of Brazil's mythic history and unfolding present. In this dramatic setting, the Brazil of myth clashed violently with the Brazil of reality. Sean Mitchell's (2017) *Constellations of Inequality* analyzes what is perhaps the most fitting ethnographic example of the contradictions and illusions of Brazilian progress: the construction of a spaceport in one of the country's poorest regions. His study of the establishment of the hypermodern Brazilian satellite launching station in Alcântara, a small rural town in the state of Maranhão that contains several *quilombos*, shows how utopian modernism at the national level intersected with more locally embedded visions of progress, producing sharp conflicts between different, and highly unequal, understandings of justice and modernity.[7] Mitchell argues that Brazilian imaginations of progress transformed in the twenty-first century. An older idea of progress, which he calls "mimetic convergence," was based on a future in which the poor were transformed the into rich, in which progress took the form of copying the wealthy and powerful nations of the world.

Contradiction or Cultural Pattern? The Dualism Debate

My descriptions of Brazil up to this point have been structured around binary categories such as illusion/reality, boom/bust, and rise/fall. The phrase "in the balance," which I include in the book's title, suggests a productive tension between two contrasting categories, and the motif of balanced forces in opposition to one another will carry through the book. Much of the anthropology of Brazil is framed around contrasts, finding insights by exploring the play of opposing categories. The dualistic perspective can be traced back to the foundational work of Gilberto Freyre, the most influential social thinker in Brazilian history. Freyre, a member of a wealthy sugar plantation-owning family from northeastern Brazil, wrote a canonical trilogy on the development of Brazilian society that was premised on dualisms, titled *The Masters and the Slaves*; *The Shanties and the Mansions*; and *Order and Progress*. The central argument of Freyre's *Masters and Slaves*, his most famous work, was that the dualistic social hierarchy formed during the colonial period rippled through Brazilian history, creating a society that was structured around what he called "dual opposition."

Two decades later, the idea of dual opposition came to define the structuralism of Claude Lévi-Strauss, an anthropological theory that was largely developed through studies of indigenous Brazil and that was premised on the idea that humans make sense of the world through contrasting pairs, such as self versus other, nature versus culture, and primitive versus modern. The theory of structuralism holds that people create meaning by making contrasts between paired categories, or by transformations from one binary category or state of being to another. The classic examples are turning something from a state of disorder into order, from a raw state into a cooked state, turning children into adults, or moving from backwardness into modernity. For structuralists, all information is formed through relations of contrast: yin versus yang, black versus white, rich versus poor—each concept is meaningless without an opposite. The dualistic legacy, from Freyre to Lévi-Strauss, is so strong that even anthropological works on Brazil that, prima facie, have nothing to do with structuralism are frequently shaped by dualistic pairings such as wealth/poverty, illusion/reality, surface appearance/inner essence, and First World/Third World. *Bovarismo* could therefore be seen as a new formulation of a more general structuralist approach—a clash between two opposing forces.

One potential problem with the dualistic mode of thinking is that it frequently posits an underlying essence, a "real" Brazil that is overlaid by a superficial facade, as if the dual personalities of *bovarismo* present a contradiction that needs to be resolved through political or social change—as if an entire nation had a treatable personality disorder. However, it should be obvious that not all contradictions can be resolved, and some insights can be gained by exploring how people balance or hold together seemingly contradictory ideas without resolving them. For example, if wealth is a relative distinction made in contrast to poverty, then there can be no wealth without poverty and any attempt to end poverty will only recalibrate the relative distinction between it (poverty) and its opposite (wealth). No one can end poverty because it is always based on a binary contrast with another implied state of being. Or, in the case of the United States, if the country is founded on the equality of all citizens yet patterns of inequality carry through its entire history, then social change will often be defined by the readjustment of the underlying tensions between equality/inequality rather than the total erasure of inequality.

This is more than just an academic debate. Dualistic thinking can unconsciously affect how anthropologists think about progress. In an essay titled "For an Anthropology of the Brazilian Tradition: The Virtue Lies in Between" (Hess and Da Matta 1995, 270–292), Roberto Da Matta argues for an anthropology of Brazil that embraces an "anthropology of the in between," describing social contradictions, without assuming a priori that they ought to be resolved. Da Matta argues that Western social thought is based on an unstated linearity, an assumption that on-the-ground social contradictions will eventually be worked out as history marches forward, usually in a straight line toward an endpoint (called a *telos* in social theory). In the liberal Western tradition, clashes between rich and poor, the powerful and the oppressed, are frequently viewed as problems that will one day be resolved as "progress" marches on.[8] This utopian faith in the redemptive resolution of social contradictions is an ethnocentric conceit, according to Da Matta. He criticizes this teleology of history, which, in his view, is inflected with a redemptive Protestant worldview shaped by the revolutions of Western Europe and the United States. He argues that much progressive social science is based on faith in a glorious future, a barely hidden utopianism that has roots in Protestant ideas of salvation: *One* nation under one God, *one* unifying vision of progress for all. Behind this lies a worldview in which one society, *the people*, is one—with one history, one present, one future. *E pluribus unum.*

Da Matta (Hess and Da Matta 1995) argues that time, space, personhood, and politics can all be reanalyzed in a nonlinear, dualistic frame that could challenge what he calls Western social logics. The most provocative aspect of Da Matta's claim is it repudiates both Marxism, which is based on a dialectical theory of history in which class conflicts eventually lead to their own resolution, *and* liberal capitalist visions of development. Despite the claims of many of his critics, Da Matta is not a nihilist. He simply believes that Western linear models of progress may not fit within "Brazilian social logics" in which dualistic modes of thinking encompass ideas of unity or liberal individualism.[9]

Da Matta criticizes the tendency to view Brazil as a bundle of contradictions that need to be resolved, arguing that a Brazilian cultural logic would embrace contradiction, ambiguity, and indeterminacy—a logic that finds comfort *in the balance.* To make his point, he recounts a story from long-time American journalist Bryant Gumbel, former host of the *Today Show* on NBC, who expressed righteous indignation over the Brazilian government's lavish spending on Rio de Janeiro's samba schools and *sambódromo* stadium for Carnival amid the city's widespread extreme poverty. In a 1986 interview, Gumbel asked Da Matta, "Why this celebration, with so much luxury and waste, when there are so many poor people here?" (Hess and Da Matta 1995, 279). Da Matta uses this question—which epitomizes a certain contemptuous puzzlement that Americans and Europeans tend to have toward Brazilian social inequality—to exemplify a Western logic that is "functional, linear, and coherent." He makes a suggestive anthropological point:

> In my opinion, the analysts have contented themselves too easily with identifying the duality and seeing it as something simply incoherent and "out of place." But why can it not be a self-referential duality, founded in "hierarchical opposition"? When we investigate Brazilian society, we are rarely able to do so from within the framework of Brazilian social logic; nor are we able to break out of the logical straightjackets we accept along with the grand intellectual designs of the West. From them we learned that ideological contradictions lead to conflict and profound social transformations. In the United States, however, the presence of two

contradictory ideas presupposes a homogenous setting wherein conflic-
tive coexistence is its own "natural" resolution. But in Brazil and in the
rest of Latin America contradiction merely engenders inflamed speeches
in public and lively sessions of anecdotes at home. (275)

Where other anthropologists see conflict and contradiction between wealth and
poverty, Da Matta sees a complementary hierarchy, a society in which inequality is
reluctantly tolerated but not necessarily valued. The "inflamed speeches and lively
sessions of anecdotes at home" suggest that people are aware of these contradictions and feel strongly about them but may not presume there will be a "fix" in the
future. Whereas a functional and coherent theory of progress would assume that
these contradictions would be resolved over time through political struggle, a
logic that embraces contradiction and indeterminacy would focus on the myriad
ways in which contradiction reveals itself in public culture—in leaning high-rises
with improvised fixes, for example. Maybe they do not need to be fixed.

While I believe Da Matta was making a provocative and important point
about Brazil, I also recognize that his theory can have morally uncomfortable
implications. His defense of hierarchy as underlying culture essence can easily be
seen as an apology for racism, poverty, and other durable structures of inequality
in Brazil. In the wrong hands, his argument could turn social exclusion into a
component of national culture. From this perspective, why struggle for equality if
inequality and hierarchy are woven into the very fabric of national culture? How
could we possibly define some kind of essentialist Brazilian social logic, anyway?
We are talking about a diverse country of over two hundred million people, with
hundreds of regional, ethnic, religious, and political subcultures. I take these potential criticisms very seriously, but I think they miss a fundamental point, central to any comparative anthropological analysis: Brazilian history has produced
a very different kind of society from that of the United States or Europe, and it
would be anthropological malpractice to ignore those differences.[10]

A second challenge to Da Matta's perspective, which I will discuss at length in
the book's conclusion, focuses on the relationship between class politics and cultural attitudes, a fundamental debate in the social sciences that is frequently referred to as the debate between materialism versus idealism, a chicken-or-egg
debate that asks whether class relationships produce cultural norms or if cultural
norms produce class relationships. In the most basic terms, are the dominant
Brazilian cultural norms that Da Matta identifies simply the norms of the dominant classes, which the powerful impose on the less powerful to support and
maintain an unequal social structure? Throughout the book, I show how changes
in political economy lead to changing attitudes about progress, but I avoid a func-
tionalist perspective that would view progress as the project of either a particular

class or a "hegemonic bloc" of classes in an uneasy alliance, to use the terms of the Italian Marxist Antonio Gramsci. While every chapter of this book has a strong materialist bent, I am more interested in the ideological forms that "progress" can take than in attributing them to specific, nameable class interests.

Past, Present, and Future in Santos

Santos is a city of about four hundred thousand people that is part of a metropolitan region known as the Baixada Santista (Santos lowlands), with a population of almost one and a half million (including the adjacent cities of Cubatão, São Vicente, Guarujá, and Praia Grande). The region is only about forty miles from the megalopolis of São Paulo, but it is separated by a dramatic wall of mountains (the Serra do Mar) and is generally not thought of as part of the greater São Paulo metropolitan area. In Brazil, Santos is famous for three things: its port, its beaches, and its soccer team, Santos F.C., where legends such as Pelé (and, more recently, Neymar) rose to fame.

When I first visited Santos, it struck me as a place from which you could write the modern history of the Americas. São Vicente, the city directly adjacent to Santos, was the site of the first Portuguese settlement in Brazil, in the 1500s, the place from which the earliest Jesuits and explorers left to scale the Serra do Mar and establish the settlement that became the city of São Paulo (see chapter 1). São Vicente calls itself Brazil's first city, and Santos was founded only a few years later (1540 and 1546, respectively). Centuries later, Santos was the port of entry for more than three million immigrants to Brazil (mainly from Europe and Japan) who, along with African, indigenous, and Portuguese-descended populations, form the backbone of modern Brazilian society. In the nineteenth and early twentieth centuries, the Brazilian government sponsored a mass migration program to bring workers from Europe to replace slave labor (after abolition in 1888) on São Paulo's booming coffee plantations (Holloway 1980). Much of the modern Brazilian population, especially in the São Paulo region, traces its heritage back to these European immigrants, who worked under a system called the *colonato*. Under this system, the Brazilian government paid for the travel of immigrants and their families and assigned them work as sharecroppers on coffee plantations. Millions of immigrants landed by boat in Santos, where they were immediately loaded onto waiting trains for the journey over the mountains to São Paulo.

Along with migration, the economic history of Santos is tied to the coffee industry (see chapter 2). The city entered an astonishing period of growth in 1867, when the Santos-Jundiaí railroad opened, scaling the Serra do Mar to form the crucial commercial link between São Paulo's coffee plantations and the Atlantic coast. From 1867 until the Great Depression, Santos was unquestionably the world's most important port for the coffee trade. This was the so-called golden age of Santos, when it became the commercial hub for the industry that dominated the Brazilian economy. At one point, as much as 80 percent of the world's coffee supply was produced in Brazil, and almost all of it passed through Santos. The city was so synonymous with coffee that "Santos #4" became the gold standard for the world coffee price, much like "light sweet Texas crude" is for oil.

It would be hard to overstate the importance of coffee in the creation of modern Brazil. From the mid-nineteenth century to the Great Depression, the production and trade of coffee dominated economic, political, and social life. The crumbling mansions, ornate theaters, and stately stone offices in the downtown center of Santos are a constant reminder of the heyday of the coffee boom, which brought with it a cosmopolitan population of workers and capitalists from around the world—bankers from London, Hamburg, New York, and New Orleans; dockworkers from Italy and Portugal; merchants from the Ottoman Empire—Jews, Catholics, Protestants, and Muslims, all brought together into the steamy Port of Santos by the market for coffee, the "black gold" of the early twentieth century. It was this commercial cosmopolitanism that first drew me to Santos. Its Rua Comércio (Commercial Street) reminded me of other Commercial Streets I have encountered in transatlantic ports such as Boston, Baltimore, and New York, with ornate art nouveau import/export houses, narrow cobblestone streets, streetcar tracks, a grand customs house, and a lavish stone coffee exchange that now serves as a museum of coffee history.

The so-called golden age, however, was not golden for everyone. This was an economy based on the importation of labor power and the exportation of a single agricultural product, coffee. Imported labor power was literally turned into export profit, with coffee beans as the mediator. Historians call Santos "the Barcelona of Brazil" because its dockworkers were at the center of the country's most significant labor struggles, and the various unions associated with the port (stevedores, mechanics, etc.) were core constituents of the Brazilian Communist Party. Conflicts between labor and capital were accompanied by an almost constant battle between humans and nature to make Santos into a livable city (see chapter 4). For much of the nineteenth century, Santos was known as *porto maldito*, "the cursed port" or "the port of death." Located in a steamy tropical lowland surrounded by mangroves, the city was subject to constant epidemics. Immigrants and visitors associated it with disease, filth, and danger, a place to be left as soon as possible. As late as 1900, nearly 10 percent of the population typically died from yellow fever, bubonic plague, or malaria in a given year. Foreign trade was periodically halted because ships refused to dock in Santos, fearing the epidemics, so sanitation became a constant concern for the government, which depended on unbroken foreign trade. For this reason, the city launched Brazil's first and most famous public sanitation program in the early twentieth century (see chapter 4). The sanitation program was also the first systematic urban planning program in Brazil, and it was the first of several centrally planned urbanism projects that would transform Santos over the next century.

Thus, strikes and epidemics were the major preoccupations of the golden age of the coffee trade, and they have something in common: both disrupted the loading and unloading of ships on the Santos docks.

After World War II, Santos became a hub for Brazil's state-driven industrialization plans. During this period, the country transformed rapidly from a predominantly rural country to an urban one, and agricultural profits were used to promote urban industrial development. People from the countryside moved to the cities to build highways and work in mines, steel mills, and oil refineries. While Santos remained an important coffee port, its economy began to diversify, with oil, another kind of "black gold," fueling its growth. The nearby city of Cubatão, which lies next to Santos on the estuary, was one of the major sites for state-owned oil refineries, petrochemical plants, and steel mills. During this period, Brazil was led by a series of military governments, and the dominant attitude was "progress at any cost." There was no attention paid to democratic process or social and environmental preservation. Santos became known as one of the world's most polluted places. By the 1970s, it was called "the Valley of Death" in the *New York Times*, for its acid rain, polluted air and water, and numerous workplace accidents. The area between the docks and the mountains became a labyrinth of oil and chemical tanks, power transmission lines, pipelines, factories, and refineries. One tragic milestone of this period occurred in 1984, when a leaky oil pipeline set fire in the *favela* of Vila Socó, Cubatão, resulting in one of the worst industrial disasters in Brazilian history. The shacks of the *favela* were built among (and, in some cases, on top of) pipes that transported oil to and from the Port of Santos to Cubatão. More than two hundred people died in a fire that is now considered an event that signaled the end of Brazil's "progress at any cost" model of industrialization. Since then the region has tried to reinvent itself as a model of "green industry" that finds a happy balance between industrial production, public health, and environmental protection. Chapter 4 describes how the relationship between economic modernization and the environment changed over time.

The 1990s and early 2000s were marked by export-led economic development, when Brazil became increasingly open to global trade and the presence of foreign capital. This was the heyday of neoliberal globalization, under the leadership of President Fernando Henrique Cardoso. During this period, Santos became more than a coffee port; it was a global logistics hub, a central node in the circuits of global trade that delivered Brazil's booming export commodities such as soy, corn, sugar, and coffee to the world. Like many other Brazilian industries, the Port of Santos was privatized in 1998, leading not only to huge increases in productivity but also to some jarring job cuts and changes in labor practices that prompted frequent strikes and unrest. Despite the problems, Brazilian incomes rose quickly from 2005 to 2016, creating a huge emerging market for consumer goods and imported "global" consumer brands.

The next major chapter in the history of Santos, which is described in chapter 5, began in 2006, when Petrobras, the state-owned Brazilian oil company, announced the discovery of the largest deposit of offshore oil in the world, called the pre-salt, off the coast of Santos. That discovery, along with a booming Brazilian economy, set off a wave of investment and speculation in Santos that became the focus of my fieldwork in the neighborhood of Valongo. The site of the first port in Santos, the neighborhood was home to many of the oldest and most historically significant buildings in the city, including a seventeenth-century church, the grandiose nineteenth-century coffee exchange, and dozens of mansions from the eighteenth and nineteenth centuries. For decades, Valongo had been a neglected, decaying neighborhood of abandoned old mansions, industrial port infrastructure, and old brick warehouses. Like Salvador's Pelourinho before it was "renewed" by urban planning (Collins 2015), Valongo was the kind of place that affluent Santos residents avoided at night. It was known for prostitution, drugs, and arson, a place where impoverished people squatted in makeshift tenements in the ruins of old buildings.

Santos was, in some senses, at the center of the "Second Miracle," and that is why I chose to base the research for this book there. During the public announcement of the oil discovery, President Rousseff announced that it "proved God is Brazilian." At the time, oil prices were near record highs. In the breathless rush to exploit the offshore oil, Petrobras built a cluster of offices in Santos to house more than two thousand employees in Valongo. Continuing a pattern that had marked Brazilian history for almost a century, the government imagined that revenues from oil sales would fuel broad-based social investment and lead to the growth of a new middle-class Brazil (Biehl 2013). With a growing percentage of people entering into the global consumer class, international corporations licked their chops over the potential for untapped emerging markets in Brazil. Real estate prices in and around Santos skyrocketed, and there was a rush to transform the Valongo neighborhood from a gritty industrial port to a modern business and leisure district, paralleling changes in other Brazilian ports, particularly Rio's Porto Maravilha, a massive real estate development plan that, at one point, was going to include a Trump Towers apartment complex and a Trump hotel. During this boom period, foreign investment in Brazil took off, and the country announced its arrival on the world stage in spectacular events such as the 2014 World Cup and the 2016 Olympic Games, which contributed to the intense building booms around the country.

Methodology

My research for the book took place over seven months in 2013 and 2016. During the first period (three months in 2013), I mainly focused on ongoing transformations in the Brazilian coffee economy, interviewing people who worked in various aspects of the coffee trade. I first visited Santos to view the archive in the city's Coffee Museum, which has a wonderful library devoted entirely to coffee, and a small collection of primary sources from the city's coffee brokers syndicate, which briefly operated out of the museum building. While I was there, I saw the Santos downtown in the midst of an incredible building spree, as Petrobras, the national oil company, prepared to develop the pre-salt oil fields. The agricultural export economy was also booming, and the Santos port was absolutely overwhelmed with the volume of exports that were passing through it. News reports focused on the need to modernize the port to prevent logistical bottlenecks, and frequent strikes by the dockworker garnered international headlines because the strikes caused a chokepoint in the flow of goods in and out of Brazil. The Santos economy was in the midst of a transition from reliance on one kind of black gold (coffee) to another (oil), and I saw the downtown as ground zero for macro-level changes that were going on in Brazil. I spent four months in Santos in 2016, and there I expanded my focus from coffee to a more holistic study of how the rise and fall of the Second Miracle took shape in Santos, with a focus on the portside neighborhood of Valongo, which exemplified many of the changes that took place in Brazil in the 2010s.

My research was based on a combination of methods: ethnographic interviews, archival research, policy analysis, and analysis of public culture (including museums, art, media, and popular culture). Conducting ethnographic research in a large city presented some new challenges compared with my previous ethnographic research, which took place in a small village. The purpose of ethnography is to get a sense of how everyday people experience the world around them, through dialogue. While some see ethnography as the defining trait of anthropology, I see it as a means to an end, primarily as a tool to understand a given social system. By living with and speaking to people, an ethnographer gathers information about their individual viewpoints, identifying broad patterns and themes across individual cases. Ethnographers can then place these findings in dialogue with more public texts. Sometimes the local view links up with national-level discourses, while other times they conflict. Nevertheless, by tacking back and forth between private and public, individual and general, micro and macro levels, ethnographers begin to get a sense of the forces that shape (and are shaped by) individual experiences. Therefore, the information gathered through ethnographic interviews is always contextualized within broader sources of information that mutually shape each other.

As a method, ethnography was developed to understand places and cultures about which relatively little had been written in the historical archive. Early ethnographers needed to collect information through participant observation because it was the only alternative to unreliable accounts from travelers, government officials, and missionaries. There are still cases where ethnography is the only game in town, so to speak. In Honduras, for example, the only way for me to get a sense of the village's past and present was to talk to people. There were very few documents about the place. I could not read about it online, in the library, or in a newspaper. In moving from the level of the individual to the collective, my sole source of textual assistance was religious services and political campaigns. These were the only settings where some sense of a collective "we" was made public. Only there did I get a sense of the stories the community told itself about itself.

Unlike the village in Honduras, Santos is a historic city of half a million people, and there were hundreds of different multilayered texts available to me in which some vision of public culture took shape. Santos has two daily newspapers, multiple local television stations, dozens of museums, constant public festivals, a vibrant arts scene, and protests and marches almost daily. There are dozens of books written about Santos by Brazilian authors from all different disciplines and genres. All of these sources are in some sense cultural artifacts. They provide texts that illustrate the stories that Santos tells about itself. This book therefore draws from an eclectic array of sources to interpret how the Second Miracle took shape in Santos.

One of the biggest challenges of conducting research in a large city, compared with a village, is meeting people. Of course, there are far more people in a city for a visiting anthropologist potentially to connect with, but the city's crowds make the individual ethnographer relatively invisible and anonymous. In Honduras, I could meet and speak with dozens of people in a day, and they would frequently invite me, a stranger, into their homes to chat almost every time I left my house. There, I was a curiosity, and people in the village led relatively slow-paced lives, making it easy to spend time chatting. In Santos, I had to work much harder to connect. I had some contacts in the coffee industry, and I was able to conduct interviews with those people during work hours or after-work meetings at cafes or hotels. These interviewees gave me tours of their businesses and patiently intro-duced me to employees at coffee export businesses and trading houses.

These were valuable sources of information, but our conversations focused on coffee and related economic issues, and rarely moved to more wide-ranging, ca-sual topics; people were busy with work or else ready to get home to their lives. I also attended Jewish religious services at a small, historic congregation in down-town Santos, which allowed me to meet people in a more informal way. This proved to be a fruitful strategy, because the members of the congregation came from a variety of social and occupational backgrounds, and they were quite will-ing to meet with me and talk. A third (and ultimately very useful) strategy was to eat breakfast and drink coffee at a busy gas station near the port. Many Brazilian gas stations have little snack bars where people sit and drink tiny espressos and eat microwaved snacks called *salgados*. For coffee, there is no Brazilian equivalent to the "grab and go" style of a US mini-mart, so people tend to linger and talk elbow-to-elbow in very cramped quarters. This particular spot, on the edge of the port and the new "modern" business district, was where the "new economy" and "old economy" came together. I would sit there and listen to conversations as port workers, coffee people, oil and gas engineers, truck drivers, cab drivers, and a host of other regular people came and drank coffee. This gas station was at a lit-eral intersection of different ways of life—the port and city, blue collar and white collar. Simply by listening, I learned a lot about how people were interpreting the events unfolding around them. For ethical reasons, I do not reproduce any of their actual conversations here, but I do use them as background context for my own descriptions.

Weber's Question

On one level, the simplest way to understand the political upheaval in Brazil is to see it as a clash between competing models of progress. Different political par-ties, social classes, and interest groups all espouse different political platforms that rest upon different understandings of what progress looks like. This ap-proach implies a series of political questions: What classes of people should have the right to live in the city? Should labor or capital in the port have the up-per hand? What rights should native Brazilians have in the context of modern-ization? What does environmentalism mean in a rapidly industrializing region? Answering any of these questions requires making a normative judgment about how things ought to be, drawing a political line in the sand about what consti-tutes progress. This is perfectly fine as an anthropological strategy, but it means defining "progress" from a particular political perspective that might not be shared by the people being studied and that absolutely cannot be shared by all in situations of political conflict. Sometimes the choice is clear, but most of the time it is not.

In one of the most foundational works in the social sciences, Max Weber (1949) asked if it were possible to define progress in a value-neutral way. His answer was no. He viewed progress in relativist terms, as a particular way of imagining a better future that would always be rooted in the cultural values of a particular social group.[11] This is progress "as a cultural system," to borrow the famous terminology of Clifford Geertz, who directly drew on Weber. The relativist approach is a reasonable anthropological strategy, but it, too, has drawbacks. It fails to define the common features that mark progress as a genre or narrative form across different contexts. Of course, progress has different meanings for people in different social and cultural positions, but the term also performs a similar function across different contexts. A relativist definition of progress is so open ended that it ultimately does not shed much light on the work that progress does as an ideological category.

The perspective that I develop in the conclusion of this work lies between these two approaches—one political and the other apolitical. I think the answer to Weber's question is yes, it is possible to define progress in a value-neutral way, by viewing it as a particular form or genre of change. In Santos, the conflict I describe in each chapter was ultimately about attempts to mark time and space as sacred—to demarcate progress from plain old change. From indigenous villages to coffee bags to sewers to decrepit old warehouses, I describe an ongoing debate about what should and should not be set apart from the normal course of life. This process of sacralization of space and time, I argue, is at the root of an anthropological definition of "progress." Through sacralization, places and events get set apart from the normal temporalities of everyday life and become woven into mythic historical narratives. Drawing on the work of Mikhail Bakhtin, Michael Herzfeld, and Terence Turner, I argue that progress can be treated like myth, as a narrative genre with a particular form or "chronotope," to use a concept developed by Bakhtin (1981, 84–258).

The word "timescape," which I introduced earlier, is, to me, a simple synonym for "chronotope," and I will use the two terms more or less interchangeably throughout the book. A chronotope is a historically and socially produced "horizon" of space and time that connects isolated events into a narrative, in a dialectical process through which parts (individual events) and wholes (a narrative of history) are connected (Lemon 2009; Irvine 2004). The word "horizon" is important for understanding why I use the term "timescape." When a painter plans a landscape on a canvas, the horizon line determines the composition of every other aspect of the work. It is the orienting anchor against which all the other elements of the painting are evaluated, scaled, and interpreted. The horizon line gives meaning to every other element of the painting: shift it an inch or two in any direction, and every other element of the painting is out of whack. The same is true with the chronotope as a way of interpreting history. A chronotope reciprocally shapes the significance of particular events, giving them meaning within a particular "horizon" of space and time. Without a "chronotope," things would simply happen in an unbroken, meaningless stream, a chaotic welter of events without any guiding order, plot, or narrative scheme.

Consider my hometown of Rochester, New York. Everyone in Rochester can tell you that George Eastman was the founder of Kodak, the giant twentieth-century Rochester-based photographic company that once employed more than fifty thousand people in the area but has since shrunk to a shadow of its former self. It is more or less impossible to go anywhere in Rochester without seeing Eastman's name: his mansion is a museum; his childhood home is preserved in another museum; there is a statue of him right outside my office. Other than Henry Ford in Detroit, there is perhaps no other American city that is as closely identified with a single person as Rochester is with Eastman. For decades, Eastman was an icon of Rochester's success and prosperity; but as the company has floundered (it filed for bankruptcy in 2013), the narrative of progress and success has begun to change. For many Rochesterians, Eastman now represents "the good old days" of economic stability and bygone middle-class industrial jobs. Eastman was once an icon of Rochester's future; now he is a symbol of the past. For others, his meaning is far from heroic. To these people, he represents discriminatory employment practices that produced stark racial inequality in the city; or he represents the environmental harm that leftover Kodak chemicals continue to cause to the city's landscapes and waterways. In Rochester, Eastman the icon remains, but the chronotope is shifting around him. As the horizon line moves up or down on the canvas of Rochester's history, the meaning of events is up for grabs.

To understand the chronotope, it is important to understand how time and space are linked in everyday speech: we are running "behind" in our work, moving "forward" with our plans, catching "up" with the news, telling "inside" jokes. Less-developed areas of a country were once called "backward," and progress has always been associated with moving "ahead." Statements about time are directly connected to relations of space. Any concept of nationalism requires a particularly strong link between time and space. In nationalist narratives, historical events tightly bind people together across space and time to create the "imagined community." For example, in the American context, events that happened in Philadelphia, Pennsylvania, on July 4, 1776, are supposed to have some sort of cultural meaning to a person in Brownsville, Texas, on July 4, 2016.

Somehow, those communities and their identities are linked across space and time. But there is nothing natural or accidental about this link. It is "produced" in history classes, through civic rituals (the Pledge of Allegiance, Independence Day fireworks, etc.), and in films, television, and other media that function to instill national identity.

The chronotope helps us to understand how events take on mythic proportions. Consider another American example: Every schoolchild learns the story of Rosa Parks as it pertains to the civil rights movement. It is in textbooks and documentaries. Her image is on a stamp. There is a library and museum in her honor in Montgomery, Alabama. These cultural products demonstrate that she is considered an icon of twentieth-century American racial progress. But the actual history of her accomplishment is less well known (besides the fact that she violated Jim Crow laws by sitting at the front of the bus in Montgomery, Alabama, in 1955). Why and how did Parks's story transform from history to myth? The story of many other activists might have performed the same historical function. What might otherwise have been thought of as a simple act of civil disobedience or resistance (an activist protesting Jim Crow) is now interwoven into the American national narrative of racial progress.

In anthropological terms, there are two ways of understanding time in play here: one is historical (the actual events that occurred at specific places and specific times) and the other is mythological (the way the events serve as a timeless narrative that a community tells itself about itself). At the individual level, Parks made a courageous political choice while, at a collective level, an entire nation was transformed. Mythologically, the country is transformed through peaceful democratic resistance. These transformations involve both time (not just something that happened in 1955, but a change in US history over a century or more) and space (not just something that happened in Alabama, but something that changed the entire country). The transformation of an individual in concrete space and time (Rosa Parks in Montgomery, Alabama, in 1955) becomes dialectically identified with the transformation of the entire nation across a very different scale of space and time.

The conclusion of this book explores these questions in greater depth, using the case of Brazil to develop an anthropological theory of progress. As is the case in many societies with high levels of social inequality, in Brazil it will always be politically difficult to define one uniform vision of progress. Perhaps a dualistic understanding of progress has emerged (or reemerged) in the present as a strategy to hold together societies that are increasingly polarized by economic globalization. In countries from India to China to South Africa (all of which are grouped with Brazil as BRICS), we see a similar pattern: progress for the elite means integration of their nation into a cosmopolitan global economy. Yet, this vision of progress has little to no meaning for people who do not have the capital or skills to participate in that system. In the context of climate devastation, older models of progress based on the expansion of capitalism are increasingly viewed as forms of civilizational decline, and new alternatives have emerged that replace chronotopes of growth and expansion with other formal patterns. The chapters that follow cumulatively illustrate the clash or play between different visions of progress in Santos. The period in which I researched and wrote this book was an exceptionally difficult time for Brazil. With each passing day, a news story broke that, it seemed, would be a turning point in the country's political history. The ways that people interpreted their own history and used it as a guide for the present and the future were present everywhere—from private conversations to newspaper stories to historic nationwide protests. Time will tell which stories become woven into the country's mythic history and how that history will be rewoven in response.

SPECTACLES OF COLONIALISM

Two Timescapes of Indigenous Presence in Santos

The first time I set foot in Brazil, I entered the country illegally. In 1996, I spent three days on a riverboat called the *Aquidaban*, which traveled from the town of Concepción, Paraguay, to Corumbá, Brazil, following the meandering course of the Paraguay River. I was part of a mixed group of Americans and Argentines. We slept on benches among dozens of Paraguayans and Brazilians who used the boat for transportation throughout the remote towns of the Pantanal, a massive swamp ecosystem that lies along the border between Paraguay and Brazil. The boat would stop and unload goods (barrels of oil, zinc roofs, bags of onions, livestock, a motorbike) and people at every little town on the Paraguayan side, and it was fairly easy to get into friendly conversations. I was a young American in a place and time when there were not many like me around, and there were no phones or computers to pull people away from spontaneous conversations. I was then a budding anthropologist who was very keen to soak up whatever I could about the local culture—what people ate, how they spoke, how they passed the monotonous hours on the slow boat ride up the river. I even got to help skin a capybara that was shot by one of the ship's crew on the riverbank, cooked up in a stew with rice, and served to the passengers and crew for a small fee.

After about a day or so on the boat, we stopped in the Brazilian town of Porto Murtinho, at the extreme western edge of the state of Mato Grosso do Sul, which was then in the early stages of a soy boom that created sharp and sometimes violent conflicts between landowners and local people, especially indigenous groups who sought to protect and demarcate their territory. I got off the boat and bought some food and a cold Brahma beer. No one checked our passports.

The boat was a regular arrival on the docks at the border, and no one paid us much attention. I could have easily stayed behind in Brazil without anyone giving it a second thought. I got back on the boat along with a few Brazilians who were heading north to the river port of Corumbá. That evening, I remember leaning on a railing on the deck, watching an incredible sunset over the river and looking at the endless jungle unfold in front of me. I struck up a conversation with a Brazilian man who, as I vaguely recall, was traveling north on some kind of sales trip. I told him I was in Paraguay as an anthropology student to learn about indigenous groups. I will never forget his response, in Portuguese-accented Spanish: "Por qué? No hay mucho para aprender. Son bichos del monte no más." ("Why? There's not much to learn. They are no more than beasts of the forest.")

Of course, I knew even then that many people around Latin America held openly hostile and racist attitudes toward native peoples. In places such as the Brazilian Pantanal, which was in the midst of rapid development, agricultural land grabbing, and population growth, indigenous peoples were sometimes seen as obstacles to progress who stood "in the way of development," to quote the title of a volume on that very topic (Blaser, Feit, and McRae 2004). However, I had never personally heard such virulent racism expressed so casually, so matter-of-factly, as if the speaker were telling me to avoid the swarming mosquitoes at dusk rather than human beings. While I am aware that similar views may have been expressed by many Americans, just as casually, for much of US history, it still took my breath away to hear those attitudes expressed in my own lifetime. I do not remember much else from the conversation, other than that I traded the man some US coins for Brazilian ones. He was especially interested in shiny copper pennies.

I did not know it at the time, but this man was expressing a current iteration of the *bandeirantes* attitude—the idea that indigenous peoples are obstacles to progress and therefore not deserving of basic human rights. On the ever-expanding margins of capitalist Brazil, places where once-isolated indigenous groups are coming into sustained contact with nonindigenous newcomers, violent encounters are not uncommon. As Vanessa Lea (2017) writes, a powerful lobby of conservative rural capitalists (*ruralistas*) "seek to unleash their power to deprive the Indigenous peoples of what land remains under their control and to prevent those groups without sufficient land from regaining the areas they have lost over the course of history" (152). This violence has been well documented for decades, from the massacre of Yanomami by gold miners in 1988 to the prolonged assault on indigenous lands by farmers and settlers that continues in the present. This contemporary onslaught against native peoples is often viewed as a modern iteration of the work of the *bandeirantes*, sixteenth-century slave raiders who are considered national patriarchs, particularly, though not exclusively, within the São Paulo region. Anthropologist David Maybury-Lewis

(1990), who founded the organization Survival International to defend the rights of Brazilian indigenous peoples, made this very point:

> Brazilian schoolbooks glorify the *bandeirantes* who built the nation, glossing over their slaving activities by asserting that the work of Indians (and later of blacks) was necessary for the economy of the colony. Similarly, elimination of the Indians in more recent times is justified in the name of civilization. The official policy of successive administrations, both military and civilian, is that assimilation is the Brazilian way. (41)

Virtually anyone who spends time in Brazil notices the historical importance of the *bandeirantes*, and they have been written about by many scholars across different disciplines. The word *bandeirante* has no precise English translation—some translate it as "expeditionary groups" (Moog 1964, 3), while others use "explorer" (Eakin 1997, 22), "pathfinder," "adventurer" (Scott 1998, 129), or "slave raider." In any case, the *bandeirantes* were men of Portuguese descent or the first-generation offspring of Portuguese men and native women (*mamelucos*); these *bandeirantes* led expeditions into the Brazilian interior from the present-day state of São Paulo to capture Amerindian slaves and find precious metals. Structurally, they occupy a similar position in Brazil's national mythology to the one Pilgrims do in the United States, in the sense that they are thought of as the ancestral founders of a small settlement from which the modern nation-state developed. Unlike with the Pilgrims in the United States, however, the encounter between the *bandeirantes* and the natives is not mythologized as reciprocal, harmonious, or peaceful; there is no joyous Thanksgiving feast here to celebrate unity and the happy birth of a settler colony. Instead, the *bandeirantes* myth often emphasizes violence, cunning, and roguish theft, while also celebrating the racial mixture of white Portuguese and natives through sexual violence. The *bandeirantes* are national heroes, but they are not pure, American-style "good guys," carrying out some kind of religiously inflected civilizational mission.

In 1964, Brazilian writer and diplomat Clodomir Vianna Moog published the book *Bandeirantes and Pioneers*, which used a comparison of the *bandeirantes* mythology in Brazil and the "myth of the frontier" in the United States to explain patterns of history and culture in the two countries. Moog's central thesis is that the *bandeirantes* myth celebrated a predatory, violent attitude and "unbridled greed" in search of wealth (155). In contrast, the North American "pioneer" spirit emphasized "colonization" rather than conquest. The American model of nation-building stressed the dignity of steady labor over time, leading to long-term upward mobility rather than rapid, predatory defeat. Moog argues that differences in "Brazilian and North American civilization" can partly be explained by this cultural history. The Brazilian state, he contends, became ideologically connected to the *bandeirantes*, and the state valorized the *bandeirantes* history of predatory, impermanent acquisition of wealth.[1]

In Brazil, the word *bandeirantes* is used in everyday language to describe ambition, opportunism, and economic success, and the *bandeirantes* are powerful symbols of national progress across the country. While the story has a particular history, it has taken on a life of its own as a catch-all metaphor for national progress, an empty container into which any specific content can be placed to narrate a story of progress. The *bandeirantes* attitude is not limited to a single political party or viewpoint. In a 2014 interview, renowned Brazilian anthropologist Eduardo Viveiros de Castro criticized the Workers' Party government for continuing the *bandeirantes* attitude of the dictatorship in a new guise:

> The Workers' Party sees the Brazilian Amazon as a place to civilize, to tame, to obtain economic benefit, to capitalize. In a sad continuity with the geopolitics of the dictatorship and of the present government, this is the old bandeirantes attitude that today forms part of the national project. The formal political conditions change, but the image of what Brazilian civilization should be—from what makes a life worth living to what kind of society is in line with that—is very, very similar.[2]

The *bandeirantes* attitude is still associated with an aggressive, predatory form of economic development that casts aside the rights of native peoples and the environment in the name of national progress. However, *bandeirante* can also be a positive term to describe ambition and opportunism. Being called "a real *bandeirante*" can be a compliment. In June 2016, the business section of the *Folha de São Paulo* newspaper referred to the fast-food chain Subway as the *"Bandeirante* Sandwich" because it was expanding so rapidly throughout the interior of Brazil.[3] As time went on, I noticed *bandeirantes* imagery everywhere: the superhighway that connects São Paulo to the interior is called *bandeirantes*; one of the largest shipping and logistics firms in Santos is called *Bandeirantes* Logistics; one of Brazil's major television networks is called TV *Bandeirantes*; and so on. *Bandeirantes* can be all sorts of people and things—coffee traders, sewer engineers, highways, slave raiders, and sandwiches. These are just superficial examples of a much deeper cultural resonance, in which the *bandeirantes* story is equated with national progress, particularly the expansion of capitalism.

The surprising thing about the *bandeirantes* myth is that it has been used to symbolize diametrically opposed political agendas. It is a narrative template that is almost completely devoid of any specific content and can mean almost any kind of transformation that, in some vague sense, moves Brazil forward. During a Santos-based insurrection against the dictatorship of President Getúlio Vargas in the 1930s (the Constitutionalist Rebellion), both the revolutionaries and the government used the *bandeirantes* myth to rally people to their cause. Vargas called his state-driven expansion of capitalism into Brazil's interior a modern-day *bandeirantes* movement, and his opponents identified their insurrectionary force as a group of tough *bandeirantes* fighting for freedom against an encroaching centralized state. Both sides of the political debate—regional separatists from São Paulo and nationalists who supported Vargas—mobilized the *bandeirantes* myth to attract support.[4] Two decades later, the builders of Brasília were once again called the modern *bandeirantes*, as were the migrant construction workers who built the highway between São Paulo and Santos in the 1950s.

The specific details of the story are not important. What matters is that the *bandeirantes* served as an ideology of progress and development that linked opposing viewpoints. In this sense, a particular vision of expansionary development derived from the *bandeirantes* myth was, and continues to be, an "encompassing value" (to use a concept from Louis Dumont that has been applied to modern Brazil by Roberto Da Matta). Encompassing values are ideas that "include their opposite at a higher level" (Hess and Da Matta 1995, 11). In Brazil, blueprints for progress across the political spectrum—even those considered to be diametrically opposed to one another—are encompassed by a higher-level vision of developmentalism that is frequently symbolized by the *bandeirantes*. In this sense, the *bandeirantes* story became a social poetic, a narrative genre that elevated certain events out of the normal timescape of history and into an unfolding mythology of Brazilian development. While the specific content of the transformation that the *bandeirantes* story is intended to express might change with the times, the form of the narrative remains more or less constant.

The Clash of Timescapes

While the *bandeirantes* timescape valorizes developmentalism and genocide, there is another—seemingly contradictory—pattern in Brazilian popular culture. Brazil has done far more to accept indigenous peoples as part of its national identity than almost any other large country in the Americas, celebrating the place of native peoples in its history and culture, and setting aside more territory for indigenous communities than any other country in the world. For many years, scholars of Brazil have identified a contradiction: Brazil celebrates and promotes its indigenous heritage, yet Brazilians simultaneously downplay the presence of indigenous people as active historical agents and victims of genocide. Native peoples are therefore set apart from the mainstream in both space and time. They exist "out there" in remote regions or as relics of a treasured past.

As Tracy Devine Guzmán (2013) writes, when native identity is "muted, distant, powerless, or invented," it is safe or "even a potential point of pride"; but when indigenous peoples become "too demanding, or too real" by making political or economic claims against the state, they become a threat and a target for hatred (11). Noted Brazilian anthropologist Alcida Ramos (2012) observed that "hyperreal" Indians are welcome participants in Brazilian history when they are part of folkloric performances and mythic histories, but Indians as real historical personages must often participate in a limited range of "authorized" scripts to be accepted by the nonindigenous mainstream.

This contradiction was visible in a clash of timescapes in São Vicente, a city directly adjacent to Santos, when a controversy emerged in 2015 over a community of Guaraní who live in a beachfront state park. The Guaraní had arrived in São Vicente in 2003 to participate in a spectacular musical reenactment of the Portuguese arrival in Brazil, recreating the "first contact" between European colonists and native Brazilians from which modern Brazil was born. Twelve years later, the Guaraní actors remained in São Vicente, living alongside some of the most expensive real estate in Brazil. The dispute over their continued presence in the middle of urban Brazil illustrates the clash of timescapes that I describe throughout this book: when indigenous people exist within the mythic timescape, performing in dramatic reenactments of history, they are outside of unfolding events and held at a distance from the ongoing struggles of social and political life; but when they occupy the historical timescape, playing an active role in actual events, their presence draws attention to the cracks in the mythic foundations of national identity. This chapter uses the ongoing conflict in São Vicente to examine the more general cultural pattern that is at the core of my argument.

Timescape 1: Indigenous People in the Contemporary City

On a warm spring night in 2015, an eighteen-year-old Brazilian man named Luann Oshiro was murdered while waiting for a bus in the city of Santos. Oshiro, who was born in Japan and came to Brazil as a child, was a recent high school graduate planning to attend the University of São Paulo, and he had been out partying with friends that night. Around 1:30 in the morning, he was waiting on a busy street near Gonzaga beach when two teenagers on bicycles attempted to rob him of his wallet and phone. Exactly what happened next is unknown, but the assailants opened fire on Oshiro, leaving him dead on the sidewalk. Months later, the police determined that one of the assailants was a sixteen-year-old resident of Bolsão 8, a public housing complex in the nearby city of Cubatão. Built by the government in the 1980s to relocate people out of a slum on the edge of the city, Bolsão 8 is one of a number of public housing complexes on the outskirts of Santos that middle-class *santistas* and the media tended to associate with crime. The complex mainly houses the descendants of migrants from northeastern Brazil who came to the Santos region to help build highways and factories during the "miracle years" of the 1960s (see chapter 5). While the complexes were constructed as a way to solve the problem of precarious housing for the urban poor, they came to symbolize the persistence of the very problem they were designed to solve. The area around Cubatão is known as a particularly dangerous place. A news article on the arrest of one of the assailants referred to the pair as *dois marginais*—literally "two marginals," but implicitly "two residents of the marginal neighborhoods" (*A Tribuna*, April 5, 2016). This usage neatly collapses social and spatial marginality into a single term: to physically live on the margins is to socially live on the margins as well.

Brazil has one of the highest levels of violent crime in the world, and Oshiro's murder, while tragic, would not be of much interest to an anthropologist were it not for the way that his family and friends responded. To honor his legacy, they created a foundation called Luann Vive (Luann Lives) to carry out community service projects, which they organized through Facebook. According to news coverage, Luann was an excellent student with a strong sense of compassion and kindness for the less fortunate. For one of the service projects, the group visited Tekoa Paranapuã, a small village of Mbyá Guaraní people located in the beachfront state park near Santos, only about three miles from where the murder took place. About ninety people lived in the village, which, as described above, was established in 2003 when Guaraní actors came to perform in a reenactment of the first meeting of Portuguese colonists and Amerindians, which took place on nearby Gonzaguinha beach in 1531.

The Guaraní came from settlements farther south on the São Paulo coast. They camped out in a forested area a few miles from the main beach where the performance was held, on the site of an abandoned juvenile detention center that the Brazilian government operated in the 1980s and 1990s. The detention center had been run by a notoriously ineffective government agency that managed Brazilian youth incarceration programs and was disbanded in the early 2000s after a series of prison riots, deaths, and corruption scandals. According to a news story, the abandoned slab-concrete building "looked like a nightmare scene," a prisonlike structure covered with graffiti, trash, cracks, and leaks, when Luann Vive's volunteers arrived to clean up in April 2016. It should be noted that this facility was only about twenty years old at the time it was abandoned, and it was nearly a ruin by 2016. The volunteers spent the day repairing the damaged building, cleaning up trash in the village, and donating school supplies to the children. Luann Vive posted hundreds of photos to Facebook of smiling volunteers doing good works, and a full-page story appeared in the local newspaper shortly thereafter.

A Kaleidoscopic History

The story of Luann Oshiro's murder and its aftermath is so rife with symbolism that it is hard to know where to begin to make sense of it. It pulls together many different threads of contemporary Brazilian society in an almost kaleidoscopic way. The story speaks to the problem of urban crime (the murder), the rising urban middle class (Oshiro's family and friends) and its relationship with the urban poor, and new strategies of policing and detention that led to the closing of the juvenile prison. At another level, it speaks to the treatment of Brazil's native peoples and the continuing legacies of colonialism as dispossessed native people struggle to survive in the midst of Brazil's economic expansion. It also is a story of immigrant assimilation, highlighting the place of Japanese-Brazilians (one of the largest immigrant groups in the country) in contemporary society. It involves real estate development clashing with environmentalism: the beachfront park where the Guaraní settled is surrounded by some of the most prized real estate in Brazil, and pressure from investors to develop new residences in the area hastened the planned eviction of the Guaraní. Finally, the story involves the legacy of failed state programs (the abandoned juvenile detention center). Years after its closure, the detention center has been repaired thanks to activist projects organized on social media, reflecting new patterns of citizenship that have emerged as middle-class Brazilians organize around political causes online to form new alliances and avenues for social change. All of these themes are part of the story, and like the pattern in a kaleidoscope, the different elements can be tilted and turned to create an entirely different picture of how and why this event happened. To me, this story was twenty-first-century Brazil in a nutshell, a palimpsest of layered historical struggles that played out in contestations over urban space.

The story, which I first read about in the Santos newspaper, *A Tribuna*, piqued my anthropological interest, so I took a bus to the stop closest to Tekoa Paranapuã, the Guaraní village, about a mile's walk away on the Avenida Saturnino de Brito (named after the sanitary engineer described in chapter 4).[5] There was a small group of Guaraní youths sitting at a news kiosk by the bus stop, playing games on their mobile phones. I walked down the nearly deserted street toward the entrance of the beachfront park. On the way, I passed an elderly indigenous woman walking in the opposite direction and carrying a selection of curios to sell, such as necklaces, bracelets, and bows and arrows. She asked if I was interested in buying something. I declined and asked her if I was heading in the direction of the village. She said yes, and I continued on. When I got to the entrance of the park, it was heavily guarded by local police. When I told them I was looking for the nature trails, the police said the park was not open to visitors. I then asked if the Guaraní village was open. They said no but there would be a special day when tourists would be able to visit. I walked back to the bus stop, disappointed.

Between History and Myth

Like many anthropologists, I first encountered native Brazilians on the beaches of Santos through the works of Claude Lévi-Strauss, the most famous anthropologist of the twentieth century, who described his arrival at the port of Santos in *Tristes Tropiques*, one of the most popular works of anthropology ever written. It is, in many senses, a mythic tale of a white European anthropologist on a quest to discover uncontacted natives in remote regions of Brazil, and the book continues to exert a powerful influence on the imaginations of anthropologists around the world. Writing in the 1940s, Lévi-Strauss first encountered Brazilian Amerindians on the beaches of Santos; yet, for him, they were already a sad relic of a bygone past. In his memorable description of the bustling Santos docks and the "serene sumptuousness" of the Brazilian landscape, Lévi-Strauss (1971) dismisses the presence of native peoples in Santos: "In 1918, the maps of the state of São Paulo, which is as big as France, showed it as being two-thirds 'unknown territory inhabited only by Indians'; by the time I arrived in 1935, there was not a single Indian left, apart from a few families who used to come to the Santos beaches on Sundays to sell so-called curios" (49).

The account of my own encounter with a curio-selling native woman is an ironic counterpoint to the heroic "arrival narratives" that were commonplace in twentieth-century anthropology. Lévi-Strauss downplayed the significance of the native people he encountered in Santos, denying their authenticity due to their presence in urban Brazil. He set off in search of indigenous groups in remote regions that were relatively "uncontaminated" by civilization. I came to Santos believing Lévi-Strauss. Despite having read extensively about indigenous peoples outside the urban core of Brazil, I wrongly assumed there were no indigenous communities that still resided in the immediate area around Santos. After all, the most famous anthropologist of the twentieth century had announced their demise back in the 1940s.

My ignorance was instructive. The anthropology of Brazil's indigenous peoples tends to focus on their experiences either as victims of an ever-expanding capitalist juggernaut or as entities who live far away from urban Brazil. They are treated, analytically at least, as separate from the underlying currents of social,

economic, and political life in the urban core. This is particularly true of anthropological accounts written outside of Brazil. Through popular textbooks and
films, many anthropologists know about the legendary political activism of
groups such as the Kayapó and their heroic yet ultimately unsuccessful fight to
stop the construction of the Belo Monte hydroelectric dams on the Xingú River.
And the treatment of the Yanomami, who live in the border regions near Venezuela, is arguably the most well-known (and controversial) case study of
twentieth-century anthropology. Yet, the complex stories of groups such as the
Guaraní in Santos, who live within, not apart from, the core of the modern, urban, industrialized world, are not as well known to outsiders.[6] For many foreign audiences, native peoples of Brazil are either positioned "out there," away
from urban life, or as somewhat tragic victims of Brazil's rapid development—
"victims of the miracle," in the words of anthropologist Shelton Davis (1977).

Therefore, many anthropologists have followed in the mistaken footsteps of
Lévi-Strauss, who discounted the presence of the curio-selling natives on the
beaches of Santos. Indigenous peoples are too often treated as living elsewhere,
both spatially and temporally, yet they are directly enmeshed in broad changes
in Brazilian society. Lévi-Strauss's depictions of native people as completely separate from processes of modernization and change are totally inadequate for
understanding the politics of colonialism in the present, a world where the curio-
selling "Indians on the beach" are pulled into networks of show business, real
estate development, environmentalism, urban crime, and volunteer projects en-
abled by Facebook. The processes of modernization and development that Lévi-
Strauss imagined as the death knell of Brazil's native cultures have advanced at
an unimaginably rapid pace, and indigenous groups continue to struggle within
and against the dominant capitalist model of progress that, once upon a time,
was thought of as the harbinger of their inevitable demise.

Timescape 2: Indigenous People in Myth

The Santos region occupies an important place in the *bandeirantes* story. It was the
site of the first permanent Portuguese settlement in Brazil, the Vila de São Vicente,
which was followed by the establishment of the Vila de Santos in 1533. As the place
where the first "economic and civil organization of Brazilian society was effected"
(Freyre and Putnam 1946, 3), it is sometimes considered the birthplace of the
nation—even though Porto Seguro, in Bahia, is thought of as the official "birthplace" of Brazil because it was the site of Pedro Álvares Cabral's first landing on
Brazilian shores in 1500 (Collins 2015).[7] In São Vicente, there is a small and rather
forlorn reconstruction of the colonial villa in the middle of the downtown, along

with a few historical sites that mark major points in the establishment of the colony; however, these places are not popular tourist attractions and, apart from the occasional school group, they tend to be empty. São Vicente is far more popular for its beaches than for its historical sites. I was the only visitor on the four occasions that I visited the villa.

While the historical sites might be empty, São Vicente celebrates its position in Brazilian history through a spectacular annual ritual, which was the reason the Guaraní came and founded the informal settlement described above. Every year between 2004 and 2015, the municipal government put on a glitzy, dramatic reenactment of the "discovery" of Brazil by the Portuguese. The "Reenactment of the Founding of the Village of São Vicente" was a major event that the municipality claims holds the Guinness World Record for largest beachfront spectacle. It was an extravagant show held at night with over a thousand actors, some of whom were well-known Brazilian soap opera stars. Throughout the economic boom of the 2000s, the municipal government of São Vicente sought to make the spectacle bigger and better. As money poured into the city's coffers, the performance became a ritual that memorialized the progress São Vicente had made. Its grand scale mirrored national ambitions of growth and power. It became something more than a reenactment of Brazil's origins: it embodied Brazilian national ambition in its production style, the "biggest and best" in the world. The spectacle of the reenactment—its massive size and cost—became the real point of the ritual. The growth of the event symbolized the rising power of Brazil. In fact, there is a museum space devoted entirely to the history of the reenactment (not to the history of the actual encounter) in the reconstructed colonial villa, exemplifying the fact that the scale of the performance was just as important as the historical events that it dramatized. The reenactment, as well as history itself, was sacralized.

Every year, the performance was based on a new original script with all-new songs and dances, headline stars, lighting, and sets. No expense was spared, and the show was broadcast live on television. Imagine a Las Vegas–style show held on a beautiful, wide sandy beach at night. This reenactment was a ritual in two different senses. The text of the narrative reproduced a particular understanding of the Brazilian nation. As a text, in the broadest sense, the reenactment resembled Brazil during the boom years in that it kept getting bigger, more expensive, and more elaborate. As is true of all rituals, the meaning of the reenactment lay not just in the message conveyed through its narrative plot but also in the effort and activity required to produce, perform, and watch it. Its meaning, therefore, cannot be separated from the social context in which it took place. The text of the drama is important, but so is the fact that it was being produced and performed in São Vicente during the boom years of the 2000s.

Below I summarize the basic sequence of the events in the reenactment, following the plot as it unfolded in one specific production.[8]

Scene 1

The performance begins in total darkness on the beach. A deep, spooky male voice booms over the loudspeakers: "In the beginning, there was nothing." Then Monan, a female cosmic force who brings everything into being, appears. Monan (also called Maira-Monan) is a Tupi-Guaraní spirit being who is considered "creator, transformer, and law-giver" (Shapiro 1987). The remainder of this scene presents Tupi-Guaraní cosmology as the "before" epoch in a simple "before and after" narrative of the colonial encounter. Here, Monan creates the earth and sky, separates water from land, blows the breath of life into the world. She creates the forest and man and woman, and teaches humans right from wrong.

A spotlight then dramatically illuminates a lone Indian in full feather regalia on the beach. He becomes the protagonist and narrator who takes us through the rest of the story. Monan creates Tupã, the figure whom the Christian missionaries called the Tupi-Guaraní "God." Tupã creates Iara, the goddess of water, and Caapora, the god of the earth and forest. Each god is represented by giant colorful puppets about twenty feet tall. This scene continues to present a pantheon of powerful god-spirits in a relatively respectful way. The aesthetics are somewhat predictable, emphasizing the natives' mystical connection with nature, but the precolonial cosmology is nevertheless placed front and center in the story. While the story is told through a Western voice and a nonindigenous perspective, it nonetheless reveres (rather than denigrates) Tupi-Guaraní cosmology.

Scene 2

The action begins to quicken. The Guaraní organize to defend themselves against their enemies, the Tupinambá. At this point, a musical number about tribal warfare and cannibalism begins, climaxing with a Tupinambá man being sacrificed and consumed by the Guaraní so that his life force is assimilated into the body of his enemies. The death and ritual cannibalism is described by one of the actors as "a sacrifice" to Tupã, or God. The initial scenes give the viewer a good idea of Guaraní religion and myth, yet they also suggest that the Guaraní were living in a state of chronic warfare with enemy groups, marked by ritual cannibalism, prior to the arrival of the Portuguese.[9] As a depiction of the mythic "state of nature," the reenactment is more akin to Hobbes than Rousseau: the Indians had their own way of life before the Portuguese arrived, and it was characterized by violence.

Scene 3

After the battle between the native Guaraní and the Tupinambá ends, the mood of the performance shifts. A shaman warns the natives that their way of life is about to change drastically, as a strange white-skinned tribe is arriving on the sea. The music shifts from deep, mystical chords to guitar-driven hard rock, and we see a flotilla of Portuguese ships on the horizon. These are the "navigators," their sails emblazoned with the red cross of the Portuguese empire. The captains of these ships are the famous explorers Americo Vespucci, Pedro Álvares Cabral, and Gonçalo Coelho. All three describe their discoveries along the coast of Brazil. As the navigators brag about their finds, a bearded, bedraggled man named Cosme Fernandes is thrown overboard for insubordination. Fernandes becomes the first white inhabitant of São Vicente. He establishes an illicit slave port, selling captured Indians to the enemies of the Portuguese—the British, French, and Dutch. He names himself the "white-skinned king" and comically parades around the beach in a tattered white blouse and feathered headdress.

Another Portuguese man is shipwrecked on the beach and encounters Fernandes. This man is the legendary João Ramalho, the patriarch and mythical forefather of the settlement that became São Paulo. In this scene, native women fawn all over Ramalho, who is lauded in the dialogue for his long beard, courage, sexual prowess, and strength. Fernandes tells Ramalho that he has arrived in paradise, and Ramalho notes how the women are "beautiful and perfumed," unlike the ugly, foul-smelling Portuguese women they left behind. Ramalho is also named a "white king," and he marries Batira, the daughter of the Guaraní *cacique* chief, Tibiriçá. Thus, "first contact" between natives and Portuguese is established by two tough, bearded *malandros* (rogues)—Ramalho and Fernandes—who are outcasts from the colonial government. In this retelling, the forebears of the *bandeirantes* are presented as opportunistic outcasts motivated by sex, wealth, and power. In no way was their mission shaped by a higher spiritual calling or a sacred civilizing duty, as would be the case in the mythology of the United States. In fact, the "official" agents of the Portuguese crown disappear from this scene relatively quickly, and the rogues are left behind as the would-be patriarchs of São Vicente, marching around the beach as proud, irreverent white kings.

Scene 4

A fleet of Portuguese ships arrive from Rio. They have been sent by King João III to establish a colony and protect the coast from invasions by Portugal's enemies. The fleet is captained by Martim Afonso de Sousa. At first, the Guaraní are threatened and frightened by the arrival of the Portuguese, and the Portuguese gather their forces to prepare for a battle on the beach. The first moments of contact are tense. Suddenly, João Ramalho, the bearded white king, appears in a feathered Indian headdress. He mediates the conflict while marching around defiantly, carrying a musket. He explains to the natives that the Portuguese are the allies of the Guaraní, and will support the Indians against their internal tribal enemies. The two groups make peace, with Ramalho breaking a warrior's arrow in half to symbolize the peace. Thus, the shipwrecked rogue who became the white chief of the Guaraní becomes, momentarily, the peacemaking hero, forming a union between colonizer and colonized.

The two groups begin to trade, and Tibiriçá, the Guaraní chief who is the father of Ramalho's Indian bride, offers up a group of young native women for the Portuguese sailors to marry. Portuguese Jesuit priests construct a small chapel and make plans to hold the first Catholic mass on the beach. Before the mass, a priest asks Ramalho if he has any sins to confess. Ramalho dodges the confession, wryly saying, "Let's talk about that later, pal." Soon, we learn that Ramalho has fathered dozens of native children, and the Portuguese sailors marvel at his virility, joking about how he probably has a lot of sins to confess to the priests. The Jesuits, therefore, stand in an awkward relationship with the *bandeirantes*, who are embodied by Ramalho, and the priests reluctantly tolerate their sins. Neither ally nor enemy, the church is depicted as a rather weak mediator, and the founding *bandeirantes* are the protagonists in the drama.

The first mass is held, with the Guaraní praying alongside the Portuguese to a large neon-lit cross that reflects dramatically off the moonlit ocean. In the final scene, a large stone *pelourinho* (pillory) is brought onshore and placed at the center of the scene. The pillory is the symbol of law and order in the Portuguese colonies, exemplifying the state's ability to punish (Collins 2015). It is found at the center of all colonial settlements in Brazil. Its arrival on the beach is one step toward the dramatic climax. The pillory is raised, and finally Captain Martim Afonso declares the colony of São Vicente officially founded. Fireworks go off over the water, illuminating the entire bay, and a grand song-and-dance finale caps off the show. Brazil is born.

Ambivalent Origins

This spectacle is a twenty-first-century ritual retelling of the *bandeirantes* origin myth, and one key feature of the narrative is that João Ramalho and his offspring are portrayed as the original founders of the colony of São Vicente. The government and clergy arrive only after both Fernandes and Ramalho have established their own informal settlements, and the colonial villa of São Vicente survives because of the relationships these two marginal figures formed with the native populations. In this drama, sexual relationships between white men and native women predate the presence of the Portuguese state, and jokes about sex (not violence) between colonizer and colonized are a motif that ripples through the performance. In the reenactment, the Portuguese state never encompasses or controls the roguish outsiders. The *bandeirantes* reach an amicable, yet unsettled, peace with the colonial government and the Jesuits, all the while remaining partly separate from the state. The people—embodied by Ramalho and Fernandes—and the state are not, therefore, positioned as one and the same. They stand in an uneasy triangular relationship. The union between the natives and the *bandeirantes*, rather than the union between that natives and the church or state, is shown as the originative basis of modern Brazil.

In popular culture, João Ramalho is almost always depicted as the founding ancestor of the *bandeirantes*. He led the first expeditions into the interior of São Paulo to capture slaves, and his offspring are considered to be the founders of Piratininga, the village that grew into the city of São Paulo. For example, a 2016 article in the popular news magazine *Veja São Paulo* calls Ramalho "the chief and founder of Piratininga." It continues, "His remains can be found in the crypt of the Cathedral da Sé [the symbolic heart of São Paulo]. He died in 1580 at an advanced age. He is the founder of the dynasty of *mamelucos* who, in the following century, would gain fame in the commercial-military endeavor called the bandeira." This mainstream version of history describes Ramalho as the literal patriarch of São Paulo, the father of the *bandeirantes* who established the city and then fanned out into the interior in search of slaves and riches. This history tightly connects the founding of São Paulo to the *bandeirantes* and their offspring. National identity begins to emerge from a combination of violent racial mixture and lawlessness, rather than a pure or uncorrupted mission.

Ramalho is a good example of the *malandro*, a rogue figure that Roberto Da Matta identifies as one of the key symbols in Brazilian popular culture. Rogues are heroes with a lawless edge, men who succeed through cunning, dodging and skirting the rules to move through the system. Recall that both Fernandes and Ramalho (the two original *bandeirantes*) are treated as outcasts by the Portuguese captains. The former is thrown overboard, and the latter is marooned. As Ramalho sings in one of the scenes in the reenactment described above, "In Portugal, I was *degregado* [degraded]; but here, I am *amado* [loved]." In this myth of national origin, the patriarchs are not the Jesuits, the navigators, or the colonial gentry. They are the rogues who married native women, became "white chiefs," and coexisted in a fragile peace with the newly arrived Portuguese.

While I recognize that this reenactment is only one popularized variant of the national origin myth, many scholars have argued that Brazilian history is marked by an ambivalent relationship between white settlers and Amerindians that makes Brazil somewhat unique among countries in the Americas. On the one hand, Brazil celebrates and promotes the contributions of its indigenous population more than many other settler countries, particularly the United States. Brazil's 1988 constitution guarantees indigenous populations rights to their own territories, and the country has set aside more land as indigenous reserves than any other in the world. The Yanomami territory alone is larger than the country of France. There is a national "Day of the Indian" on April 19, the day before the Portuguese discovery is commemorated, and children learn about the country's indigenous peoples throughout their education. The reenactment, though simplistic in many ways, spends more time on the dramatization of indigenous cosmology than it does on either Christianity or Portuguese history. It places the histories of a number of indigenous populations front and center in the narrative of national origins. The natives do not appear as victims or passive "helpers" on the path to modernity. While one could certainly criticize how the native Brazilians are portrayed, they are far from invisible or marginal to the drama. Moving from the level of ritual to politics, the politics of indigenous peoples are part of everyday Brazilian discourse (in newspapers, on television, etc.) in a way that makes them highly visible in public culture.

On the other hand, there is a glaring silence about the genocide committed against native populations and the ongoing dispossession and destruction of their ways of life that has occurred as Brazilian capitalism encroaches ever more on indigenous territories in the Amazon and elsewhere. Brazilian national identity is founded on what Da Matta calls the "fable of three races," a narrative that produces a unitary Brazilian-ness out of a set of three different yet complementary races—white, black, and Indian. Da Matta (Hess and Da Matta 1995) argues that this "ideological pact hides or disguises differences" (273), making Brazilian race relations more harmonious than the "exclusionary" system found in the United States.[10] His analysis is based on an implicit comparison with the United States, where assimilation means the creation of a unified body politic out of differences (*e pluribus unum*). Historically, this attitude has created an exclusive racial logic that denies or downplays racial mixture in the United States. At a deeper cultural level, Da Matta argues that American identity emphasizes unity and oneness over contradiction and ambiguity. In Brazil, on the other hand, the encompassing cultural value is complementary hierarchy, in which fundamental differences (based on race and class) are never assimilated into "one" body politic. Instead, underlying differences are coordinated into a stable, yet fundamentally hierarchical, relationship. The Indian is therefore an important part of Brazil's mainstream national identity, but Brazilians can simultaneously deny the presence of Indians as active historical agents and victims of the civilizing process. Indians are not invisible, but they are set apart from the Brazilian mainstream in both space and time. They exist "out there," in remote regions or as relics of a treasured past.

Alcida Ramos (2008) puts it brilliantly:

> Brazil's origin myth indulges the Indian with the honor of ancestor of its citizenry. Together with African slaves and Portuguese colonizers, autochthonous [indigenous] Indians added their blood to the melting pot that boiled down to a unique Brazilian identity. It should not go unnoticed that this myth or fable of the three races is mute about the toll the Indians paid in territory to the new country. Touchy as it has been and continues to be, the issue of indigenous territories is no subject for fables. With the government having set aside about 13 percent of the country's territory for the exclusive and permanent use of the Indians, a national cliché has it that there is too much land for so few Indians. In the past, as in the present, the national economic frontier respects no borders, and invasions of indigenous lands are a recurring strife in the countryside. In turn, Indian blood as heritage is somewhat of an abstraction with no material cost and is even cause for a certain folkloric pride inscribed in the common gag that one's Indian grandmother was caught in the woods with a lasso and then had her blood transfused to generations of Brazilians. (13)

Ramos's analysis highlights the fact that violence against Indians by the *bandeirantes* is assimilated into a mainstream narrative. The joke about the lasso—and the "folkloric pride" it indexes—is a direct reference to the *bandeirantes* story, in which Indians were literally captured, tied up, and brought into white "civilization." As Ramos points out, this founding moment of violence is not repressed or viewed as a shameful historical inheritance—it is referenced in everyday conversation. As recently as 1935, Claude Lévi-Strauss wrote that "a favorite pastime [of Brazilians one generation older than he] was to collect infected garments of smallpox victims from the hospitals and hang them, together with other gifts, on the paths still frequented by the Indian tribes" (49).[11]

A major difference between the United States and Brazil is that racial mixture is almost invisible in American national mythology, whereas it is present in the earliest stages of Brazil's origin myth, and powerfully reproduced on the beaches of São Vicente each year. It would be hard to imagine a popular reenactment of the story of the Pilgrims in Plymouth or John Smith and Pocahontas in Virginia, in which intermarriage between Europeans and Native Americans was placed front and center in the narrative. It would be almost unthinkable within the cultural logics of American race relations, which tend to downplay or avoid the fact of racial mixture, and would be unlikely to contain the ribald references to sexual conquest found in Brazilian popular culture, where stories of the violent capture of native peoples and sexual violence against them are woven into the *bandeirantes* story and reproduced with folkloric pride.

From Myth to Reality

With the founding of Tekoa Paranapuã by native people who arrived from all over Brazil and Paraguay to participate in the ritual retelling of a myth, these natives now occupy the timescape of history, actively participating in political and social life in São Vicente. It would be hard to imagine a more apt setting for a clash between the Indians of myth and the indigenous peoples of reality. After the first large-scale performance of the reenactment ended in 2004, the Guaraní who were hired as actors remained in Paranapuã, a vacant area that had been demarcated as a park by the state of São Paulo in the 1990s and was, at that time, managed by the state forest service. The village was settled by members of two Guaraní subgroups, the Mbyá and the Nhandeva, who are classified by anthropologists as distinct populations yet have intermarried and resided together in villages throughout São Paulo state over the past twenty years. The Guaraní are historically a nomadic population, so it is difficult to define a specific territory as their "ancestral homeland." In fact, this is a matter of great debate among anthropologists. Some argue that the Guaraní homeland follows a pre-Columbian pilgrimage route from Central Brazil to Cuzco, Peru, a distance of several thousand miles. It is possible, though by no means certain, that some of their ancestors once resided in the area around Santos before the arrival of the Europeans. However, both the Mbyá and Nhandeva populations were mainly located in Paraguay and the western edge of the Brazilian state of Paraná until the past thirty years, according to the extensive record of ethnographic studies of the group. This record goes back almost a hundred years and includes work by some of the most influential scholars in South American ethnology, including Curt Nimuendajú, León Cadogan, Alfred Métraux, Hélène Clastres, James Howe, David Maybury-Lewis, and Egon Schaden. Both the Mbyá and the Nhandeva have progressively moved east from the interior of Brazil and Paraguay toward the coast over the past hundred years (Shapiro 1987). Nimuendajú (born Curt Unkel), a German who became one of the founding figures of South American ethnology, helped to establish a reserve for the Guaraní in Bauru, a city in the interior of São Paulo state, in 1912. Bauru was a small outpost in the middle of coffee plantations at that time, and now it is a bustling city of more than three hundred thousand inhabitants (and, as described in chapter 5, is also the hometown of Pelé). Many Guaraní bands left the reserve over the years and moved eastward toward the coast. At present, there are more than twenty-five Guaraní villages scattered throughout the São Paulo coastal region, more than five hundred miles from the Paraguayan border area where they resided a century ago.

The question of whether the Santos and São Vicente region could be considered an ancestral home of the Guaraní became a hotly contested issue. In general, the politics of indigenous land claims are extremely fraught in contemporary Brazil. The 1988 Brazilian Constitution guarantees native populations the right to lands that were necessary to reproduce their cultural and physical way of life (Carneiro da Cunha et al. 2017). The national indigenous agency, FUNAI, was responsible for the demarcation of indigenous territories, and it relied on professional anthropologists to help determine the territorial boundaries. One problem was that the system relied on a concept called "temporalization," which required indigenous populations to have a documented history of habitation in a particular territory prior to the passage of the 1988 constitution. This policy put two categories of indigenous people at a legal disadvantage: nomadic groups, who did not inhabit any ancestral territory for long periods of time and therefore did not formulate their identity around a connection to land; and groups who had been forcibly settled into small reservations in the twentieth century, had already suffered a violent loss of land, and were now fighting for the preservation of small patches of land that were in no way proportional to the lands they occupied under their precolonial way of life. Without claims to continuously inhabited territories or a pristine, traditional way of life, nomads and forcibly assimilated peoples faced legal challenges in their attempts to make land claims.

The Guaraní in São Vicente belonged to both of these disadvantaged categories. They had been resettled into reservations as Brazil expanded in the early twentieth century, and, more recently, they lived a seminomadic existence, moving from settlement to settlement around São Paulo state. This history placed them in a precarious position with regard to land claims. How could a nomadic group that had only inhabited the land in São Vicente for about a decade make a claim to demarcate their land as an indigenous reserve? Adding to the problem was the physical setting of their village. Paranapuã was directly across a small bay, less than a thousand feet wide, from Millionaire's Beach on Porchat Island, home to some of the most prized real estate in all of Brazil. Separated from the rest of São Vicente by a small causeway, Porchat Island is home to expensive apartments and the exclusive Porchat Island Club, which was a famous symbol of Brazilian glitz and excess in the 1980s, when the club's South Seas Ball would be televised nationwide and attended by celebrities such as Pelé. Atop Porchat Island's summit sits Oscar Niemeyer's dramatic high-modernist sculpture commemorating five hundred years since the European discovery of Brazil, adjacent to an elegant mountaintop restaurant with a terrace overlooking the ocean. The sculpture, an abstract concrete sail that recalls the sails of the arriving Portuguese ships, is in a state of crumbling disrepair. It looks out over the very place where the "discovery" (and the reenactment) took place. Symbolically, it is as if the Brazilian modernist project is itself looking down on its past. This modernist memorial in the middle of luxury high-rises looms over a village of Amerindians who are in the process of being dispossessed.

During the boom years of the 2000s, there was an explosion in real estate development along the São Paulo coast, as high-rise towers sprouted up on almost every available piece of land. The cities of Santos and São Vicente made big investments in infrastructure and services to support tourism, a large part of which was devoted to the cleanup of their notoriously polluted beaches (see chapter 4). This was part of a broader effort to promote environmental quality throughout the region and to change its image as a heavily polluted area that was, to say the least, not known for pristine natural beauty. As the bay was cleaned up and more people (especially retirees) began to buy up land around the region, residents and tourists began to use the small beaches and coves around Paranapuã for surfing, kayaking, and other aquatic recreation. A neglected space that only a decade earlier had been home to a juvenile prison was transforming into a leisure space. The trash around the village, as well as the ugly and unsettling abandoned prison, became a major cause of embarrassment. In the mid-1990s, the small peninsula around the village was established as a São Paulo state park, which protected about two thousand acres of land from future development. By the mid-2000s, when the Guaraní arrived, the park had not yet been developed for visits by the public (it did not yet have trails, signage, or facilities), but it was protected from private construction by law. In practice, it was essentially vacant land, yet it was legally designated as a park, to be built in the future.

As the value of and demand for coastal real estate skyrocketed in the mid-2000s, the problems of pollution, aesthetics, indigenous peoples, and the environment became oddly linked in public accounts of Paranapuã. In 2015, FUNAI issued the report "Reflections on the Trash in Paranapuã Village," which stated that the Guaraní, a nomadic people, did not place a high cultural value on disposing of garbage because they were not accustomed to a sedentary lifestyle and had only been utilizing consumer products that created trash for a short period of time. The municipal government of São Vicente and the state of São Paulo saw this as a problem because the village was in the middle of a "zone of environmental protection" that was being harmed by organic and inorganic refuse left behind by the villagers. The Guaraní were also accused of cutting down trees and using natural resources from a protected zone for homes, firewood, and crafts. In 2015, the designation of the land as an environmental protection zone became the linchpin in an ongoing legal case to forcibly evict the Guaraní from the land. When I tried to visit the park in June 2016, the case was still not closed. In January of that year, a judge had issued an order of eviction ruling that the Guaraní had to leave the park, but the removal had not yet been carried out when I was conducting my research.

In contemporary Brazil, much of the debate around the rights of indigenous populations focuses on land rights. As the economy boomed, fueled by the production of agricultural commodities such as soy, sugar, coffee, and beef, demand for land also boomed. Land values went up everywhere but especially in the exploding frontier regions in the Cerrado and the Amazon. Indigenous territories were being invaded or illegally violated by settlers and investors, and the legal demarcation of indigenous lands (*demarcacão*) became the most effective way for Indians to fight off the invasion of Brazilian capitalism.

In 2008, the wealthiest man in Brazil, Eike Batista, sought to build a high-tech "superport" to improve shipping logistics on the São Paulo coast. He planned to invest several billion dollars in the project to create a port that was as large as Santos and could accommodate oil tankers and larger ships, to speed the flow of goods in and out of the region. At first, Batista planned to construct the port in a coastal town to the north of Santos. Later, he changed the plan to a small town about twenty miles to the south. Both towns were home to Guaraní villages. Indeed, they were the places from which some of the actors in the reenactment had come. In both towns, the indigenous communities, along with allied activists, successfully resisted Batista's project. Working with FUNAI, these communities attained legal demarcation of nearly three thousand hectares of land. President Dilma Rousseff signed the order in May 2016.

April 19, the Day of the Indian, is a Brazilian national holiday during which many indigenous groups hold public marches and protests in defense of land rights. In 2016, at the height of the legal drama over eviction from Paranapuã, local indigenous groups planned for a march in front of the Santos municipal government building. On the day of the march, construction crews working on the new light-rail system to link Santos and São Vicente ruptured a water main, flooding the street where the march was to take place, and the march was cancelled. On the one day that native peoples are given center stage, they were pushed out by the construction of infrastructure. This time they were not flooded by a dam or evicted from a park, but instead, they were obstructed by the newest, most modern train system in all of Brazil.[12]

Challenging the *Bandeirantes* Attitude

There is no doubt that the myth of the *bandeirantes* retains cultural significance in contemporary Brazil, but at the same time, there is an increasingly visible movement for indigenous rights that explicitly challenges the hegemony of the *bandeirantes* narrative. Anthropologists are often at the forefront of this movement to decolonize Brazilian history, playing an important public role in the indigenous rights movement in Brazil as advocates for land claims and as recognized legal experts in matters of cultural rights. Many Brazilians I met assumed I was working with native populations (though I was not) because the role of the anthropologist as an advocate for indigenous rights is widely recognized in public discourse.

In a "Sunday chat" in a Santos newspaper in 2015, Cristiano Hutter, the regional representative for FUNAI, assessed the situation:

> Indigenous lands are hyper-coveted by the real estate sector, which includes the majority of local mayors of municipalities on the coast. It's natural that municipalities would be opposed to these indigenous lands. That is to say, the Indians are really nice and cute when they are at a distance, near the mountains, but when they start to come to the side of the highway, alongside the beaches, that won't work because of the real estate questions. But the people have their lands because they invaded indigenous lands.[13]

In a 2016 public hearing on the status of the Paranapuã case, a protestor held a sign that said, "Yesterday, Bandeirantes. Today Alckmin," a reference to then governor of São Paulo state, Geraldo Alckmin. In 2013, a group of about four thousand people led by a Guaraní advocacy organization marched from Avenida Paulista, in downtown São Paulo, to a large stone *bandeirantes* monument in Ibirapuera Park. This granite sculpture, over sixty feet in length, was commissioned in the 1920s but not inaugurated until 1953. It depicts a group of people, including whites, blacks, and Indians, pushing and dragging a ship while chained to two figures on horseback who lead them. During the protest, the Guaraní group painted parts of the statue red: "Que representa o sangue dos nossos antepassados, que foi derramado pelos bandeirantes, dos quais os brancos parecem ter tanto orgulho." ("That represents the blood of our ancestors, which was spilled by the *bandeirantes*, about whom the whites seem to have so much pride.") The protest was against a proposed change in the legislation of indigenous land claims that would shift the authority to approve the demarcation of Indian lands from the executive branch (the president and appointed cabinet ministers) to the legislative branch, which was dominated by the interests of *ruralistas* (large agribusiness interests), who were constantly (and often violently) opposed to Indian land claims. The proposal passed in 2017, and it was widely seen as a move that weakened the authority of FUNAI and other allies of native peoples. The *ruralistas* frequently and proudly associate themselves with the *bandeirantes*, as the modern incarnation of people who expanded the frontiers of Brazilian capitalism by subduing nature and indigenous peoples in the name of progress.

Another Maracanã Village?

The story of Paranapuã is eerily similar to one of the most famous cases of eviction in recent Brazilian history, which took place at Aldeia Maracanã (Maracanã Village) in Rio de Janeiro during preparations for the 2014 World Cup. Maracanã Village was "the occupation of an abandoned public building in Rio de Janeiro evicted in 2013. The crumbling nineteenth-century palace, next door to the iconic Maracanã football stadium, had served as the headquarters of the first organ of the Brazilian government dedicated to indigenous policy and then as Museum of the Indian" (Danowski and Viveiros de Castro 2016, 150). The museum had been relocated and the building had been occupied by indigenous people in 2006. After the government falsely claimed the building needed to be demolished to comply with demands from FIFA (the governing body of international soccer), the occupiers were evicted. In both cases (Maracanã and São Vicente), indigenous people occupied spaces in coastal cities that celebrated Indians as parts of Brazilian cultural heritage (in the museum and the reenactment, respectively). The Guaraní in Sao Vicente were, in essence, evicted from their own commemoration, and the indigenous people of Aldeia Maracanã were evicted from the very site that had sought to celebrate their place in Brazilian society. Both groups occupied spaces that became valuable for real estate development and grand nationalist spectacles, making the groups targets for eviction. It makes sense, therefore, that Danowski and Viveiros de Castro would assert "Brazil is an enormous Aldeia Maracanã" (122). The entire country was being developed for capitalism on a spectacular scale, and small groups of people who were trying to find spaces to live differently were considered out of place and treated as obstacles to progress.

The rejection of the *bandeirantes* attitude, viewed as part of a broad movement to decolonize Brazilian history, exemplifies my central argument about progress. It is a movement to resignify certain historical events that have been placed within a mythic chronotope. This movement, which might be considered a politics of temporality or "chronopolitics" (Innerarity 2012), takes place alongside the unfolding everyday struggles of the Guaraní to survive in modern Brazil. Certainly, there are moments of unity between the chronopolitical struggle over the meanings of progress and the political struggle over how to live, but it is also true that the two struggles occupy two different levels of temporality. In the next chapter, I apply a similar template to Brazil's coffee economy, showing a clash between ongoing changes in the coffee industry and a historical understanding of coffee as a part of Brazil's past that has been surpassed on the march to progress.

COFFEE OF THE PAST, COFFEE OF THE FUTURE

Two Timescapes of Export Agriculture

"The origin of the Port of Santos is linked to coffee. From the mid-1870s on, the culture of coffee was growing constantly, moving and promoting the economic development of the State of São Paulo."

—Promotional flyer from the Port of Santos, 2016

In the previous chapter, the presence of indigenous people as political actors disrupted a myth of national origins in which the Guaraní were relegated to the past. In this chapter, the presence of the contemporary, high-tech coffee economy disrupts the myth that the "era of coffee" was an episode in Brazil's agricultural past that has been left behind by the new, modern Brazil. Once again, two timescapes exist alongside one another, rarely in dialogue, and sometimes in conflict. Santos, as both a historical port and a twenty-first-century hub of the coffee trade, is a contact zone between these two chronotopes: the coffee of the past versus the coffee of the present. Nowhere is this clash more visible than in the Santos Coffee Museum and the surrounding industrial port, where the disjuncture between the "coffee of myth" and the "coffee of reality" is analogous, with almost exquisite symmetry, to the example of the Guaraní on the beaches of São Vicente. With both coffee and the Guaraní, a continuously evolving, dynamic presence in contemporary Brazil is symbolically transformed into an outmoded historical stage in Brazil's epic march to modernity. With coffee, as with the story of the Guarani, a variant of the *bandeirantes* myth has served as the framing trope of progress. Coffee production in Brazil has changed dramatically over time, but divergent modes of production are assimilated into the *bandeirantes* plot—different content, same form.

It makes sense for a chapter on coffee to follow a chapter about Brazilian colonialism, because the rise of Brazil's coffee economy is often thought of as the next major episode in the country's great drama of historical development after the end of Portuguese colonialism. When Brazilian students learn about their country's history, they study a series of economic cycles. The "cycle of coffee" is a stage that comes after the "cycle of cotton" and the "cycle of gold," running from about 1830 until the Great Depression. Look at any Brazilian history textbook (or even Wikipedia) and you will find the "cycle of coffee" as a defining element of the nineteenth and early twentieth centuries, a pivotal stage in the country's march to progress.[1] The coffee cycle is always followed by the "cycle of industry," beginning with the development of national oil and steel industries under President Getúlio Vargas in the twentieth century. The irony of chopping up history into these discrete episodes is that Brazil has continued to be the world's dominant coffee producer well into the twenty-first century, and large-scale coffee production is constantly expanding into new, peripheral regions. The cycle of coffee did not end with the onset of industrialization, despite the "fields-to-factories" vision of modernization, which sees agriculture as a stage that must be surpassed on the march to modernity. In both popular memory and school curricula, coffee is a thing of the past. Agriculture defines the nineteenth century, industry the twentieth. But from the vantage point of the world's coffee industry, Brazilian coffee is very much a thing of the present and the future, and profits from big agriculture continue to drive urban growth in Santos.[2]

Coffee as Object of Production or Consumption?

Brazil remains the world's largest producer of coffee by volume. In 2018, the country produced more than sixty million sixty-kilogram bags of coffee, enough to supply about one pound of coffee to every person on earth. Brazil produced almost double the amount grown in Vietnam, which is the world's second largest producer. As an old pop song by Frank Sinatra ("The Coffee Song") put it, "They've got an awful lot of coffee in Brazil." Yet it would be a mistake to view Brazilian coffee through a simple twentieth-century "dependency" lens, under which relatively poor countries in the Global South toil to meet the needs of relatively wealthy countries in the North. The export market is certainly important to Brazil, but Brazilians consumed twenty-two million bags of coffee in 2018, placing the country just behind the United States (twenty-six million bags) in the ranking of national coffee consumption by volume. Brazil has developed a new form of superproductive agribusiness that is now at the core of the coffee industry. Plantations located in immense frontier regions have become extraordinarily efficient since the 1990s, a development that popular observers have referred to as a second Green Revolution. The first Green Revolution, which took place across the developing world during the Cold War, relied upon technological inputs like fertilizers and hybrid seed to rapidly improve agricultural productivity. The second Green Revolution has used biotechnology and soil science to make Brazil the dominant force in the twenty-first-century coffee trade. In the process, Brazilian producers have combined the scale and productivity of agribusiness with the traits and qualities of high-end specialty coffees.

The Port of Santos is where the vast majority of this coffee is exported from, yet, as a physical commodity, coffee is almost completely invisible in Santos except as a drink to be consumed. The technological sophistication of the logistics industry, including containerization and the mechanized loading and unloading of trucks and ships, means all objects that pass through the Port of Santos are more or less homogenous. Scanning the port, an observer would have no way of knowing whether a warehouse holds coffee, corn, sugar, or grain. I spent four months in the port, and I only saw physical coffee once, stacked in a warehouse. You can smell roasting coffee constantly, because a large domestic coffee roaster, Café Floresta, is located very close to the port, but physical unroasted coffee beans are hard to come by.

In the days before container shipping, unroasted "green" coffee would be visible everywhere. Jute bags would be stacked on trucks and wagons, moved by mules and men onto ships. Huge warehouses would hold coffee in sacks until it was ready to be loaded on board. An entire economy of bag stitchers, carters, stevedores, brokers, traders, and inspectors interacted in the port. These days, coffee rarely touches human hands from the time it is harvested until the time it is roasted. For that reason, coffee is ubiquitous as a consumer product, but it is almost completely invisible as a tradeable commodity in the present.[3] However, as an artifact of history, the story of coffee is almost unavoidable in Santos.

The Coffee Museum is the most well-known tourist attraction in downtown Santos. Housed in the historic Santos coffee exchange, a lavish Beaux Arts building that opened in 1922 and functioned for a mere seven years before closing after the 1929 stock market crash, the museum tells the story of how Brazil came to be the world's leading coffee producer in the late nineteenth century. The Coffee Museum opened in 2008 as part of the Alegra Centro urban redevelopment plan, a multimillion-dollar program to revitalize the Santos downtown by transforming decaying old properties and slums into a zone for historical tourism. Alongside the museum sits the 15th of November Street, a narrow cobblestone corridor that was converted into a pedestrian-only street with a plan to develop bars and restaurants to attract crowds at night. Prior to the redevelopment, the downtown area was mostly empty after businesses closed for the day, except for sex workers and a small number of people living precariously in buildings in various states of neglect. In addition to the new development, the old streetcar system, the *bonde*, which had been out of service for decades, was restarted for historical tours rather than transportation. Tourists could ride the old-time trolley around the neighborhood while a guide in an old-fashioned uniform pointed out the historical sites. The Alegra Centro redevelopment plan sought to repackage the Santos downtown as a historical relic that harkened back to a golden age of coffee capitalism in the city, and the museum was the centerpiece. Cobblestone streets, a quaint streetcar, and restored Beaux Arts buildings would give a patina of history to the revived downtown—a future with a clear reference to the past.

These days, most downtown redevelopment plans across the world involve coffee shops, which have become icons of upper-class consumer capitalism and urban gentrification. The cafeteria in the entrance to the Santos museum sells a variety of high-end coffees from around Brazil to a mixed crowd of tourists and local businesspeople, many of whom work in the international coffee industry, which is centered in the streets around the museum. Several of the world's major coffee trading companies have small offices near the museum, including Mitsui Foods, Neumann Kaffee Gruppe, Volcafé, and Louis Dreyfus Commodities. These are companies that trade and ship large volumes of coffee to supply all the major consumer brands. Employees of the nearby coffee firms frequent the museum coffee shop, which is the only specialty coffee purveyor in the neighborhood and one of the few contemporary-style coffee shops, as opposed to the blue-collar bars and *lanchonetes* found on every block. At these establishments, people can buy a simple *cafezinho* made from Brazilian "industrial" coffee, but downtown Santos is not a place where they can find specialty coffees. The only Starbucks is located in Praiamar, the huge shopping mall about a mile from downtown, in an area that caters to wealthier residents of beachfront neighborhoods. For workers in downtown Santos who want something other than the "industrial" coffee that is available everywhere, the museum coffee shop is the place to go. It is open to the public, and the museum itself is sparsely attended, so the coffee shop functions more like a local gathering spot for businesspeople than a tourist trap.

In this space, there are three different timescapes of coffee intermingling with each other. In timescape one, the mythic timescape, coffee is a part of Brazil's national drama. It provides subject matter for the museum, where it is presented as a prior stage in Brazil's history. Coffee is also a part of the future, with the museum serving as a tourist attraction that will anchor a redevelopment scheme designed to make downtown Santos part of a "new economy," with the help of professional middle-class consumers and tourists. In timescape two, coffee is an object of consumption or production in the present. It is a drink that provides pleasure, sustenance, community, and cultural capital. It is also an instrument of production, a tradeable commodity upon which an entire economic system depends.[4] When I describe coffee as part of Santos's imagined future, I am referring to something more abstract and metahistorical—the idea that the presence of specialty coffee shops and the Coffee Museum will serve as attractions to make the Santos downtown more appealing to upper-class consumers. In this third timescape, coffee will help move Santos into a future in which consumption replaces production. Coffee as a part of capitalist work is turned into coffee as a part of capitalist play. Tourism, leisure, and consumption, alongside a "new" knowledge economy, will replace the work, production, and manual labor of the "old" economy.

Coffee *Bandeirantes*

The *bandeirantes* are at the center of the Coffee Museum. The main salon of the building once housed the coffee trading floor, where brokers met to establish the daily market price for both physical coffee lots and coffee futures. The original marble trading floor and an old chalkboard used to mark prices sit at the center of the room. The salon's ceiling (fig. 4) is covered by a lavish stained-glass tableau based on a painting by Benedicto Calixto, the most famous landscape painter of Belle Époque São Paulo. There is no better illustration of how coffee fits into the story of national progress than this ceiling.[5]

FIGURE 4. "Epic of the Bandeirantes" stained glass (Photo by author, 2016)

The ceiling is called "The Epic of the Bandeirantes" and is divided into three panels, with each representing a "cycle," or an episode of the epic. The central panel is "The Colonial Period, The Conquest of the Backlands by the Bandeirantes" (1560–1721). It shows a vision of Anhanguera, a legendary *bandeirante* named Bartolomeu Bueno da Silva (1672–1740) who left São Paulo to find gold, precious stones, and Indian captives. According to legend, Anhanguera (also called the "old devil") went searching for the mines of Goiás, which were guarded by nymphs and the "mother of water," who would not let the white Brazilians enter the mines. According to the legend, the *bandeirantes* used their knowledge of fire to scare the natives into revealing the location of the mines, and they returned to São Paulo with untold riches. In some tellings, these riches were confiscated by the colonial treasury, leaving the *bandeirantes* destitute and solidifying their position as roguish rivals of the colonial government. It is this fiery legend that is depicted in the central panel of the ceiling, showing a terrified Indian fleeing in fear from the flames, a central episode in the Anhanguera myth. Thus, the first scene in the *bandeirantes* myth is about the violent capture of Indians and the pursuit of gold and jewels.

The second panel is "The Cycle of Agriculture and Abundance" (1822–1889). It begins when coffee was introduced into São Paulo state and ends with the abolition of slavery. According to the artist's 1922 description of his work, the *bandeirantes* returned from their adventures to settle down and establish plantations. Using slave labor, they learned to cultivate "all the rich products of the farm: coffee, cotton, alcohol, sugar, corn, beans, rice, etc."[6] The artwork depicts sacks overflowing with these products, while the new plantation homes sit in the background surrounded by verdant fields. Sacks of coffee, flour, sugar, cotton, and beans surround a treasure chest of gold. One of the sacks reads, "Gold is what gold is worth," a line from Saint Paul's letters to the Corinthians. In this episode of the *bandeirantes* epic, the source of wealth transforms from Indian slaves and precious metals to the new "treasure" of agricultural products.

The third cycle depicts the period of "Industry and Commerce." It shows the climax of the epic of progress, with steamships loaded with coffee and the new coffee exchange building representing the triumph of industry. It includes symbols of capital (a safe and a bank note) as well as labor (white dockworkers and the wheel of a cart). In the background, flying above the docks is an airplane, representing the achievements of one of the fathers of modern aviation, Alberto Santos Dumont, a Brazilian from Santos who was heir to one of the world's largest coffee fortunes. At the time the ceiling was made (1922), Santos Dumont would have been one of the most famous people in the world, and the age of aviation was considered the pinnacle of progress. The fact that he came from a family of Brazilian coffee barons cemented the link between coffee and progress. In the ceiling's depiction, coffee wealth literally created modern technological innovations. In this final episode, modern export agriculture replaces the old plantation system. Piles of money replace sacks of gold and agricultural products. The era of capital had arrived in Santos, and coffee was its source. Condensed into a simple formula, coffee equals capitalism equals modernity equals progress.

In the era of "national" coffee, in which foreign capital became associated with dependency, the *bandeirantes* narrative was used by President Vargas to promote Brazilian nationalism. He called the process of colonizing the interior of Brazil the "March to the West" and frequently invoked the *bandeirantes* as a model for the development of new agricultural regions. During the first Green Revolution, the high modernist government used the *bandeirantes* myth to describe the builders of Brasília, who were "collectively called bandeirantes of the twentieth century, after the adventurers who had first penetrated the interior. The label was intended as a compliment, inasmuch as [President] Kubitschek's Brasilia was also a symbolic conquest of the interior in a nation that had historically clung to the shoreline" (Scott 1998, 129).

In the present, there is no doubt that the spirit of the *bandeirantes* continues to inform the expansion of coffee capitalism into the interior. As Viveiros de Castro put it in the 2014 interview mentioned earlier:

> Brazil continues as a peripheral country, a "high tech" plantation that supplies central capitalism with raw materials. We live by exporting our land and our water in the form of soy, sugar, beef, to industrialized countries. . . . In an unfortunate continuity between the geopolitics of the dictatorship and that of the current government, this is the old "bandeirantismo" that is now part of the national project.[7] The formal political conditions have changed, but the image of what Brazilian civilization is or should be, of what a life worth living is, of what a society is in tune with itself is very, very similar.

Viveiros de Castro bluntly makes the case that the attitude of *bandeirantismo* continues to reverberate through the present stage of agro-industrial expansion. My central assertion is that this new *bandeirantismo* in the countryside is paralleled by a new model of urban developmentalism that pushes agriculture into the past. The tension between these two models of progress—one urban and one rural—creates the clash of timescapes between coffee of the past and coffee of the present.

Colonial Coffee

The story of coffee in Brazil is indeed epic. It is one of the most significant political economic transformations in the history of transatlantic capitalism. In a mere 150 years, Brazil went from having not a single coffee plant to being the world's dominant coffee producer. This was a transformation that created commercial connections across the Atlantic world. Coffee turned São Paulo from a backwater into one of the world's great cities. Coffee grown in the interior of São Paulo was shipped from Santos across the globe, making the port one of the most important nodes in the network of global capitalism. Immigrants poured into Santos, seeking work in the coffee fields. Money flowed from London, New York, and Hamburg to finance the coffee business. The city of São Paulo became Brazil's financial and industrial hub, largely due to the fact that the air and climate on the plateau atop the Serra do Mar was far more "sanitary" than the swampy, tropical lowlands of Santos. But while São Paulo may have been the financial hub, the port was the nexus for the movement of goods and money, connected by rail to the city. Without Santos, there would be no São Paulo, and coffee was the commodity that launched the region into modernity.

Coffee is not indigenous to Brazil, and there is a well-known fable about how it arrived. As the story goes, in 1727 a staff sergeant in the Portuguese colonial army named Francisco de Mello Palheta was sent by the governor of Maranhão (now a state in northern Brazil) on a secret mission to the French colony of Guyana. Palheta's official charge was to map and explore the boundary between Portuguese and French colonial holdings that had been established by the Treaty of Utrecht, but his other mission was to steal a treasured coffee plant from the French. At that time, France was the world's leading coffee producer, chiefly in its colony of Saint Domingue (now Haiti). The French were beginning to establish coffee plantations in Guyana, and they strictly prohibited the exchange of coffee plants with the rival Portuguese in Brazil. Using his bravery and cunning, Palheta supposedly seduced a beautiful daughter of a French colonial administrator into giving him an illicit coffee plant and seeds. He brought them back to Belém, the capital city of Pará, and coffee eventually found its way to the gardens of the colonial aristocracy in Rio, from which it propagated around the Paraíba Valley, the original center of the Brazilian coffee economy. Until the 1850s, Rio de Janeiro was the primary coffee port in Brazil, and it was a crop that was mainly produced by slaves on lands that were owned by colonial elites.

During the colonial period, Santos was a small settlement with relatively little commercial importance. It was separated from the rest of Brazil by the Serra do Mar, so people and goods could only be transported by boat along the Atlantic coast. The muddy estuary was not suitable for large international ships, so most trade within Brazil was conducted via small vessels. The ports of Rio and Bahia were then the focal points for foreign trade, and the main hubs for the export of sugar from the north and the importation of foreign goods. After its initial period of growth in the sixteenth century, led by the original *bandeirantes*, Santos fell into a period of decline through the seventeenth and eighteenth centuries. There was some small-scale commerce in mining, sugarcane, and the slave trade, but, for the most part, Santos was a sleepy colonial town with an economy based largely on fishing and small-scale agriculture, including the production of sugarcane liquor. Gonçalvez and Nunes (2008) write, "Without land for cane cultivation, far from the mining districts, abandoned by its own local population, Santos fell into stagnation that lasted until the 19th Century" (29). In the 1825 census, Santos had a population of fewer than five thousand people, 45 percent of whom were slaves (Read 2012, 47).

Two major changes occurred that catapulted Santos into modernity. First, in 1792, the governor of São Paulo constructed the Lorena pathway (*calcada lorena*), a cobblestone mule trail that scaled the mountains and connected Santos with Brazil's interior. This seemingly minor development was in fact a major milestone, allowing products from the interior to be shipped from a port other than Rio or Bahia. It was "a true 'export corridor' of its times, enough to move, with the support of teams of animals, the sugar produced in the interior" (Gonçalvez and Nunes 2008, 29). Sugar exportation from Santos began to grow, and other products began to move through the port of Valongo, which was then little more than some small wooden docks designed for fishing boats. The first shipment of coffee left for Lisbon in 1797 (ibid.), and some ships began to stop in Santos as they traveled along the Atlantic coast between Buenos Aires, Montevideo, and Rio. Keep in mind that all transcontinental commerce required a trip around Cape Horn during this period, so the small ports along the Atlantic were never truly isolated from global trade, as ships would frequently stop on the journey to the Pacific.

Nevertheless, Santos remained a port of minor importance until 1867, when the second major change occurred. The São Paulo Railway opened, linking the port with the rural hinterland and turning Santos into the central hub of the world coffee trade within twenty years. The pace of change was incredible—in only seventy years, Santos went from not even having a mule trail connecting to São Paulo to having a railway. In 1856, the imperial government issued a concession for the construction of a railroad to connect the coffee-rich interior of São Paulo with the Port of Santos. In 1867, after a decade of work, the Santos-Jundiaí railroad was completed by the São Paulo Railway Company. This engineering feat was financed by the Baron of Mauá, founder of the Bank of Brazil (and the so-called Rothschild of Brazil), and a consortium of Scottish investors. The railroad "tied the hinterland to the coast" and made export-coffee agriculture feasible at a large scale (Holloway 1980, 6). The railroad led to an astonishing period of growth in coffee production, as well the rapid deforestation of the interior of São Paulo state, and the death and displacement of native populations as coffee capitalism roared like a steam locomotive through the sparsely populated countryside.[8] In the years prior to abolition in 1888, these plantations shifted from the labor of enslaved people to a sharecropping system sustained by millions of immigrant sharecroppers from Europe and Asia, who were brought to Brazil as indentured workers of the coffee planters. Labor recruiters working on behalf of the coffee barons hired these workers from abroad and paid for their passage, which was then repaid through their labor on the share of the plantation for which they and their families were responsible. These sharecroppers were also given housing and small plots of land for household production.[9]

The construction of the railroad almost instantly made the São Paulo region into the world's coffee hub. By 1880, Brazil accounted for 65 percent of the world's total coffee production, and the vast majority of Brazil's crop passed through Santos. The decades between 1880 and the economic crash of 1929 are often thought of as the "golden age" for Santos, a time of unprecedented prosperity, urban growth, and modernization. Indeed, during those years, fortunes were made that played a powerful role in the history of transatlantic capitalism. This was also the period in which foreign capital came to dominate the coffee economy, with British, German, and American firms becoming the dominant force in the coffee trade. The rising power of foreign firms set the stage for their own undoing, however. In the early decades of the coffee boom, foreigners provided an influx of capital and technical knowledge to facilitate trade. Trading houses bought coffee from Brazilian plantation owners and exported it to affiliates throughout the world. This required capital (held in foreign currency), insurance and collateral against losses, and relationships with shipping firms and importers in ports all over the world. The first century of Brazilian coffee was highly dependent on this foreign capital. During the so-called Belle Époque of coffee, this dependency was thought of as something positive—a stepping stone to progress and a sign that Brazil was participating in the modern world of global commerce. By the twentieth century, the presence of foreign capital shifted from being the sine qua non of progress to its opposite—an obstacle to Brazilian autonomy.

Elite Transnationalism in the Belle Époque of Coffee

Before the abolition of slavery, the Portuguese colonial elite dominated the coffee trade. Owners of plantations in the Paraíba Valley and the northeast financed the early stages of coffee in São Paulo state. In this sense, wealth that originally was produced by slave labor in the colonial sugar plantations funded investment in the early stages of the coffee boom. Historians Warren Dean (1997) and John Monteiro (1985) have extensively documented the early stages of coffee in São Paulo, describing the incredible levels of forced labor and violence that were employed against native populations to transform a sparsely populated wilderness into a "sea of coffee." From the vantage point of Santos, the nineteenth century was an incredible boom period during which progress came in the form of foreign capitalists, who largely replaced Brazilian colonial elites as the major players in the coffee trade or entered into joint ventures with the old aristocracy to finance new investments in coffee. The German firm Theodor Wille and Sons was the largest coffee trader in Santos until World War II. After the war, the American firms Leon Israel and Anderson Clayton were the two largest trading houses, but there were hundreds of other exporters from all over the world with shipping offices in Santos. While there were certainly some points of conflict between foreigners and Brazilians in the upper echelons of society in Santos, both groups were part of a headlong rush toward modernity.

Santos and Wall Street: An Origin Story

Over the course of my research in Santos, I spent many hot, lonely days pouring through the archives of the Santos Commercial Association. The association was completely dominated by the demands of the port and the coffee industry for much of its history. The newsletters, yearbooks, and reports from the association provided a fascinating viewpoint on what life was like for the coffee elite of the Belle Époque, documenting how foreign capitalists profited off of Brazilian coffee and just how central Santos was to the transatlantic coffee trade, creating wealth that helped to form some of the world's most powerful financial institutions, including Goldman Sachs.

The year was 1920, and Leon Israel and his brothers Adolph and Achille were living like royalty in Santos. Leon, an American, was the son of a French coffee merchant who had immigrated to New Orleans and started a coffee business there. Leon and his brothers in turn founded Leon Israel and Brothers Exporters, which grew to become one of the leading coffee traders in all of Brazil, exporting five hundred thousand sacks of coffee from the docks of Santos to their affiliated import houses in New Orleans and New York by 1920. A second company, A. C. Israel, was led by Adolph Israel. A third man from New Orleans, Jacob "Jack" Aron, was married to Leon Israel's sister Hortense, and he, too, ran a successful coffee import/export business in Santos named J. Aron, with import branch offices on New York City's Wall Street and in New Orleans.

Jack Aron held a seat on the New York Coffee and Sugar Exchange, allowing him to combine his knowledge of the supply side (Brazil) and the demand side (New York) of the coffee market. The extended Israel-Aron family therefore had both sides of the coffee business covered: Aron would receive information about coffee supplies from his relatives in Santos, and they, in turn, could learn about market conditions and demand in New York from Aron. The famous "Santos-to-New York run" (Roseberry 1996, 767) for the physical transport of coffee along the Atlantic seaboard had a financial analog between firms in downtown Santos and Wall Street. Between the two Israel family companies and J. Aron, the extended family accounted for about one million bags of Brazilian coffee shipped to New York in 1919 (*Tea and Coffee Journal* 1920, 184). After World War II and the embargo on shipping to the Axis nations, Leon Israel became the leading coffee exporter in Santos, moving three million of the five million total bags shipped from Santos in the 1941–1942 crop year (Bacha and Greenhill 1993, 282).

The family eventually became a major force in the creation of the commodities futures industry in New York. Aron's company still exists as the commodities trading arm of Goldman Sachs, which acquired J. Aron in 1981.[10] Leon Israel's company eventually joined with his brother's firm and became ACLI, which was one of the largest commodity trading companies in the world until 1981, when it was acquired by the investment bank Donaldson, Lufkin, and Jenrette. By that time, ACLI owned commodities businesses all over the world and had branched off into private equity investing, acquiring the Lane Drug and Peoples Drug store chains in the United States. After the sale of ACLI, members of the Israel family continued to run a private equity firm, which still operates today.

In those early days of the coffee boom, Santos was a melting pot for the transatlantic mercantile elite and home to a casino, a golf course, and dozens of emporiums selling fine French wines, Italian silks, Cuban cigars, and even Neapolitan pizzas (Pedro 2015). With a steady stream of cargo ships unloading imported goods at the Valongo docks and reloading with coffee for export, Santos was a hub of global trade. However, the fault lines between Brazilian capital and foreign capital were beginning to emerge by the end of the nineteenth century. In the early decades of the coffee boom, Brazilian firms with roots in the colonial aristocracy were securely in control. The difficulties of transporting large volumes of coffee from the interior of Brazil to the port made it difficult for non-Brazilians to work independently. They needed a network of Brazilian intermediaries to facilitate the complicated movement of coffee from field to port.

This began to change by 1890, when the British trading firm E. Johnston and Sons created a modern "warehouse-warrant" system of purchase and sale, in which a coffee trading agent could give a grower a "warrant," or bill of sale, for a certain volume of coffee and then trade or use that warrant as collateral for financial transactions. This system introduced liquidity and facilitated financial speculation in coffee, making it easier for foreign firms to finance and trade coffee without relying on personal ties to Brazilian elites. The new system required financing in foreign currencies (stable cash reserves to back the warrants), which Brazilian elites generally did not have. German, British, and American firms began to take over, and Santos became a hub of both shipping and finance, with coffee as the source of virtually all the wealth.

In the early years, foreigners simply extended capital to the Brazilian growers in the interior. The foreigners purchased the coffee that moved in and out of Santos, but actual farming remained firmly in the hands of Brazilian landowners who worked through intermediaries to connect with foreign buyers. By the end of the nineteenth century, foreigners began to purchase land or directly finance plantations that they owned in the interior, integrating their operations from plantation to export. The Brazilian Warrant Company, Leon Israel, and the American cotton company Anderson Clayton were innovators in this regard. They started their own plantations in the interior, creating vertically integrated coffee operations that reached far into the Brazilian countryside. Foreign investors purchased land in western regions of São Paulo, eventually pioneering large-scale, capital-intensive coffee agriculture in the state of Paraná, particularly around the city of Londrina, in the 1940s and 1950s.[11] Between 1935 and 1953, the state of coffee production in Paraná increased tenfold, to five million bags per crop year (Dozier 1956). The vertical integration of the coffee trade created a tremendous boom in Brazilian coffee production, leading to severe overproduction that crashed the world market, and prices were ultimately regulated by the International Coffee Agreement.

Coffee Royalty

At the beginning of the twentieth century, the Santos coffee bourgeoisie was truly part of a transatlantic commercial elite, with strong connections throughout Europe and North America. Beyond their role in the actual trade of coffee, families like the Israels worked to transform Santos into a modern city with all the amenities of their hometowns. These tycoons brought the latest technologies to Santos, including automobiles, movie theaters, and hotels, and even built the city's first radio transmitter, which was created by a private group led by Achille Israel in 1925. The site of the radio transmitter is now a neighborhood called Radio Club (written in English), which is home to some of the largest informal settlements (*favelas*) in Santos. (One of my favorite examples of the presence of coffee's past in everyday life in Santos is the bus line that ends at the Radio Club neighborhood. Buses pass by at all hours of the day with "Radio Club" written on illuminated route signs on the front of the buses. Few locals know this bus route refers to a private club started by foreign coffee elites in the 1920s.)

In October 1920, three members of the Belgian royal family, King Albert I, Queen Elizabeth, and their son, Prince Leopold, made an official visit to Santos (*A Tribuna* October 13, 1920). The Leon Israel coffee company donated a brand-new car, the elegant Cole Aero Eight coupe, for the royal family to travel in during their visit. The Israels were the sole vendor of the Cole automobile in Brazil, and they advertised their Indiana-made vehicle as "The King of Automobiles—An Automobile for Kings" in a full-page spread in the Santos newspaper, *A Tribuna*, to coincide with the visit.

The Cole rumbled through the muddy streets of Santos in the rain, and crowds formed to welcome the royals, showering them with flowers as a military band played. (See chapter 4 for a description of sanitary conditions in downtown Santos during this period.) The procession traveled from the port to the brand-new Parque Balneario (Bathing Park) hotel on the beach, which was the most opulent hotel in South America at the time. To celebrate the visit of the Belgian royals, lunch was served in the grand marble dining room of the hotel. As the guests dined on *chateaubriand a la Valois* and *robalo a la bresiliénne*, an orchestra performed the symphony *Il Guarany* by famed Brazilian composer Carlos Gomes. In attendance were the Brazilian president, Washington Luis, a host of decorated military leaders, the president of the Santos coffee exchange, and the chamber of commerce (the Commercial Association). Members of the Israel family were not invited, nor were any of the other German, French, or British members of the commercial elite. The guest list, which was published in *A Tribuna* on October 13, 1920, shows that the crowd was composed almost entirely of Brazilian government officials and military officers.

Only two weeks later, a groundbreaking ceremony was held at the hotel to launch a major expansion. A member of the Israel family (Achille) was part of a group of investors who funded the project, adding a casino, skating rink, and movie theater next door. The group also included Roberto Simonsen, one of Brazil's leading engineers, and Luis Suplicy, a wealthy coffee capitalist whose family has since become one of the most well-known lineages within the São Paulo commercial elite (and the owners of a chain of twenty-first-century specialty coffee shops that carries their last name). At the groundbreaking for the casino in October 1920, a poet delivered the following homage:

> It was in São Paulo, source of our national civilization, the land of the remote and heroic bandeirantes, the cradle of our immense fatherland, that is this rippling tangle of forests, this serpent of rivers, this harmony of colors . . . it was in São Paulo that, for the first time in Brazil, an actor had the honor of . . . publicly affirming on the blessed land of Santos that a heart beats within me that loves this blessed earth, that saw us born, that we work as you do with our eyes fixed on the great ideal of a strong country. (*A Tribuna* October 20, 1920)

The poet wove the construction of the casino into the great epic of progress, connecting it to the spirit of the *bandeirantes* and defining São Paulo as the source from which Brazilian civilization emerged. While foreigners such as the Israel family may have been excluded from the grand dinner for the Belgian royals, they were positioned at the forefront of Brazilian modernization, helping to finance and build the latest and greatest developments. They grew fabulously wealthy by trading coffee. They sold automobiles and built grand hotels, skating rinks, and movie houses. They even helped to transport royalty. Yet, this wealth was created with their "eyes fixed on the great ideal of a strong country." The wealth created in Santos was fueled by foreign capital, but when fused with the *bandeirantes* myth, it was undoubtedly on the side of national progress.

National Coffee

It would be hard to overstate the importance of coffee to Brazil in the early twentieth century. For the coffee oligarchs and the government that they controlled, world coffee prices were directly tied to national well-being (Eakin 1997, 33). In 1906, the Brazilian government initiated one of the most ambitious agricultural price support programs in modern history, a "valorization scheme" under which the government bought coffee directly from planters to control supply and stabilize prices. Coffee planters did not have to worry about ups and downs in the market; the government kept exchange rates favorable for export crops, and it purchased, burned, or destroyed excess coffee to keep it out of the market.

The heyday of the Brazilian coffee economy lasted until the crash of 1929, which sent coffee prices spiraling downward almost 60 percent. The crash abruptly sent the Brazilian economy into crisis, leading to the military coup d'état of Gétulio Vargas in 1930, which ultimately broke the political power of the coffee barons. By this time, the tide had turned against foreign capital. What was once seen as a harbinger of modernity—the presence of foreign firms— became a problem that needed to be controlled on the path to progress. Under Vargas, Brazil embarked on a period of rapid, state-driven industrialization. Celso Furtado, who is arguably the most important intellectual of the dependency school, which sought to minimize Brazil's reliance on foreign capital, described how the mindset of development shifted after the 1929 crash. He wrote:

> It was in the decade of the Thirties when the model of an "essentially agricultural" economy, defended by the Brazilian ruling class, began to be questioned. I was among the first who denounced ruralism as a cause of backwardness in the country. With its territorial extension and its social heterogeneity, Brazil's development could not depend upon extensive agriculture. What today looks obvious, a half century ago was the theme for heated polemics. The truth was that more than nine tenths of her exports were comprised of unprocessed agricultural products, and that the interests tied to exterior trade were those who ruled the country. (Furtado 2007, 4)

Plantation agriculture, once the path to progress, abruptly became "a cause of backwardness." President Vargas created the Estado Novo, premised on a philosophy of industrial developmentalism that viewed the coffee industry as an anachronistic obstacle to Brazilian progress. The future was to be located in the city and based on iron and steel, not coffee and sugar. Profits from those export industries would temporarily be used to finance investments in heavy industry, but eventually Brazil would leave agricultural dependency behind. As Verena Stolcke (1988) writes, the guiding belief from the Vargas period on was that "industry should lead economic development; the agricultural sector was assigned a supporting role" (70). In the Brazil of the mid-twentieth century, coffee was spatiotemporally associated with backwardness and dependency. Coffee profits may have been strategically utilized as a temporary source of funds to pay for national industrialization, but, if successful, national development would eventually make coffee agriculture obsolete.

This close relationship between coffee agriculture and the Brazilian state is what made it a foundational example for theories of dependency, which, in the simplest terms, were built on the idea that economies based on export agriculture created a neocolonial relationship between producer states in the Global South and consumer states in the Global North. Dependency theory developed many variants and offshoots over the years (ranging in their political viewpoints from state-centric Keynesianism to postcolonial Marxism), but the key foundations of dependency can be traced back to the ideas of Argentine economist Raúl Prebisch, who led the UN-sponsored Economic Commission on Latin America from 1950 to 1963 (Edelman and Haugerud 2004). Prebisch trained and mentored a group of thinkers who would indelibly shape public policy in Latin America in the twentieth century. Nowhere was the influence of dependency theory greater than in Brazil, where noted *dependentista* Celso Furtado became one of the country's leading architects of public policy in the 1960s and where sociologist Fernando Henrique Cardoso, the coauthor (with Enzo Faletto) of the classic 1973 text *Dependency and Development in Latin America*, was president from 1995 to 2002.

Green Revolution Coffee

The philosophy of developmentalism affected plant breeding, leading to the modernization of agriculture via Green Revolution techniques. By the 1930s, the Brazilian coffee sector had been protected from competition for such a long time that its levels of productivity were exceedingly low. It continued to be the world's top producer due to the sheer volume of land devoted to coffee, but countries such as Colombia and Costa Rica were catching up. The mid-twentieth century therefore brought efforts to modernize or "renovate" what had become a stagnant industry. *Cafezeis* (coffee fields) that had been planted during the boom of the late nineteenth century were unproductive, with exhausted soils and aging plants. In 1939, the Campinas Agronomy Institute (IAC), the leading coffee research station in Brazil, developed a scientifically improved coffee cultivar to improve productivity, vigor, and resistance to various diseases, resulting in the bourbon variety that was widely introduced around Brazil and the rest of Latin America. Stolcke (1988) describes the role of the IAC: "The Agronomic Institute of Campinas demonstrated that it was perfectly possible to obtain yields on old coffee land comparable to those achieved traditionally only on virgin soil. The so-called 'Campinas System' required the introduction of high-yielding coffee varieties, the regular use of chemical fertilizers, closer spacing of coffee trees, control of soil erosion through contour farming, and partial mechanization" (89). This process was supported by the Brazilian Coffee Institute, which offered funds for fertilizer and other aspects of crop modernization, including paying farmers to destroy old cultivars such as *típica*, to be replaced with the improved varieties. In 1957 and 1958, seventy million coffee trees were destroyed (Stolcke 1988, 92). From the 1950s on, the IAC created productive cultivars that could be densely planted in large, level fields under direct sun and treated with chemical fertilizer.

There was also a major shift in labor patterns on coffee plantations as they modernized. The mid-twentieth century saw the end of a semifeudal system of rural labor called the *colonato* and the creation of a wage labor market on coffee farms (Stolcke 1988). Under the *colonato*, families lived on plantation land and owners paid them a fixed amount for tending a set number of coffee trees, coupled with a separate payment for the harvest. The families—most of whom arrived in Brazil via subsidized mass immigration programs—were provided land for food production. As Brazil modernized, rising wages, rural-to-urban migration, and modern labor regulation led to the demise of the *colonato* and its replacement with seasonal wage labor. Sharecroppers and wage laborers who lived on the farm were replaced by *boias frias*, temporary day laborers who migrated to work in the fields. According to Margolis (1973), it "is essentially a system which employs day laborers as a group rather than on an individual basis. On most mornings, announcements are made on a loudspeaker advertising jobs available on a number of *fazendas* in the county" (239–40). These flexible crews of temporary workers allowed farmers to avoid paying social security benefits, as workers who are employed by a farm for less than ninety days were not eligible.[12]

In 1979, the first mechanical harvester was introduced, and mechanized harvests became the norm on Brazilian farms. This led to more changes in coffee agriculture: plants could be packed together in rows with wide lanes in between for the harvester to pass through; large land areas could be harvested with relatively little manual labor, so that a hectare of coffee could be mechanically harvested in about five hours, compared with about five days for manual labor (Bliska et al. 2009, 12). The development of mechanical harvesting set the stage for the next major change in Brazilian coffee production, allowing it to become a modern agribusiness in the 1990s.

The Second Green Revolution: Rise of the Cerrado

The Cerrado is a massive region of Central Brazil, covering parts of the states of Minas Gerais, Goiás, and Bahia. Until the 1960s, the Cerrado was considered to be unfit for agriculture due to high acidity and toxic levels of aluminum in the soil. While the region began to develop in the 1960s, it remained an agricultural frontier until the 1980s. As late as 1997, legendary plant breeder and Nobel Peace Prize recipient Norman Borlaug referred to Brazil's Cerrado region as one of the "last frontiers, the last sizable blocks of arable land to be put into production" (Easterbrook 1997, 82). Thanks to a chemical soil treatment developed by Embrapa, Brazil's government-funded agricultural research agency, the Cerrado is now one of the most productive agricultural regions in the world, the heart of the boom in agricultural commodities such as soy, sugar, and corn, a boom that has transformed Brazil. "The Cerrado region now provides 54 percent of all soybeans harvested in Brazil, 28 percent of the country's corn, and 59 percent of its coffee."[13]

The early period of coffee agriculture in the Cerrado was devoted to the cultivation of cheap robusta coffee, but since the late 1990s, the Cerrado has become the world's largest producer of high-quality arabica coffee. The region also has the most capital-intensive system of coffee production found anywhere, utilizing mechanical planters and harvesters, sophisticated irrigation systems, and large amounts of inorganic inputs like chemical fertilizers and pesticides. In the Cerrado, machines have largely replaced human labor power. Economists estimate that five people can be as productive in the Cerrado as a thousand people on a Guatemalan farm. Here, coffee is a pure commodity, commensurate with any other. The same land that could be devoted to soy, corn, or other commodities is "put into production" as a coffee farm based on market conditions, including the cost of land, labor, and chemicals. Some of the large agribusinesses in the Cerrado hold portfolios of commodity crops to manage risk in the market. These might include holdings in coffee, oranges, soy, sugar, and rubber, which as a group are less risky than investment in one single commodity.

Before 1990, there was very little irrigated coffee in Brazil (or anywhere in the world). Now there are over two hundred and fifty thousand hectares under irrigation in Brazil. The IAC has developed techniques for huge, mechanized plantations using both center-pivot and drip irrigation, chemical "fertigation," and heavy use of chemical pesticides, fungicides, and herbicides (Bliska et al. 2009, 7). The main challenge for farmers is resistance to coffee leaf rust, a fungus that can destroy entire plantations. Farmers apply huge amounts of fungicides to stop it, which is both expensive and environmentally damaging. A second focus is resistance to heat and drought. The Cerrado is an extremely hot and dry region, and the São Francisco River is the only water source for thousands of square miles. The main cultivar planted in the Cerrado until recently was *catuaí*, which is quite productive with ample fertilization and water; but intensive agriculture is threatening the sustainability of the entire region due to water shortages. Production costs in the Cerrado are among the highest in Brazil, largely due to the cost of irrigation and chemical inputs, so farmers are interested in new varieties of coffee that might be less resource intensive. The end result of the development of the Cerrado has been a significant increase in Brazilian coffee production since 2000, as well as tremendous gains in productivity per unit of land area. For example, in 2005–2006, the average yield of arabica coffee in Brazil was twenty-six bags per hectare (more than double the world average). In western Bahia state, yields averaged forty-five bags per hectare and were as high as seventy bags per hectare in some areas. In 2013, there was talk of farms yielding one hundred bags per hectare, which would be about a tenfold increase from an average coffee *fazenda* a century ago.

Merging Quantity and Quality

While consumers experience coffee as a product with specific sensory qualities (taste, aroma) and symbolic attributes (price, brand, packaging), there is a world of coffee traders who view it as a commodity to be traded, plain and simple. Brazilian coffee, which constitutes about 40 percent of the total world coffee supply in a given year, is vitally important to the overall movement of coffee prices worldwide. What happens in Brazil affects growers around the world, so there is an entire industry focused on analyzing the state of Brazilian coffee production. A contact of mine in the commodity trading world once unsuccessfully urged me to work as a consultant to traders in New York. He said,

> This business is all about having information that the rest of the market does not have . . . knowing things before everyone else. If you know about what's happening on the ground in Brazil, that information can be very valuable to an analyst at a trading firm. Let's say that you are hearing that there is some kind of new variety that's being planted before it is being reported in the media, and that variety yields more than people expect. That gives people a valuable edge that they can trade on. It's all an information game.

On the other end of the business are the people for whom coffee is not primarily about information and price movements. These people buy, sell, and transport the physical product that ends up being consumed around the world. While price and supply are, of course, vitally important to them, the sensorial and physical qualities of the coffee matter greatly. These two ends of the coffee business, financial speculation and supply-chain management, are not inseparable, but they do have different objectives and require different sets of skill and expertise. This is where the coffee broker comes in.

The basic function of brokers is to connect coffee buyers with coffee sellers. (Think of the job of a real estate broker, for example, who connects buyers and sellers in the marketplace.) In practice, this can mean many things. There are small-scale speculators who buy and sell coffee based on minor fluctuations in the market. Their office might be a single desk and computer connected to a trading platform. There are supply-side offices of major commodities conglomerates that purchase and ship millions of pounds of coffee at a time, with multiple floors filled with cubicles and staff managing the logistics of shipping. There are offices that provide cupping services, testing specific samples from around Brazil to identify suppliers that will fit a certain price point and flavor profile. I had the opportunity to spend time in the offices of two very different kinds of coffee brokers that illustrate how the two ends of the coffee market—bulk commodity and specialty market—function differently.

I met an American executive from a major international commodities corporation in the lobby bar of a Santos hotel. He connected me with coffee brokers from the company's Santos office, who gave me a tour of the facility, allowed me to test (or "cup") some coffee samples, and spoke to me at length about their business. The office is housed in a Beaux Arts building near the Coffee Museum. The entrance looks a bit like an old post office or bank teller window, with a small well-worn desk and a scale to weigh coffee samples that might be delivered in person. Behind the desk are shelves with small coffee cans, each labeled with the date and the name of the producer or intermediary that delivered them. Behind this public-facing front window is the main cupping and sample area, which is not visible to the public. This room is lined with hundreds, if not thousands, of sample cans of green coffee from all around Brazil. There is a roasting area for samples and a cupping laboratory where workers, all of whom are speaking Portuguese and appear to be Brazilian, can test the quality of the samples following a more or less scientific protocol (Besky 2021).

This company buys coffee in large volumes for two different markets: the Brazilian "industrial" market and the international export market. Brazilian consumers tend to buy inexpensive coffee, mainly robusta, which is then heavily roasted, ground, and sold in inexpensive bricks to be served with ample amounts of sugar. For this market, the main concern is the price and reliability of the supply. In this market, coffee "quality" does not conform to international standards of flavor or aroma, which tend to favor mild arabicas. Brazilian industrial coffee would be a cheap filler coffee that might be used to blend with higher-quality beans to lower the unit cost of a mass-market blend, but it would not be sold on its own abroad.

From a global perspective, the coffee market is segmented. There are customers who, like the Brazilians, want cheap robusta. Instant coffees are still popular in many parts of the world. Large food companies want arabica with a relatively neutral flavor profile. For them, a reliable supply at high volumes, a steady price point, and good traceability protocols is a top priority. For large multinational buyers, it is crucial to be able to trace the supply chain back to origin in the event of some kind of contamination or mishap in the handling of the product. For this brokerage firm, volume and consistency of supply was the top priority. The firm was able to match the coffee supply with the demands of a truly global commodities market. From the company's perspective, the so-called specialty market was an afterthought—a tiny branch off a much larger tree.

When I spoke to the executive about his major concerns for the future of coffee, he was focused on getting enough coffee to supply a growing international market. He thought about securing enough coffee to supply divisions of his own company in Asia, the United States, Brazil, and Europe. Quantity, reliability, and traceability were his major concerns. His other concern was matching up the demands of specific national markets with supply. "In Korea, they like to drink instant coffee," he told me. "As that market grows, I need to find enough coffee to supply it." I asked him if he was concerned about oversupply, and he responded, "No. There's a market for all the coffee in the world. Every bean of coffee ends up somewhere—good or bad. As long as new consumers continue to come along in emerging markets, there will be a need for more coffee—just like soy, sugar, or any other commodity. These markets probably won't want the same kind of product that we can sell in the US and Europe, so I'm not worried about the future."

For multinational companies like this, coffee brokerage is essentially about matching supply and demand in multiple markets simultaneously, and predicting the movement of prices through hedging. While these companies have hedging operations, their primary purpose is not financial speculation or profiting off of futures trading. For traditional commodities brokers that move physical products, hedging is used as a risk management strategy so that the company has some cost stability in a volatile market. For example, if you need to deliver several tons of coffee to a customer by a certain date, locking in a futures contract is an insurance policy in case prices move sharply. A futures contract is simply an instrument that allows the holder to purchase a specific volume of coffee at a certain price by a specified date. The contracts get bought and sold with marginal profits and losses, but rarely do they lead to an actual transaction involving a shipment of coffee (a process known as "AA-ing," or "adding to actual" shipments). In most cases, it is a simple financial transaction: a contract for, say, a shipment of January coffee at $1 might be worth about three cents if coffee moves to $1.03, and brokers might pay more or less than that if they predict that the market will move in a different direction before the date of delivery.

The second brokerage firm that I spent time with is oriented toward the specialty market and the high end of the retail market, working with boutique roasters and major multinational customers such as Nespresso and Dunkin' Donuts. This brokerage may be too big to work with third-wave coffee buyers who want microlots of a few bags, but it does work with Cup of Excellence winners and other high-quality producers around Brazil. In this office, which is just down the street from the larger firm described above, there is a tiny area for cupping and samples, and a small staff who generally speak English rather than Portuguese. The Santos office mainly works with satellite offices that are located closer to the interior coffee regions and have close relationships with producers. The main priorities of this brokerage are to find coffee suppliers that fit the very specific needs of customers in terms of reliability of supply, price, flavor profile, quality control, and traceability. Higher-end retail buyers have very stringent demands for traceability, particularly regarding the use of fertilizers, postharvest handling, and, in some cases, labor standards. Nongovernmental certification systems such as UTZ and 4C are quite common in Brazil because the standards set by these regulating bodies tend to be equal to or less strict than those set by Brazilian regulators at the state or federal level. This makes it easy for large growers to comply with these regulations, whereas small growers in places with lax labor regulation find the criteria to be quite strict and burdensome. In addition, large coffee operations with over five hundred hectares (roughly twelve hundred acres) in production will always have a professional system for bookkeeping, auditing, and tracking and tracing the movement of their crops. Larger farms already have the management systems that are required by large buyers such as Starbucks or McDonalds. From the perspective of a big multinational brand, these producers are easy to work with and low risk compared with, say, a small family farmer in Central America who may produce a coffee of exceptional quality but does not have the professional infrastructure to comply with quality control/assurance and traceability requirements. This brokerage firm uses the point system of the Cup of Excellence program, which judges coffees based on a hundred-point scale, with coffees scoring eighty-seven or higher being considered exceptional. I asked about Brazil's emerging place in the high-end specialty market, and a broker told me Brazilian producers can easily produce coffees that score in the high eighties in massive, consistent quantities, but buyers tend to look elsewhere for the more "interesting" and unique ninety-point-plus coffees. At this firm, my contact was interested in hearing from me about what I thought the emerging trends were for high-end consumers in the United States. My contact's job was to work with producers to find what demanding customers wanted before it became mainstream.

Making "Big Coffee" Small

Coffee is amazing because it is both a commodity and a noncommodity—something that can be both homogeneous and heterogeneous, depending on your perspective. It is one of the few commodities in the world that continues to be produced by small-scale family farmers yet is traded on a global scale. A single bag of coffee can contain products from dozens of countries—figuratively, the world in a bag. While huge agricultural conglomerates produce coffee in Brazil and elsewhere, it has yet to become totally commoditized like sugar or corn. And unlike with tea, which is perhaps the closest comparative example to coffee, the family farm rather than the large plantation is the standard form of production. There is coffee from small growers and cooperatives from all over the world in almost any high-end coffee shop. It amazes me that the Honduran coffee farmers I met who had an acre of shade-grown coffee in their backyards were part of the same global market as the large, multimillion-dollar coffee farms in the Brazilian Cerrado, with their own optical sorters, sophisticated irrigation systems, mechanical harvesters, and computerized milling operations.

In Santos, I discovered that the two ends of the coffee commodity chain— the "big" homogenous coffee of the plantation and the "small" heterogeneous coffee of the specialty market—were becoming one and the same. In 2014, the Cerrado Mineiro, located in the western part of Minas Gerais state, was granted Certified Denomination of Origin (CDO) status by the Brazilian government. The CDO is a form of intellectual property that legally protects products based on the unique attributes of the geographical location in which they are produced and is often associated with artisanal food products such as wine and cheese. Given the inexhaustible interest in the locality of high-end coffee among consumers around the world, it should come as no surprise that a coffee-growing region has attained CDO status. But the Cerrado is ground zero of Brazil's agro-industrial boom, home to some of the largest and most capital-intensive, high-tech coffee operations in the world. Far from being a region associated with "tradition," artisanal production, and other qualities that might symbolically particularize Brazilian coffee in a homogenous commodities market, the Cerrado is the epicenter of "big coffee" in Brazil. Surprisingly, this modern, highly commoditized coffee region has branded itself as "local" and particular.

The Cerrado's CDO status illustrates recent transformations in the global coffee economy. On the one hand, the world is producing more coffee than ever to meet demand from growing consumer markets in China, India, Korea, and Brazil itself, which is now the world's second-largest consumer of coffee. On the other hand, the global oversupply of coffee requires producers to "particularize" their product to sell it at a premium in a deregulated global market. For Brazil, which has been the world's largest producer of coffee for a century, the challenge is to make big coffee something more than a homogenous commodity. Once known for producing massive amounts of relatively cheap bulk coffee regulated by a global price control system (the International Coffee Agreement), Brazil now needs to "move up the value chain" to compete with countries (mainly Vietnam) that can produce even cheaper coffee. As one Brazilian farmer put it to me, "Brazil is not a coffee boutique, or a discount store. We are the world's coffee supermarket—consistent, high-quality, and reliable."

Me, Dr. Doom?

What does the rise of big coffee in the Cerrado mean for the future? In March 2016, I spoke at a panel discussion on the history and future of the coffee industry, hosted by Vanderbilt University. The event was held at Barista Parlor, a high-end third-wave coffee shop in Nashville, Tennessee, that sourced and roasted its own coffee in small lots from around the world. It was a beautiful industrial chic building in a booming neighborhood downtown, where the young and trendy could gather and enjoy spectacular coffee, food, and general pre-COVID urban bonhomie. Surrounded by an audience of local coffee connoisseurs, I was asked by my host, Edward Fischer, an anthropology professor at Vanderbilt who studies coffee in Guatemala, what I thought the future of the coffee industry was. I responded (paraphrasing from memory): "I think we will see genetically engineered copies of the highest-quality specialty coffees in the world, produced on a massive scale in places like the Cerrado of Brazil and possibly China—places with extremely capital-intensive agriculture and relatively few restrictions on GMO crops. The specialty coffee industry won't disappear, but it will need to seek out greener pastures, so to speak, as very good genetic copies of specialty coffees become mass-produced in places where yields are far higher than anything that small farmers can produce in places like Honduras or Guatemala."

My prediction was, and still is, this: if every botanical and chemical aspect of the coffee bean can eventually be sequenced and recreated in a lab with gene editing technologies such as CRISPR, then the unique, heterogeneous qualities of coffee (such as *terroir* and the flavors of unique varietals) can be replicated and mass-produced with relative ease. (And that is leaving aside, for the moment, the many benefits that GMO coffee could potentially provide from the perspective of coffee producers, such as drought and disease resistance, herbicide and pesticide tolerance, and labor savings.) In the past, there was almost no incentive for anyone to invest heavily in GMO coffee. Coffee plants can survive for almost a hundred years. They are easy to propagate in nurseries and can be crossbred through simple techniques such as cutting and grafting. Coffee research centers around the world have used traditional techniques of selective breeding, crossing, and experimental field trials to develop new varietals of coffee for centuries, so genetic research was slow to catch on. There is essentially no market for commercial coffee seed, and this has limited the investments made by biotech companies. Now the price of sequencing and gene editing is within reach for government coffee research centers and other nonprofits, even in the Global South, and the high end of the coffee market has become sufficiently lucrative for it to make sense for different groups—besides multinational companies—to invest in genetic research. What is stopping GMO coffee from taking hold?

It is not just the high end of the market that will be affected. As global demand for coffee increases, supply will have to keep pace. China has been working on developing coffee production for the past two decades (mostly in the province of Yunnan), and coffee consumption there also continues to grow rapidly, due to not only general economic growth (more consumers mean more coffee drinkers) but also an aggressive effort by the coffee industry (particularly the National Coffee Association in the United States) to turn young consumers across tea-drinking countries into coffee drinkers. Most of the increases in coffee consumption in the past decade have been driven by increases in Asia and in coffee-producing countries such as Mexico, Indonesia, India, and Brazil. In the future, the world will demand more coffee, and genetic research will drive new shifts in production. Bradley Wilson, a colleague in geography from West Virginia University who was also on the panel, responded to me, "You're saying that coffee could become Iowa corn?

"In Brazil," I said, "it already has."

From the perspective of the people who work and shop at places like Barista Parlor, this was a decidedly dour forecast. If you love coffee for the unique, craft-like aspects of connoisseurship—millions of varieties to explore, taste, and enjoy as an educated consumer—then the idea of mass-produced GMO clones is disheartening, like when your favorite local brewpub is bought by a conglomerate and its beer shows up on the shelves at Target. What could be worse for artisanal coffee than the looming specter of GMOs and mass production, something that could take the "specialty" out of specialty coffee? Only half-joking (I think), my friend Professor Fischer called me "Dr. Doom" after I made my prognosis.

Broken Brokerage

Just in front of the Coffee Museum sits a sculpture called *Homage to the Coffee Broker* (fig. 5). It was made in 2012 as part of the downtown restoration project. The statue is a life-size depiction of a white businessman in a suit and tie, carrying the coffee cans that are used to hold samples of beans for export. The statue is somewhat deceptive—it is made of fiberglass and covered in a painted veneer that makes it look like bronze. In the image shown here, the arm that normally holds the beans has been broken off, revealing the hollow inner core. In the decade since it was built, the statue has been frequently vandalized (in fits of *broke*

FIGURE 5.   *Homage to the Coffee Broker* statue (Photo by author, 2016)

rage?), requiring dozens of repairs during its short lifespan. As I show in chapter 3, the construction of the coffee broker statue on a new pedestrian-only street was part of a broader transformation that would gentrify the port area in a way that valorized a shift away from blue-collar work and production toward white-collar work and consumption. While I can only speculate about what actually motivated the vandalism, the presence of a broken broker seemed to symbolize the conflict over the attempted gentrification. At another level, the broken broker symbolizes the occupation's changing function within the Brazilian coffee industry. As the center of gravity shifted toward the megafarms in the Cerrado, there was less of a need for brokers to connect producers with Santos exporters. The industry was becoming more of a computerized logistics business, and the old days of the hustle and bustle around the coffee exchange were no more. The statue was commemorating a dying occupation at the very moment that the city of Santos was hoping to create a white-collar business district in and around the port.

The parallels between coffee and the example of the Guaraní in the previous chapter should be clear. In both cases, there was a clash of timescapes between an unfolding present and a mythologized past. In both, the icons of mythic history—statues of *bandeirantes* and brokers—were vandalized, but it would be misleading to assert that the popular rebuke of the golden age of coffee is as prominent as the decolonial challenge to the *bandeirantes*. There is no doubt that a reconsideration of the place of plantation agriculture in Brazil's history is underway, and, as I have shown in this chapter, there is a strong link between rural capitalism and the *bandeirantes*. In Santos, a city whose history and present are so indelibly shaped by the export of coffee, the resignification of this history produced something of a cultural identity crisis. Nowhere was this crisis more visible than in the port itself, the interface between Santos and the global economy. The next chapter will describe how the clash of timescapes in the Port of Santos, which is directly adjacent, geographically, to the neighborhood described in this chapter, yet is socially a world apart.

PORT OF THE PAST, PORT OF THE FUTURE

Two Timescapes of Labor and Capital

In this chapter, the clash of timescapes takes place in the Port of Santos. Is it a dynamic industrial port of the present or a white-collar "historical" district for the future? As is the case with coffee, these two timescapes are rarely in dialogue with each other.

The idea for this chapter came from a bus ride. Although I rarely take buses at home, I love riding buses while doing fieldwork abroad. One of my fieldwork strategies in Santos was to take every one of the fifty or so city bus routes from the main terminal to the end of the line, walk around and explore for a bit, get something to eat or drink, and then wait for the next bus back to where I started. This strategy gives you the lay of the land in an urban space, taking you into neighborhoods off the beaten path and industrial areas where you would be unlikely to go if you walked through the urban core or stuck to a preset itinerary. Buses force you to interact with people of all social classes, especially when the buses are crowded or slow. They are always good for overhearing interesting conversations (although the popularity of headphones, mapping apps, and texting has quieted buses down a bit). Physically, I do not stand out in Brazil, so I never attracted much attention, and my Portuguese was good enough to understand most of what was going on around me. In both Honduras and Brazil, I made some of my best spontaneous connections on buses, and I observed things looking out the window that led to some important discoveries. There was the time in Honduras that I was stuck on a school bus for four hours sitting next to a Pentecostal evangelist who was determined to save my soul; and the time in Brazil that I listened to a couple in the seat in front of me fight for five straight hours before deciding to break up. If you are new to a place, buses are a great way to absorb the local culture.

The main bus terminal in Santos is an aging, open-air structure right in the center of the downtown. Some Brazilian bus terminals are incredible—equal to modern airports in their amenities and use of the latest technologies. The Santos terminal is not one of them. It houses little more than ticket booths, a few news kiosks and luncheonettes, and some benches. My first trip to Santos in 2013 was on a bus from the city of Campinas, a journey that should take about three hours but took nearly eight hours due to traffic standstills on the road down the mountains. I ended up talking for a while with a man in the seat next to me, and just before we finally got to the station, I noticed an old sign on a decrepit building that said "Armazen Generais Theodor Wille SA." I knew that Theodor Wille had been one of the world's largest coffee traders prior to World War II (see chapter 2), and I asked the man if this building was still a functioning coffee warehouse. He told me that it was one of several old buildings being redeveloped as office space—part of a big project by Petrobras to build a research and development complex in Santos. What the man told me was not exactly correct. By the time I returned to Santos in 2016, the old coffee warehouses were part of another office building development, eventually housing a business processes outsourcing firm called Atento. The new Petrobras offices were just down the street, and the two projects were linked as part of the general overhaul of Valongo.

In some senses, my simple question on the bus was the origin of this entire project: what happens when an important coffee port is redeveloped and old warehouses are repurposed to serve a new "knowledge economy"? I came to Santos with an interest in coffee, but I saw that a new kind of "black gold"—oil from offshore reserves—was beginning to transform Santos, and this transformation was most visible in the port of Valongo, the neighborhood around the bus station and the Coffee Museum, where the research and development offices for the offshore oil industry were located. My basic argument is that the underlying goal of the transformation of Valongo was to change the neighborhood from a space of production to a space of consumption—a goal where progress meant erasing the "old economy" of physical and industrial labor and replacing it with a new mode of production tied to knowledge work and other kinds of immaterial labor, such as call center work and research and development for the oil industry. As a consequence of this transformation, the meanings of "labor" and "capital" were changing. The redevelopment plan for Valongo, which was promulgated by the city government, the state of São Paulo, and a consortium of private investors, had an unstated goal that rippled through the entire initiative: physical labor in the port would eventually disappear altogether—or to be more precise, it would become invisible in the postindustrial economy of the "new" modern port. The new port would house office workers, tourists, and consumers in restaurants and bars, but the hard, dirty work of the port would be banished to history.

The trouble, of course, is that Santos remained the busiest port in Latin America, and it was the linchpin in the commodity-fueled Brazilian boom of the 2000s. At the very moment when modern port infrastructure was vital to the economy, the Valongo port was being shifted into the timescape of myth—a historical relic of a period that had been passed on the road to progress. Downtown coffee warehouses could house call centers, but the actual warehouses still existed: they were just shifted off site. There is an interesting historical parallel here with the rise of the coffee economy at the turn of the twentieth century, described in chapter 2. Scholars such as Lanna (1996) have showed how urban space in Santos became sharply divided along class lines as a coffee bourgeoisie developed. The coffee capitalists developed social spaces such as casinos, theaters, and country clubs that kept them from interacting with the working class. During this period, the wealthy moved to newly built neighborhoods along the canals as the city sprawled out from the port to the beach. The port and the adjacent downtown neighborhoods became "popular" areas (to use the Brazilian euphemism for "working class") as the wealthy came to inhabit new spaces of home and leisure, which were sharply separated from spaces of work.

During the redevelopment, a similar process was taking place in an even more pronounced form. As the working industrial Port of Santos became increasingly important to Brazil's export economy, it was simultaneously being redeveloped as a historic downtown district that would appeal to tourists and postindustrial workers in the new Petrobras office complex and the surrounding neighborhood of hotels, condos, and office buildings. This created an irresolvable contradiction: industrial, working-class Santos was an outdated relic but the port was always chugging along as Brazil's most important hub for the export of the commodities that were fueling its growth. All of the development in Valongo was premised on the bright future of the pre-salt oil, and, on a national scale, the most ambitious plans of the Workers' Party were based on expected revenues from oil profits that did not materialize. But it was more than just oil: coffee, soy, orange juice, sugar, steel, and basically every other primary commodity produced across the country was transported through Santos. The redevelopment of Valongo depended on the profits being generated in the countryside or in the oil fields hundreds of miles out to sea, but the material processes that generated this wealth were being pushed to the margins, as if the city could have the wealth without the labor. Nowhere was the contradiction more apparent than in controversies over parking and traffic.

Labor as an Inconvenience

One day in May 2016, I wandered through downtown Santos and found that traffic was completely blocked by a protest organized by the local truck drivers' union. In the central plaza, named after the Baron of Mauá, a fabulously wealthy Brazilian who financed the first railroad in São Paulo, the truckers assembled to voice their concerns. While setting off firecrackers, playing loud music on a huge PA system, and having a good time, little side groups of men assembled to drink coffee and beer in the *lanchonetes* around the plaza. I asked one of them what the protest was about. "The city doesn't want trucks," they said. "We have no place to park, no place to rest, no place to wait." This comment surprised me, because if there is one thing that downtown Santos has in abundance, it is tractor trailer trucks, rumbling through the streets and belching diesel fumes at all hours of the day and night. How could the port function without a never-ending stream of trucks? They are the main conduit for goods that move from the interior of Brazil to the port.

The bottleneck at the Port of Santos is an ongoing problem that the Brazilian government has invested billions of dollars in solving. To understand the problem, you must begin with geography. Santos sits at the bottom of a steep mountain range that plunges three thousand vertical feet to the sea in only a few miles. Almost all goods that enter or leave Santos must cross the mountains by one of two main roads or a single rail line. One road is an old two-lane highway named after José de Anchieta, the Jesuit priest who left São Vicente with the *bandeirantes* to establish the settlement that became São Paulo. The Anchieta is a slow, frightening, twisty road that all commercial traffic must follow down the mountains, through hairpin turns, dark tunnels, and dense cloud forest. When the Anchieta highway was completed in 1947, it was considered an engineering marvel and a great national triumph. It was largely constructed by another group of so-called *bandeirantes*, the migrant laborers who left rural regions of the country (mainly the northeast) to build a modern Brazil in Brasilia or São Paulo (Holston 1989, 209). Seventy years later, what was once a marvel of modern civil engineering had become a pitifully overburdened relic of the past. To deal with the choke point getting goods to the port, there are a few "logistics patios" at the top of the mountains where trucks could wait to receive electronic clearance to move to the port. These helped the situation somewhat, but the patios were filled to capacity and the wait times could last for days. Waiting trucks are charged by the hour for the delays at the patios. Add the driver's hourly pay to that cost, and it is easy to see why shipping costs in Brazil are the highest in the world. The costs can be directly traced to the bottlenecks on the roads to the Port of Santos.

Just west of the Anchieta highway lies another road, a modern superhighway named in honor of the millions of immigrants who arrived in Santos and crossed the mountains by rail to arrive in São Paulo.[1] The beautifully maintained Immigrants Highway is for private vehicle traffic in the downhill direction from São Paulo. While trucks and buses take the old, slow road, tourists and residents can take the newer, faster one. Because all commercial traffic is banished to the old road, there are almost constant traffic jams caused by trucks laden with shipping containers that must descend the mountains. Brazil is one of the world's leading exporters of agricultural commodities, and, depending on the year, Santos accounts for about 65 percent of all exports. A huge percentage of the world's soy, sugar, coffee, and orange juice has to be transported down an old, dangerous, narrow road to get to the port. At the bottom, in Santos, the truckers face an even worse bottleneck when the highway turns into a narrow urban street that is crisscrossed by railroad tracks. (It once took a bus that I was on more than an hour to travel a half mile on this stretch.) Trucks must pass through the bottleneck to get to the port terminals to load and unload shipping containers. During the boom of the 2000s, the slow pace of traffic to and from the Port of Santos was frequently mentioned in international reports as an obstacle to Brazil's economic growth. The two highways—a new modern road for private vehicles and an old rundown one for commercial shipping—illustrate the conflict that led to the truckers' protest: a "new" Brazil oriented toward middle-class consumerism versus an "old" Brazil oriented toward the export of agricultural commodities. Pardon the pun, but the new Brazil was clearly in the driver's seat.

In 2012, Reuters published a feature article called "The Long, Brutal Haul from Farm to Port in Brazil" (Murphy November 1, 2012). The story followed a trucker who hauled a cargo of corn from the town of Rondonopolis, in the booming agriculture belt of southern Mato Grosso state (the ancestral home of the Mbyá Guaraní described in chapter 2), to the Port of Santos, a distance of about a thousand miles. The journey, which Google Maps tells me should take eighteen and a half hours, took seven days, including a day and a half to cover the final fifty-mile stretch over the mountains from São Paulo to an Archer Daniels Midland terminal in Santos. The cost of the transport was $3,800 for a cargo worth $10,200. In other words, the transport cost was more than 35 percent of the value of the corn being shipped.

The Reuters article reads as follows:

> "Logistics are jammed up," says Glauber Silveira, head of Mato Grosso's association of soy growers, who lose a quarter of their revenue to transport. "The buyer is losing out and the producer is losing out." With ample land, plentiful water, and high-tech farms cultivating its vast in-

terior, Brazil is now the world's biggest producer of sugar, coffee, cit-
rus, beef, the leading exporter of poultry and on the verge of becoming
the top soybean grower. . . . Economists struggle to quantify the impact
of Brazil's infrastructure woes on the economy. But most agree that a
poor transport network, saturated ports and other deficiencies prevent
the economy from consistently growing more than 4 percent a year, a
rate analysts say must be sustained over time for Brazil to attain developed nation status.[2]

One could find hundreds of news stories making a similar case in business and
trade publications. Traffic in Santos was not a mere inconvenience; it was a problem with national and, indeed, international consequences. Brazil's economic
progress depended on international trade, which required efficient ports, which
required a smooth flow of traffic to and from Santos. On the other hand, the presence of tractor trailer trucks was a major problem for the renovation and revitalization of a "new" downtown Santos. It is the same dynamic I describe in
chapters 1 and 2: the unsettling reemergence of something—an event, a group of
people, a commodity—that was thought to be surmounted on the path to progress. The city and the port needed the trucks, but the presence of the trucks also
signified the country's failure to achieve its fantasy of progress. It is also very
clearly a clash between two kinds of capitalism: one, rooted in the production and
trade of commodities for export, is framed as a thing of the past; the other, rooted
in the consumption of commodities by people who earn their wealth through
managerial or knowledge work, is framed as a thing of the present and future.[3]

Valongo

Valongo is the historic birthplace of the Port of Santos, the home of the oldest
shipping terminals and the last stop of the first railroad in Brazil. The city is the
site of the Pelé Museum, the Coffee Museum, the Ibis Hotel, and almost all of the
other new tourist and business infrastructure that was constructed in Santos
ahead of the 2014 World Cup, including the new Petrobras office buildings. To
recreate Valongo as a place of leisure with sidewalk cafes, walkable cobblestone
streets, and renovated historic attractions, the municipal government of Santos
sought to cut down on the truck traffic that rumbled through the city. To that
end, they placed severe limitations on where trucks could park, idle, load, and
unload. No-parking zones were enforced in all of the places where the truckers
used to stop. As Brazil's commodities trade boomed—in coffee, soy, orange juice,
sugar, oil, and all sorts of other goods—more trucks than ever were coming to the

Port of Santos; yet, at the same time, the city saw the presence of these trucks as an impediment to its own progress. This was more than a conflict between truckers and bureaucrats—it was a clash of two different political economic systems: an "old economy" of physical export commodities loaded into noisy trucks and container ships, and a "new economy" of office workers and tourists enjoying themselves as consumers in the "historic center," having arrived swiftly in private vehicles on a brand-new superhighway. The clash pitted industry against postindustry, producers against consumers, the present against the future of Santos. Like the trucks, all of these issues came together in Valongo, and the drivers were literally stuck in the traffic—of vehicles, goods, and timescapes.

The presence of the truckers illustrates that there really was no "old economy" and "new economy." The old economy of export agriculture could not disappear because the new economy depended on the wealth it generated. The truckers saw this problem clearly. In their opinion, Santos needed their goods, but the city did not want the workers who brought these goods. In other words, the city was utterly dependent on the profits generated by international trade but wanted to make heavy industry as invisible as possible. The city needed the port but also saw it as something of an embarrassment, an impediment to Valongo's reinvention as a twenty-first-century city.

Trucks in Santos were a nuisance, but as instruments in the production of wealth taking place elsewhere, they were celebrated. In 2016, Mercedes-Benz launched a television ad for its new Actros model of tractor trailer. The ad shows a working-class Brazilian truck driver who picks up a passenger on the side of a dirt road. The driver has a slightly darker complexion than the passenger and is dressed in work clothes with a *caipira* (country) look. The two men banter back and forth about how modern, comfortable, and spacious the truck is ("Like a ship," one says) as it bounces through a seemingly endless field of soy, outpacing a freight train on a parallel track. The driver has religious icons on the dashboard, and he repeatedly thanks and kisses a small photograph that he pulls out of his pocket. The hitchhiking passenger assumes that the driver is thanking a Catholic patron saint for his good fortune and asks the driver which saint he is praying to. The man replies that he is not thanking a saint, he is thanking the ranch owner (*dono da fazenda*) who bought this beautiful new Mercedes truck. The camera shows a picture of a stereotypical white Brazilian ranch owner, an older man who is the embodiment of *ruralista* appeal, standing proudly alongside his horse. The camera pans out to an image of the truck and the Mercedes logo.[4]

The ad perfectly sacralized the figure of the plantation-owning *fazendeiro*, putting him in the position of a saint to whom the workers must express their gratitude. Here, infrastructure and the movement of commodities is tied to the overall project of national prosperity, as if everyone should thank the plantation owner for buying the latest and greatest truck. The ad is obviously paternalistic in a way that is quite jarring to American viewers, who are accustomed to advertisements that associate trucks with rugged individualism and freedom rather than plantation agribusiness and deferential patron–client bonds. In fact, US television programs rarely show nationwide ads for commercial farm equipment. Personal vehicles, such as pickup trucks, are always the focus of US ads. More to the point, the ideological juxtaposition between Brazil's two views of shipping is clear: when commercial trucks create traffic, noise, and parking problems, they are obstacles to progress; when they are "out there" in the countryside, they are agents of progress.

This is just one example in a long historical pattern in which the port and the city stand in a tense, ambivalent relationship. The relationship maps closely onto other structural pairs: port and city, labor and capital, work and play, past and future, clean and dirty. The port–city relationship developed over a century, and that history is absolutely relevant to the conflicts in the present. Today, Santos continues to be the world's most important port for the export of coffee. Yet, like the presence of Indians on the beaches of São Vicente, the contemporary presence of the coffee industry disrupts the dominant historical narrative of Brazilian progress. The mythic narrative of coffee as a historical period that was surpassed by the new, industrial Brazil of the First World denies (or at least occludes) the continuing importance of coffee to the Santos region. Coffee is present as a stage in the city's history that has been surpassed and is now memorialized, yet many of the contemporary political and social tensions in the city are still, to a certain degree, structured by the political economy of coffee. Here, there is a familiar pattern: like the Guaraní in Paranapuã village, coffee in Santos is treasured as a relic of the past but somewhat invisible as an active presence in everyday life. And like the unsettling presence of real Indians on the beaches, the contemporary realities of the coffee industry pop up time and again to destabilize the mythic narrative of progress. Whereas chapter one looked at the relationship between white Brazilians and Amerindians, this chapter looks at the relationship between labor and capital.

The Heroic Capitalist Mythology

There is no doubt that Brazil tends to mythologize titans of industry. The shipping docks of the nineteenth century were the Mercedes trucks of the twenty-first. In 2016, the Brazilian affiliate of the History Channel television network produced a series called *Giants of Brazil*. It was almost identical in style to a US version called *The Men Who Built America*, which was also produced by the

History Channel. Each episode was a dramatic retelling of the life story of a major industrial tycoon of the early twentieth century. As the titles would suggest, these were entertaining exercises in hero worship, not critical documentaries. In the United States, the episodes were devoted to Cornelius Vanderbilt (shipping), Henry Ford (automobiles), John D. Rockefeller (oil), Andrew Carnegie (steel), and J. P. Morgan (banking), depicting each as a heroic patriarch in the story of American capitalism. In Brazil, the series profiled four titans of Brazilian industry: Giuseppe Martinelli, Francesco Matarazzo, Percival Farquhar, and Guilherme Guinle, who are often considered the robber barons of Brazil. Martinelli was a shipping magnate, Matarazzo an industrialist, Farquhar a financier, and Guinle the president of the Santos Dock Company, which was cofounded by his father. Guinle's place in this pantheon of industrialists gives a sense of how important the Santos port is to the history of Brazilian capitalism. The opening sequence of the entire series shows Guilherme Guinle standing proudly alongside a steamship in front of a Santos Dock Company warehouse. In the 1970s, the Brazilian fifty-cent coin showed a crane loading a container ship with sacks of cargo. In Brazilian history, the Santos docks are a key part of the mythic history of Brazilian capitalism, on par with the steel mills of Pittsburgh or the auto factories of Detroit in the mythic history of US capitalism. The lionization of the Dock Company is visible throughout Santos. Just behind the customs house sits a huge monument to Cândido Gaffrée and Eduardo P. Guinle (Guilherme's father), the two businessmen who established and owned the Santos Dock Company (fig. 6). In the statue, they sit on a high pedestal cast in bronze. Both men have mustaches and embody a certain image of the nineteenth-century bourgeoisie: they wear business suits and bow ties, and carry rolled-up documents. Their serious faces peer down on the viewer with a look that is somewhere between smug superiority and disdain. Far below them, at the base of the stone pedestal, are two clusters of coffee workers straining under the weight of heavy sacks of beans. In the front of the statue, just under the watchful eyes of the bosses, are muscled men who strain to load the bow of a ship with coffee. To the rear of the statue is a long line of stevedores that disappear into a ship on the horizon, each one shouldering a sack of coffee—an endless stream of workers hauling an endless supply of coffee. In this monument, the homogenous labor of coffee plantations is literally the foundation atop which the heroic capitalists are perched. Gaffreé and Guinle (G&G) are portrayed as larger-than-life historical figures looming above the workers. While G&G are depicted as specific historical personages, labor is depicted as a smaller-than-life homogenous mass that supports the capitalists. In an apt continuity with the myth of conquest, Gaffreé and Guinle are standing on top of a colonial-style Portuguese caravel rather than a modern steamship.

FIGURE 6.   Gaffreé and Guinle monument (Photo by author, 2016)

The G&G empire began in Rio de Janeiro, where the two ran an emporium called Aux Tuileries, which specialized in imported fabrics, mainly from France. Their business coincided with a period of major economic growth in Rio as Brazil's early coffee economy began to take off in the mid-nineteenth century. They expanded their business into coffee, railroad construction, and other import/export businesses. Gaffreé and Guinle arrived in Santos in 1892 with a concession from the Brazilian government to modernize the port facilities. Their company, the Santos Dock Company, was given an exclusive monopoly over port operations, one that lasted until 1980. Needless to say, with a century-long monopoly over the busiest port in Latin America, G&G became fabulously wealthy and powerful, controlling the entry and exit point for the movement of goods that circulated throughout the continent.

When the railroad arrived, the Port of Santos was still a technologically primitive colonial outpost, with a disorganized network of old wooden piers (*trapiches*) equipped with hoists and moorings suited to the days of mule trains and sailboats, not the era of railroads and steamships. While the railroad was an engineering marvel, the old port was an embarrassment and an impediment to the efficient flow of goods in and out of Brazil. Built on the soft, muddy banks of the Santos estuary, it was impossible for the port to support the large machinery and bulk goods that the new ships were capable of carrying. This was where G&G stepped in. In 1888, working with foreign engineers and a small group of investors from around the country, G&G developed plans for the improvement of the Santos docks. Between 1890 and 1892, they constructed almost a mile of continuous heavy concrete docks and warehouses, lining the shore of the Santos estuary almost to the foot of the Serra do Mar. Gaffreé and Guinle modernized the port to facilitate the movement of goods from ships to the railroad and constructed huge, bonded warehouses to store the goods that moved on and off the docks. In 1892, the first foreign steamship arrived at the port of Santos, an English vessel called the *Nasmyth*. The golden age of foreign trade in Santos had begun. As steamships moved millions of bags of coffee off the Santos docks, the Brazilian government filled its coffers with receipts from the Santos custom house. The Santos Dock Company enjoyed a complete monopoly on one of the busiest ports in the Atlantic region.

The rapid modernization of the city was astonishing. A December 28, 1909, profile in the *Times of London* heralded the city's progress:

> Those who knew the port of Santos 18 or 20 years ago will certainly be amazed at the improvements now apparent. In those days, the loading or unloading of merchandise was effected by means of wooden piers leading to the bonded warehouses. Sailing vessels were often kept for 3, 4, 6 or more months until their turn came to moor along the pier . . . the handsome granite quay is equipped with the latest and best of hydraulic and electrical machinery . . . the City of Santos, in 1892 a plague-ridden vestige of colonial times, has now become a noted health resort, with well-laid out streets and avenues, fine buildings and electric trams, all of which owe their existence to the Santos Dock Company. (56)

A few statistics give a sense of just how fast Santos changed after the new docks were built. The population tripled from 1890 to 1900 and doubled yet again by 1920, when it reached over one hundred thousand (Teixera da Silva 2011, 70). Coffee exports went from about two million bags in 1889 to fourteen million bags in

1907. Much of the growth of the population was driven by Brazil's government-sponsored immigration programs, which paid for the passage of European immigrants to work in the coffee fields. "In 1913, no less than 42.5 percent of Santos's inhabitants were foreign born. The main 'foreign colonies' were Portuguese, Spanish, and Italian" (ibid.).

The Santos Dock Company, which journalists called "the dockopolis," came to be known as *o polvo* (the octopus) due to the spread of its powerful tentacles throughout every aspect of life in the city (Teixeira da Silva 2011, 73). But there was constant opposition to the power of the dockopolis from two different groups: port workers, who resisted monopolistic control over labor, and coffee exporters, who resisted monopolistic control over dockage fees, loading and unloading, transport, warehousing, and all other aspects of trade from which the Dock Company could potentially profit. While one would think that there was an alignment of interests between the Dock Company and the coffee barons, it was in fact far more complicated. The company wanted to charge more money to the exporters and tighten its control of workers, while the exporters wanted lower costs and a port that was free from strikes and worker conflicts. This triad—port owners, coffee barons, and workers—shaped the development of the city from 1892, when the Dock Company took control, until the mid-twentieth century.

Two Visions of Labor

About a mile away from the Gaffreé and Guinle monument, but almost out of sight, is a massive monument to the Santos stevedores (fig. 7). If the G&G monument is a shrine to capital, then the latter is a shrine to labor. One of the most significant aspects of the two monuments is that they depict the exact same activity—stevedores hauling sacks of coffee—from entirely different perspectives. The monument to the stevedores shows the muscular, shirtless torso of a man straining under the weight of a coffee sack.[5] Standing over thirty feet high, the worker's body is depicted with sharp angles and a grave expression. The exact same activity—shirtless laborers hauling sacks of coffee—literally supports the capitalists in the Gaffreé and Guinle memorial. In the stevedores monument, labor is not in a supporting, inferior position—it stands alone, at the center of the action, atop the pedestal.

Everywhere in Santos (and São Paulo State in general), the shirtless stevedore hauling a sack of coffee is an icon of a particular era in Brazilian history in which coffee reigned supreme. Micol Seigel (2009) describes how this image was mobilized by advertising agencies to sell Brazilian coffee around the world: "Advertising in coffee trade journals overwhelmingly featured barebacked manual laborers.

FIGURE 7.   Monument to coffee laborers (Photo by author, 2016)

The basic elements of dark-skinned laborers, generally muscular men in some state of undress; doing work, usually carrying" (57). To illustrate this pattern, Seigel includes an image of a 1921 ad from All America Cables called "Santos, Brazil: Where Your Coffee Comes From." This advertisement, like so many others, uses the shirtless stevedore as an icon of productivity in the tropics.

Despite the similar iconography, there is an important difference between these two monuments. While the G&G monument commemorates two specific people, the stevedores monument is a generic depiction of a nameless, faceless worker out of time. Labor may stand alone, no longer supporting the success of the "heroic capitalists," but it remains homogeneous. It is possible that this depiction is done in the spirit of solidarity, but it is still nameless and impersonal. While capital is represented as a historical actor in the form of Gaffreé and

Guinle, the stevedores monument celebrates workers in the abstract—as a class. Furthermore, the G&G monument is cast in bronze and stands prominently at the center of a busy commercial plaza, while the workers monument is a work of polystyrene foam painted to make it appear to be bronze. It was not built until 1996, long after the privatization and modernization of port operations had made stevedores less important to the actual labor of the port then they had been in the golden age of coffee. By the time the monument was erected, the famous image of the shirtless stevedore was already a reference to the past. Whereas the shrine to capital is solid, grand, prominent, and permanent, the shrine to labor is made of foam, hidden out of sight, and moveable.

It is only fitting, then, that the monument to labor became an inconvenience to capital in 2007, in the midst of the commodities boom. A grain silo was built on the site where it stood, which was owned by a Brazilian subsidiary of a Dutch commodities company that was later taken over by China's largest commodities company. This silo would be used to store cereal crops from all over Brazil before they were exported. In the midst of the construction, the stevedores statue was damaged and neglected. The monument was eventually moved to its new home on the side of the highway, where cars speed by at sixty miles per hour, their passengers hardly noticing the monument to the labor that created the wealth of Santos.

Solidarity and Unrest in the Red Port

In Brazil, the history of labor in the Port of Santos is legendary, and journalists often referred to it as the *porto vermelho* (red port) due to the centuries-long presence of communists, anarchists, and syndicalist movements. Yet, it would be a mistake to view the port workers as a political monolith. There were important economic and political divisions between workers in different operations at the port, the most important being the divide between stevedores (workers directly responsible for the loading and unloading of ships) and dockworkers (all other classes of workers who do not enter the ships), which includes longshoreman (who transport cargo on the docks), carters and porters (who move cargo to and from the docks to warehouses), baggers and bag stitchers, mechanics, maintenance workers, painters, cleaners, office staff, and dozens of other jobs that are essential to the operation of the port. In essence, there was a distinction between those who entered the ships (stevedores) and those who had to remain on shore. The Santos Dock Company had almost complete control over all the workers on their docks, but the stevedores remained fiercely independent from the Dock Company for ninety years. They never succumbed to attempts to absorb them as company employees, and thereby the stevedores proved to be one of the most powerful and effective labor unions in Brazilian history.

In the era of the container ship, cranes and forklifts replaced human labor to transport goods from land to sea. By the time the stevedores monument was built in the 2000s, it referenced a bygone era of the shirtless worker hauling coffee sacks on his shoulders. By the 1980s, the standardization of the shipping container meant that the loading and unloading of ships could be done without much manual labor. Stevedores and longshoremen became crane operators and forklift or truck drivers. Yet, prior to containerization, stevedores played an incredibly important role in global trade. They were the people who physically moved the commodities that were the lifeblood of the global economy. The stevedores' speed, organization, and skill determined how long a ship would remain docked in port and whether its cargo would arrive intact. "Most of the work was not structured by the rhythm of a machine, and neither the cargo nor the dimensions of the ships were standardized. The efficiency of the work depended in large part on the skill of the workers" (Texeira da Silva 2011, 70). Prior to containerization, ships were loaded with pulleys and hoists, cargo nets, and teams of workers manually carrying sacks of cargo on and off the boats via gangplanks.

Like the Indians in São Vicente, laborers play an important role in the mythic history of the port, but the mythic history tends to erase struggle, turning the workers into the instruments of Brazilian capitalist modernization rather than its adversaries. The history of Brazil's labor movement can be told through the story of the Santos docks. As early as 1877, coffee workers went on strike, and violent confrontations between stevedores and export houses became more frequent throughout the late 1800s (Gonçalves and Nunes 2008, 35). The country's first general strike took place in May 1891, with over four thousand strikers shutting down the operations of the customs houses and paralyzing movement of goods in and out of the warehouses (Gitahy 1992, 79). Workers began to organize through immigrant mutual aid societies based on national origin (Spanish, Portuguese, Italian, etc.) around this time. As traffic in the port increased, the Dock Company attempted to control and monopolize the labor market.

> CDS [Santos Dock Company] expanded its tentacles into ship maintenance, electrical generating, and warehousing, and it operated its own railway around the docks. . . . The company held power over workers in loading and unloading gangs as well as warehousing, crane operators, railway yardmen, foremen, locomotive engineers, firemen, and sailors for harbor vessels. It also employed workers in mechanical and electrical maintenance and in the paint shop, as well as brick masons and helpers, office staff, guards, and inspectors. After the strike for the

eight hour day, in 1908, only the stevedores—who worked inside the ships and were the most important category—escaped the absorption of their services. (Texeira da Silva 2011, 73)

Santos became known as one of the most concentrated sites for labor activism in the Americas, with the stevedores union leading organized opposition to the power of the Dock Company. Teixeira Da Silva (2011) quotes the anarchist Manuel Marques Bastos describing the city in 1913: "The workers had their Federation. . . . Next to the Federation operated the Union of Construction Workers, the Coachmen's Resistance, the respective Unions of Stone-Masons, Railroad Workers, Coffee Sackers, and Dockworkers" (82). Unlike in many ports, workers in Santos were not divided along racial and ethnic lines, and organizers were quite successful in building worker solidarity against the power of "the octopus." Workers were organized into independent gangs that were hired by import/export houses or shipping lines. The Dock Company tried to employ its own stevedore gangs, offering better rates, but the workers preferred the arrangement in the independent gangs, and the shipping companies preferred not to cede more control to the Dock Company.

The Revolution of 1930 was a turning point. Gétulio Vargas came to power, ushering in an era in which some of the country's most important industries (oil and steel) were nationalized, and the government forged close ties with organized labor through a system called corporatism, in which "labor would accept discipline . . . in return for a share of the fruits of future economic growth" (Rock 1994, 12). Under this system, the industrial labor unions of the cities were incorporated into the mainstream politics of the revolutionary government. Vargas's Estado Novo "moved to establish and to oversee universal health care, maternity leave, a national system of labor unions, free and compulsory public education, a pervasive system of censorship, and a well-oiled and intrusive police force" (Collins 2015, 122). From 1930 on, the stevedores union had "absolute control" over the labor market (Teixeira da Silva 2011, 78). During the Vargas years, labor unions (*sindicatos*) had unprecedented political power, particularly in cities such as Santos, Rio, and São Paulo. In the Port of Santos alone, at least seven *sindicatos* were formalized between 1930 and 1939, including stevedores, port workers, foremen, administrative workers, guards, roadway workers, and terminal operators, all of whom had their own occupation-specific organizations to articulate their interests to the corporatist state through the Ministry of Labor (Gonçalves and Nunes 2008, 46).

Vargas was removed from power in 1945, and the end of the dictatorship opened up space for the Communist Party to exert influence in Santos until the party was banned in 1947. A Communist Party candidate for president won the

Santos vote in 1945, and the communists had especially strong support among the stevedores (Gonçalves and Nunes 2008, 47). Vargas returned to power as the elected leader of the Brazilian Labor Party in 1951, consolidating the support of the trade unions while neutralizing the threat of communism. During this period, the Brazilian government solidified a model of state-led industrialization, in which strong corporatist ties between organized labor and the state were accompanied by an outright ban on communism. The modernization and industrialization programs of the 1950s changed Santos irrevocably. What had been mainly a coffee port became a hub of industry. By 1947, the Anchieta highway connected Santos to São Paulo. The construction of the highway had attracted thousands of migrant laborers, many from the rural Brazilian northeast, who settled in and around Santos, first as temporary workers and then as residents. The roadway connection to São Paulo spurred a period of rapid state-driven industrialization in the Santos region, mainly in the town of Cubatão (see chapter 4), where Brazil's largest oil refinery was built in 1955 and a state-owned steel mill was built in the early 1960s. Cubatão became Brazil's petrochemical hub, with at least sixteen different factories producing fuel, fertilizers, industrial gas, and plastics. New products meant larger ships, more modern terminals, and a constantly expanding volume of cargo in the port.

As the port transitioned from the old patterns of coffee work to the new patterns of petrochemical work, there were frequent strikes and work stoppages led by the stevedores. The workers understood that the country's development depended on the flow of goods in and out of the port, and the "indispensability" of their role gave them a great deal of leverage (Teixeira da Silva 2011, 83). This political power was checked in 1964, when a coup d'état ushered in an era of military dictatorship that would last until 1985. The deposed president, João Goulart, had been minister of labor under Vargas and was a strong proponent of the minimum wage and the corporatist labor unions. The coup, which was backed by the United States at the height of the Cold War, was motivated by a fear that Goulart was moving too far to the left and was leading the country toward communism. The military government almost immediately suppressed radicalism in organized labor. In the days after the coup, the most active leaders of the Santos *sindicatos* were fired, threatened with violence, or held prisoner in a downtown jail. While labor unions continued to exist and to exert influence throughout the dictatorship, their power was neutralized by severe restrictions on political speech, on public protests, and on strikes. The unions became corporate groups whose power was dependent on good relations with the state. The military government therefore gained control over labor at the exact moment the port began to modernize and transition to container shipping. The history of Santos as a "red port" became a "stigma, above all for the city's middle classes, who closed their eyes to what they considered to be the subversive and uncivilized world of the port" (Teixeira da Silva 2011, 84). When the Santos Dock Company concession finally ended in 1980, the docks fell under the control of the state government of São Paulo through their agency CODESP (São Paulo State Dock Company). The dockopolis was no more. A state agency assumed control over the port, and a century of conflict between labor and private capital ended with an arrangement that would have been unimaginable at the outset.

Corporatism to Privatization

Brazil has a notoriously labyrinthian system of labor laws that offer some of the most worker-friendly protections in the Americas, including a forty-four-hour maximum work week, thirty days guaranteed vacation, a bonus of one month's pay for Christmas (called the thirteenth month), and (until recent reforms) an official retirement age of fifty-five for women and sixty for men. Santos is a very popular place for people from the São Paulo region to live in retirement, and I was always surprised (and a bit envious) to see how many youthful people would gather on the beach in the middle of the workday or sit under beachside tents sponsored by local retiree clubs, which would provide food, drinks, and shade for their members. A walk down the beach reveals the entire economic structure of Santos materialized in retiree club tents: the coffee brokers retiree club, the stevedores club, the truck drivers, the iron workers, the schoolteachers, and so on. Among many other things, Santos is a city of retirees.

Many of the labor laws can be traced back to the corporatist system created by Vargas in the 1930s and 1940s. Corporatism was a political philosophy based on the idea that social harmony could be created by the hierarchical organization of corporate groups into a single unified "social body." In practice, this meant that all labor unions came under the control of the state, which actively sought to mediate the conflict between labor, capital, and itself by establishing representative bodies coordinated by the federal government. In the Port of Santos, it is easy to see the historical legacy of corporatism. There are ten separate unions that represent the port workers based on their specific roles in the work of the port: the stevedores union (established in 1930); the port laborers and operations staff union (SINTRAPORT, established in 1931); the cargo clerks union (1932); the administrative workers union (SINDAPORT, 1933); the guards and security workers union (1938); the drivers union (1939); the terminal operations union (SETTAPORT, 1939); the repairmen union (1950); the crane operators union (SINDOGEESP, 1964); and the cleaners and janitorial workers union (1979). Historically, the stevedores union was the largest, most powerful, and most militant union in the port. The stevedores still operates a large, ornate union hall and a hospital, although their union membership has declined significantly as the port has modernized.

In addition to these ten unions, there is yet another more important division between two main categories of workers in the port: *avulsos* (freelancers) and *celetistas* (salaried workers). In 1943, Vargas passed the Consolidation of Labor Laws (CLT), which put the federal government in charge of regulating employment, recognized the right to form unions, and established a minimum wage, a fixed workweek, paid holidays, and other benefits for workers. Workers who are formally employed, follow a predetermined schedule, and are contractually guaranteed a fixed salary and benefits are called *celetistas*, or CLT-ists, a reference to the Vargas-era labor code. In contrast, workers who are self-employed and paid a negotiated daily rate are called *avulsos*. One might assume that the CLT workers would be given preferential treatment, given that their working conditions are formalized and they are protected by the labor laws, but in fact the opposite is true. *Avulsos* are controlled by the unions that manage work assignments and pay scales based on a rotational hiring system called the *rodizio*. The union assigns jobs to *avulso* workers based on a preference system, in which *registrados* (registered workers) have priority over *cadastratos* (listed workers), who have completed job training but do not have extensive experience. The unions are in control of hiring, training, and managing the "gangs" of workers, who enjoy far more independence and a less rigid operational structure than the salaried CLT workers. Historically, the self-employed freelancers were the backbone of the port and its labor movement. They fiercely guarded their independence from managerial control and used slowdowns and strikes to achieve their goals. They were also blamed as the cause of the somewhat notorious inefficiency of the Santos port, which was known as one of the slowest and most inefficient major ports in the world prior to the 1993 modernization laws, which drastically shifted power away from the unions.

The privatization of the port in 1993 was a watershed that fundamentally altered work patterns (Gonçalves and Nunes 2008, 109). The law ended the monopoly of CODESP, the state of São Paulo's port-operating company, and awarded concessions to private companies that now operate the port terminals. Each private port operator controls a certain number of the port's hundreds of terminals, some of which handle grains and other bulk commodities such as soy, coffee, and sugar, while others handle liquids, including oils and juices, or focus on gasses or petrochemicals. Each terminal operator has its own employees, fragmenting the old corporatist system, in which the ten occupational unions were all working under the corporatist umbrella of CODESP and were therefore public employees. The unions continued to function after privatization, but the major axis of organization was no longer the type of work being performed. Rather, workers were organized by the conditions of their employment, with salaried *celetistas* taking control from the freelance workers. Where the most important relationship prior to modernization was union–worker, the new primary relationship is employer–employee; where all employees were union members before the 1993 modernization laws, 44 percent were non-union workers by 2006 (Gonçalves and Nunes 2008, 148).

According to Alcindo Gonçalves and Luis Nunes (2008), there was "strong resistance" to the new system of employment, largely because the unions lost control over workers' pay scales. The stevedores union, which had always been the largest and most powerful *sindicato* in Santos (and possibly Brazil as a whole), is now surpassed in membership by SETTAPORT, a union that includes salaried operations workers, managers, longshoreman, and other workers; SETTAPORT had thirteen thousand members in 2016. Unlike in the old system, the unions no longer set pay and assign work to their members through the "rotation." Instead, SETTAPORT provides benefits such as dental care, a private retirement and disability program, and legal and grievance assistance, as well as an array of professional development courses in partnership with local universities. These changes reflect the shift toward the development of professional skills that give workers the possibility of upward mobility and movement across a range of occupations; again, this is unlike the old system, where a stevedore, for example, would be able to move up through the ranks of the union but would be unlikely to search for a new occupation elsewhere in the port. Workers can now shift from company to company and job to job depending on their skills and experience, reflecting a shift toward a new "generalist" model of work in the modern port. The new era of productivity and efficiency in the port has made training in new technologies and processes an essential part of work. As workers need to position themselves to compete in a liberalized labor market, flexibility, skill, and productivity have become dominant values.

As this change in organizational structure was occurring, the mechanization and containerization of loading and unloading ships continued apace, so the raw number of stevedores required to do manual labor continued to decline. By 2006, the stevedores union still had sixty-three hundred members, but less than half of them were active—the majority had retired (Gonçalves and Nunes 2008, 110). In contrast, the terminal operations union SETTAPORT had four thousand members versus 150 retirees, and by 2016 its active membership had tripled. Freelance workers continued to operate, but the total process of modernization had fragmented their political power at the same time that mechanization and containerization made their actual labor less important to the work of the port.

Invisible Labor

In 1978, Brazilian filmmaker Aloysio Raulino made a short black-and-white documentary, *The Port of Santos*. He went on to become one of the country's premier documentarians, and the film was restored and made available online by the Brazilian government in 2009. The documentary beautifully illustrates how much the port has changed since the 1970s—most notably in the visibility of physical labor. The film shows workers, shirtless and sweating from the heat, moving goods off ships onto forklifts and trucks, working together under the watchful eye of a foreman. Sometimes they stop and casually talk to each other; other times they move swiftly. One scene introduces the importance of coffee in the port, and it shows men lifting jute sacks and loading them onto a truck while women sweep up the coffee beans that have spilled out onto the sidewalk and street, gleaning the detritus for their personal use. Later, there is a scene from the now-defunct nightlife district, glittering with neon signs, where a sailor from Morocco introduces himself, and sex workers who work in the bars mingle with sailors from around the world.

This kind of rich social interaction between the port and the city is no more. The rise of the shipping container totally transformed a way of life. The first container terminal in the Santos port did not open until 1981, so the work of loading and unloading cargo was still done by humans when the film was made. Now, 90 percent of all cargo in the port is shipped in standard steel containers, either forty by eight feet or twenty by eight feet in size (Gonçalves and Nunes 2008, 106). The port is now closed off from the city by forests of piled-up steel containers, and massive cranes (including the new supercranes) load the ships directly from trucks or trains. There are also new "ro-ro" (roll on, roll off) ships that allow trucks to drive right into them to deposit or load cargo. Fewer workers are needed on the boats and on shore, and machines operated by one or two people have replaced the manual labor of the stevedores and longshoremen depicted in Raulino's film. In the months I spent in Santos, I never saw an individual person working in the port who was not operating a machine. Work with cargo was completely mechanized, while humans performed the labor of safety inspection, security, and logistics management.

In addition to replacing manual labor processes with mechanized work, the container also made cargo into a homogeneous commodity. The contents of the ships are measured in TEUs (twenty-foot equivalent units). One small container is one TEU; a normal-size container is two. From the perspective of a cargo loader, the qualities of the cargo no longer matter at all—it is simply a matter of quantity, which is tracked in MPH, or "movements per hour," a measurement of how many TEUs are moved in an hour. No one knows if a container holds sacks of coffee, barrels of ammonia, or washing machines—the content is measured and expressed only as a quantity of TEUs. Electronic barcode readers track the contents of the containers and the rate of movement from trucks to ships. Productivity in the port is then measured and ranked against that of other ports in the world. The Santos port is far behind places such as Shanghai, Yokohama, Long Beach, and Rotterdam in terms of efficiency, and the local newspaper publishes data on improvements in MPH to show progress in the port.

Santos does not just compete against other ports in the world; there is also a competition among the private operators of the port's terminals to demonstrate that each is more efficient than its competitors. For example, a 2016 special issue from the newspaper *A Tribuna* carries the headline, "National Leadership: In the Biggest Port Complex in the Country, the Keywords Are Innovation and Efficiency." The story contains reports from each of the major private operating companies about its improvements in speed. For example, one company states that "in 2011, the company registered 38 movements per hour. Now, they are, on average, 85 movements-per-hour. According to the Director of Operations, a port terminal of 50 to 70 movements per hour is considered a first rank installation, over 70 is world class. In 2014, five South American records were broken in our terminals" (*A Tribuna* April 5, 2016, 40). Tecon, one of the more modern and efficient terminals in Santos, averaged 113 MPH, which is nearly twice as fast as the "world-class" standard defined in *A Tribuna*. Despite these improvements in efficiency, Santos is well behind the most efficient ports in the world and is not even among the top twenty most efficient ports in the Americas according to industry reports. For comparison, in 2005 the Port of Santos was the thirty-ninth busiest port in the world, roughly the size of the Port of New York and New Jersey in terms of cargo movements, according to global rankings of port productivity from the shipping industry.

I am reluctant to fetishize the patterns of work shown in Raulino's 1978 film: there's nothing romantic about hauling drums of fuel on and off a ship in hundred-degree tropical heat. Nevertheless, there is a certain kind of wistful appeal in the film. It depicts a time when the labor processes that made the port function were visible and deeply interwoven into the life of the city. It bothered me that I lived in the world's biggest coffee port but never saw physical coffee being moved. I had an app on my phone that allowed me to trace the itineraries of the ships in the port. I would follow them up and down the coast of South America—from Buenos Aires to Santos to Rio—and then on to New York and to Europe. But the time in port was short, and sailors tended to stay on board, using WhatsApp to communicate. There was no longer a nightlife area where international visitors would mingle with locals. I would always eat lunch in working-class restaurants where port workers would gather. They wore uniforms and safety vests that indicated which terminal operator they worked for, but I never heard a language other than Portuguese being spoken. The lunch spots were filled with professional port workers, but there was never any interaction with any of the ships' crews.

The loading of sixty-kilogram jute sacks of coffee by teams of men is, without a doubt, the most enduring image of the Santos coffee labor. Yet, even the sack itself is becoming obsolete. In 2016, the largest Brazilian coffee plantations began to phase out the jute sacks, instead using synthetic fabric "super sacks" or "big bags" that hold one ton of coffee (about fifteen sacks' worth) each and are hoisted by cranes. Other producers are using synthetic bulk liner bags that cover the entire inside of a shipping container and hold twenty-one tons of coffee each. With this technology, the containers can be loaded or emptied in a single movement, creating significant cost savings. A Reuters article quoted Carlos Roberto Lima, a union leader at a Santos coffee warehouse: "We used to have 59 lifters on a shift, now we have nine" (Ewing 2015). According to the same article, "one worker with a forklift can fill a container with super sacks in 25 minutes, while 9 men need nearly an hour with jute. Loading a liner is even faster as beans are dumped in loose" (ibid.). This technology was relatively new in 2016, but now about 40 percent of Brazil's coffee is shipped in big bags or bulk liners. This has changed the scale of the warehousing facilities needed to store coffee. While there are still a few small coffee warehouses in downtown Santos, including the one depicted in Raulino's 1978 film, most of the action has shifted to processing sites near the coffee plantations, where the beans are dried and packed onto containers on trucks without ever touching human hands. The trucks ship to large, modern terminals on the outskirts of town, in multimodal logistics centers that are off the highway, where the containers are stowed and ultimately loaded onto ships for export.

Returning to chapter 2's discussion, the export commodities boom was driving growth in Santos, but the modernization of the supply chain made agriculture almost invisible—or only visible as a uniform stack of shipping containers that was in the process of moving elsewhere. Port labor also became invisible— or only visible as a process that used machines to streamline the movement of containers. When the trucks entered the downtown or made too much noise, they become a nuisance.

The Discovery of Oil and the New Independence

Recall that in 2006, Petrobras announced the discovery of one of the world's largest offshore oil fields. It was found in the Santos Basin, an extremely deep part of the Atlantic that lies about a hundred miles off the shore of Santos, running from the southern edge of São Paulo state northward toward Rio de Janeiro. Using new technologies that allowed offshore oil rigs to drill deeper than ever before, Petrobras was able to access oil reserves located under seven thousand feet of water and an additional six-thousand-foot-thick layer of salt, which functioned like a cap sealing off a deep reserve of hydrocarbons. By drilling into this pre-salt layer, Petrobras was able to produce astonishing amounts of oil. By 2016, the pre-salt reserves were producing more than one million barrels of oil per day.

When the first oil field was discovered, President Luiz "Lula" Da Silva referred to it as a "new Independence Day" for Brazil. Dilma Rousseff famously declared that it "proved God was a Brazilian." The new discoveries were regulated in a way that allowed the Brazilian government a cut of all oil profits, which would be used to create a social fund, following the model of Norway's national oil company, Statoil. The key policy decision was to ensure that Petrobras was guaranteed at least 30 percent of all the oil rights, the rest of which were auctioned off to private corporations such as Shell and Repsol, which paid concessions to Brazil. The discovery and subsequent development of the pre-salt was in some ways the linchpin of the new model of hegemony for the Workers' Party: the government would use the profits generated by primary commodities to fund new social programs, working together with private capital—even foreign capital. This was the twenty-first-century version of Vargas's "The oil is ours!" nationalism. The Brazilian state knew that it could not succeed in profitably exploiting the oil if it cut itself off from the companies that were well equipped to produce it efficiently, so the government worked in close partnership with private capital. It did not want to become an oil-dependent petrostate like its neighbor Venezuela.

The giddy optimism of Lula and Dilma came from the fact that they imagined oil would create an almost unlimited supply of funds that could help the poor. In a 2009 speech that announced the state's plan for generating revenue from the oil, Lula said he planned to "make Brazil become richer, more developed, from the scientific point of view, from the educational point of view, from the point of view of social policies. All of this because of oil" (Lyons and Kiernan 2015). Critics of the Workers' Party mocked the messianic tone of its leaders, who seemed to promise everything they could have imagined to the people of Brazil— free housing, high-speed rail, new infrastructure, universal health and education, all paid for by oil profits.

In Santos, the discovery of oil off the coast promised a new kind of transformation. The Valongo neighborhood was chosen as the site for a new Petrobras office complex devoted to administration and research and development for the Santos Basin. The port facilities could not handle the large tankers that carry crude oil, nor was the estuary deep enough for the tankers, so crude oil would have to be shipped from the nearby ports of São Sebastiao and Angra do Reis. Offshore oil is in some ways analogous to big agriculture in the Cerrado, in that the production of wealth takes place far away from population centers and at a massive scale that requires large capital investments but relatively few humans to work. The workers on offshore oil rigs tend to travel back and forth by helicopter from remote ports that are far away from Santos. This allows for the illusion of a society where the dirty, material labor of capitalism is largely invisible, and where the work of administration, management, and consumption can proceed as if it were disconnected from physical labor.

During the oil boom, Santos would become a hub for the administration and management of the oil, while the material production would take place elsewhere. Initially, a huge cluster of seven office towers were planned to house white-collar jobs, but the plan was later cut down to two. The initial promise was between two thousand and four thousand professional jobs coming to Valongo, which would anchor the development of the port district. In addition to the Petrobras offices, a 350-room Ibis Hotel was built across the street, along with several office buildings and mixed-use residential apartment buildings. A light-rail system was planned to connect the port with the beaches and other residential areas. In some ways, the plan was modeled after other successful port renovations in South America, such as Puerto Madero in Buenos Aires and Porto Maravilha in Rio.

The Chimera of Postindustrial Progress

I began this chapter recounting a conversation I had on a bus in 2013, when the flush of optimism around the pre-salt and the redevelopment of Valongo was in full bloom. By 2016, the signs of trouble were already clear. Crude oil prices had crashed from a high of $140 per barrel in 2008 to about $40 per barrel in 2016. Most of the projects that were deigned to be funded by oil revenues were pared back or cancelled. The Ibis Hotel was mostly empty. Only a couple hundred of the thousands of promised jobs at Petrobras had materialized, and many of those workers ended up commuting from metro São Paulo rather than moving to Santos. The Valongo area was often a ghost town. However, Atento, the business processes outsourcing firm that moved into the old coffee warehouse, was still thriving. Hundreds of workers came and went throughout the day and night, and lines of motorbikes and scooters clogged the parking area in front of the entrance. The firm had been purchased by the US private equity firm Bain Capital in 2012, and it had an IPO on the New York Stock Exchange in 2014. In 2019, Atento was the largest private employer in Brazil, with seventy-three thousand employees nationwide.

In 2019, the conservative news magazine *Veja* published a postmortem of the Santos downturn called "Decay by the Seaside: Santos Region Faces Problems." It listed a number of "white elephants" that resulted from the expected pre-salt boom that had failed to materialize:

> In the historic district of Valongo, which houses Petrobras' headquarters, projects that were built in the wake of promises to explore the pre-salt at the site ran aground. . . . The hotels are only full even between New Year's and Carnival. The rest of the year is a long, melancholy low season. . . . The Ibis Hotel, located in the Valongo district, is part of the Valongo Brasil complex, built by Odebrecht Realizações and completed in 2015. There, in the same structure, there is also a commercial building. Of the 329 rooms for sale at the site, at least 100 are for sale by the construction company and have never been used. There are still the seven existing stores on the ground floor of the development, which until now have no floor. A little further on, Cyrela's Wave Offices building faces the same problem. With 210 office units available at the property since 2014, at least thirty have never been occupied. Both constructions were built amid Petrobras investment promises in the region, which did not materialize. (Prado and Rosario August 18, 2019)

By 2020, even Atento had to shut its location in Santos, terminating 480 employees and shifting the rest to other locations. The company's profits had plummeted, and Bain Capital sold its stake in the company for a loss.

It would be a mistake, however, to view Valongo as a copy of the famous neoliberal port developments that David Harvey (1989) first described as harbingers of postmodernism in his study of Baltimore's Inner Harbor. The difference is that Valongo would remain an industrial port as well as a tourist district. It would be blue collar as well as white collar. A space of work as well as play. A place where Chinese container ships would intermingle with wealthy residents of São Paulo who stopped at the Pelé Museum on their way home from the beach. It was a perfect illustration of the Workers' Party version of hegemony, a place where all class contradictions would be resolved.

Ruralistas and the New Horizontalism

Let me now return to the clash between the truckers and the city government over traffic, which I described at the beginning of the chapter. It might be tempting to see this as a simple story of a failed attempt at gentrification, with noisy trucks spoiling the downtown experience for new urban consumers. My argument is that this clash was really a conflict between two sets of class interests, one tied to agricultural production and the other tied to urban redevelopment and consumption. Each class produced its own chronotope of progress, and the two appeared superficially to be in conflict but were in fact directly connected. The disruptive presence of agricultural commodities shattered the myth of a new, modern Santos, revealing its connection to big agriculture in the interior.

In the introduction to this book, I mentioned a canonical theory of Brazilian civilizational development put forth by Gilberto Freyre in *The Masters and the Slaves*. Freyre (1946) argued that Brazilian history was shaped by two great "foci of energy" that he called horizontalism and verticalism (16). Horizontalism was a form of expansionary movement into the interior of Brazil epitomized by the *bandeirantes*, who were rooted in São Paulo (which Freyre called "the South," as opposed to the sugar-producing regions of the North, where he was from). Verticalism was a form of agrarian patriarchy based on slavery and the colonial sugar plantations of the North, which were the economic core of Brazil under colonial rule. Freyre argued that much of Brazilian social structure, politics, and culture could be explained by the development of the patriarchal agrarian system (verticalism) as it developed over more than three centuries, creating a hierarchical society with roots in racial inequality and rigid hierarchies of class and status.[6] The two foci of energy were chronotopes describing two types of development—predatory capitalist expansion into the interior, and the consolidation of social hierarchies in the cities and towns. In this respect, the presence of traffic in Santos reflected the uneasy compromise between these two chronotopes, revealing that they were in fact two sides of the same capitalist coin. Santos may have banished the trucks to the old highway and built a brand-new road for personal vehicles, and wealthier residents may have distanced themselves from sites of production and manual labor, memorializing it as a thing of the past; but the truck traffic brought country and city together in a troubling way.

Mention the term *ruralista* in Brazil and people will know exactly who that means. In simple terms, the *ruralistas* are "the rural lobby" (Stolcke 1988, 76), but in a broader sense, they are a group of wealthy landowners who used their political influence to dismantle environmental regulations and roll back protections of indigenous land rights throughout the 2000s (Ferrante and Fearnside 2019). *Ruralistas* were the strongest supporters of Jair Bolsonaro's rise to power in 2018, and he strongly identifies with their interests, at one point even saying, "This government is yours," to a group of *ruralista* leaders at the presidential palace (Rodrigues 2019).

Critics of the *ruralistas* see them as the new *bandeirantes*, a group who is obsessed with profit and the expansion of agribusiness at any cost—the new avatars of horizontalism. The *ruralistas* have systematically halted all the progress Brazil made on sustainable development, deforestation, and indigenous rights over the past two decades, and have "thrown the country's status as an environmental beacon into doubt" (Viscidi and Graham 2019). The *ruralistas* and Bolsonaro have denied the reality of anthropogenic climate change (and, more recently, downplayed the seriousness of the COVID-19 pandemic). They fiercely resist agrarian reform and virtually every other reform movement proposed by Brazil's social movements. Yet, the power of the *ruralistas* cannot be dismissed as simply a cabal of moneyed landowners. The Brazilian middle classes have supported them at the ballot box. In 2018, conservative *ruralista* politicians earned sweeping victories in congressional elections. What is frequently overlooked in the criticism of the *ruralistas* is that much of Brazil's economic growth and social progress during the boom years was based on the expansion of agribusiness in the Cerrado and the Amazon, and even during the years in which the Workers' Party was in power, it was able to tie its own interests to the cause of national progress. During the commodities boom of the mid-2000s, the growth of agribusiness became associated with national progress, not just in rural areas but in places like Santos.

The term *bancada ruralista* (agribusiness bench) emerged during the Lula years as a direct response to the rising power of the Movimento Sem Terra (MST), a militant social movement devoted to aggressive agrarian reform through the occupation of farmland around the country. In the early 2000s, the MST was probably (along with the Zapatistas in Mexico) the most famous grassroots social movement in Latin America. The relationship between Lula and the MST is complicated, and it in some ways reflects his political genius. He was supportive enough of its radical agenda to achieve the MST's electoral support, but he distanced himself from that agenda just enough not to alienate his more moderate supporters and the *ruralista* power brokers. However, pressure from the MST mounted in 2005 and 2006, and Lula began to accelerate the pace of a resettlement program for landless people. Although the *bloco ruralista* (rural bench) was officially formed in 1955 in the Brazilian congress (Stolcke 1988, 76), according to a Google trends search, the more recent term *bancada ruralista* began to appear in the Brazilian media in 2006 to describe the bloc in congress that opposed agrarian reform and was the arch enemy of the MST. By 2010, there were hundreds of articles in the Brazilian press that used the term *bancada ruralista* to describe the bloc of politicians who were opposed not only to agrarian reform but also to basically all new regulations to slow the pace of deforestation or limit the use of GMOs, as well as any other legislation that might curtail the unchecked power of agribusiness. It is important to note that the MST's agenda reached far beyond land reform, conducting direct action against biotech companies such as Monsanto and Syngenta and occupying farms owned by multinational commodities companies. While the MST stepped up its pressure, the economic power of agribusiness increased at an incredible rate. Between 2005 and 2015, Brazil's economy boomed on the heels of increases in trade with China. The *Wall Street Journal* reported in a 2015 article, "How Brazil's China-Driven Commodities Boom Went Bust," that "looking back, it is easy to understand the frenzy of optimism. If the biggest economic story this century was China's rise, Brazil was uniquely poised to benefit from it. Rich in iron ore, soybeans and beef, not to mention oil, Brazil was positioned as a supplier of many things China needed. Its annual trade with China, only around $2 billion in 2000, soared to $83 billion in 2013. China supplanted the U.S. as Brazil's largest trading partner" (Lyons and Kiernan 2015).

There is no doubt that the boom in commodities exports was driving urban growth in Santos. The 2016 Mercedes-Benz ad perfectly symbolized how this new horizontalism was ideologically transformed into a project of national progress. The figure of the ranch owner was positioned as a national patron, someone to whom the people should be not only deferential but also grateful. The endless fields of soy may have been off in the distance from Santos, but the point was clear: if you are going to need trucks to bring products to the port, it is best to ride in comfort and style. The horizontalism of the plantation and the verticalism of the city were neatly synthesized. If only they could do something about the traffic.

SACRALIZING THE SEWER
Turning Pollution into Progress

> **"It is a mistake to believe that sanitary science is a new progressive science, or that its progress has been always upward. Like the human race itself, it has had and will have its ups and downs and may degenerate again, for a long time to come, even though the secular progress tends towards higher planes."**
>
> —Estevan A. Fuertes, Cornell University Professor of Civil Engineering, in *Sanitary Improvements for the City and Port of Santos, Brazil* (1894)

Chapter 3 described the relationship between labor and capital in Santos. That relationship has been mythologized and woven into the story of Brazilian national progress through museums, monuments, and popular culture. This chapter applies the same template to the history of sanitation and public health, focusing on two different moments when the Santos region overcame health disasters and turned them into triumphs. In both examples, an economic boom was halted by a health emergency. The ensuing crises were overcome by engineering, and the technological solutions to the crises were memorialized as a triumph. All along, these triumphs were assimilated into the *bandeirantes* narrative.

The two crises hit about a century apart. In the late nineteenth century, as the coffee economy boomed and the Santos docks were modernizing, the city was struck by an epidemic of yellow fever that killed an astonishing 12 percent of its population in one year. Many Atlantic ports had fallen victim to yellow fever around that time, including New Orleans, Havana, New York, and Philadelphia. The cause of the epidemic, mosquitoes, had not yet been identified, but all of these ports instituted major urban sanitation programs according to the best scientific theories of the day. The municipal government of Santos became preoccupied with urban sanitation, not only because people were sick and dying but also because the disease was interrupting the flow of trade and turning the city into an international embarrassment. Modern ports were sanitary ports, and Santos was, at that time, one of the least sanitary ports in the Atlantic world. In the frenzied culture of progress during the nineteenth-century coffee boom, sanitation became a defining marker of modernity.

About seventy years later, during the petrochemical boom of the "miracle years," Santos again became an international embarrassment. The rise of an essentially unregulated petrochemical industry during the military dictatorship of the 1960s led to an environmental disaster. The city was plagued by acid rain, oil spills, industrial fires, and poor public health. The problem was so bad that a 1985 *New York Times* article described Cubatão, an industrial boomtown on the outskirts of Santos, as a living hell, a "valley of death," with the highest known levels of pollution on earth. Similar stories were published around the globe, placing Santos alongside Bhopal, India (site of one of the biggest industrial disasters in modern history), as symbols of industrialization gone wrong (Fortun 2001). Santos, which had been maligned as a yellow fever–infested "cursed port" in the nineteenth century, became a valley of death in the twentieth century due to industrial pollution. For the sanitation campaigns of the nineteenth century and the environmentalism of the twentieth century, the Brazilian government turned to civil engineers to develop solutions, and then it celebrated the triumph of engineering as a step on the national march to progress.

Beautiful Sewers

The idea for this chapter came to me when I saw a painting by Benedicto Calixto, the same artist who created "The Epic of the Bandeirantes," described in chapter 2. Much of Calixto's work depicts idyllic, postcard-like images of Santos and its environs, particularly the ocean, beaches, and the lush green landscapes that surround the city. These were the paintings that would be hung in the parlor of every São Paulo coffee baron worth his salt. The paintings memorialized the transformation of Santos into a modern city, depicting scenes from the port and its surroundings to develop a powerful visual iconography of Santos.

One painting called *The Beach of São Vicente* (fig. 8), shows a sewer pipe crossing the very same bay that separates the Guaraní village (described in chapter 1) from the rest of the city. The undated canvas, which is probably from about 1910, shows a black cast-iron pipe running across a narrow salt marsh and disappearing into the horizon at sunset.[1] The sewer pipe is set against a backdrop of islands and lush tropical forest. Why would a landscape painter known for bucolic images of the Santos coast paint a picture of a sewer pipe? Wouldn't that spoil the beauty? Was this a criticism of an encroaching modernity that would spoil pristine nature—or was it something else?[2]

This pipe was built in 1910 and 1911 as part of the comprehensive sanitation program in Santos. For Calixto, the rapid development of the modern city of San-

FIGURE 8.   Benedicto Calixto, *The Beach of São Vicente* painting, from the collection of the Fundação Pinacoteca Benedicto Calixto, Santos, Brazil. Used with permission.

tos in the previous twenty years was the realization of a utopia that began with the divine vision of the early *bandeirantes* on the beaches of Santos (Antonio Ferreira 2002, 278). It was to be the city that led Brazil's march to progress, with profits from the coffee boom fueling a furious period of modernization and development. As described in chapter 2, the coffee boom that transformed Santos during the Belle Époque turned the city's elites into heroic agents of progress. Ferreira (2002) describes the giddy sense of exhilaration that São Paulo's intellectuals felt as they abandoned themselves to "rhythms brought with modernity" (132). For example, in a 1910 poem about Santos, the poet Júlio Conceição compares the growing port to New York City:

> And just as the portentous New York has the unveiled affection of the Yankee and constitutes his pride, Santos, will soon be, without a doubt, the Brazilian pride, demanding merit, esteem, and patriotic attention from all of us. (Ferreira 2002, 132)

From this point of view, Santos was on its way to becoming one of the world's great cities, and its modernization was another iteration of the *bandeirantes* myth. "A period of adventure and an intrepid collective spirit were revived, and the bandeirantes were considered as architects of regional progress, who continued in coffee-growing, in locomotives, in the metropolization of capital and in industries. The bandeirante activity was thus taken as the vehicle of the São Paulo territorial formation and of the very construction of the country" (Ferreira 2002, 133).

Within this context of giddy modernization, Calixto the artist did not, perhaps could not, see the sewer pipe as a blot on the landscape. He saw the development of modern industrial infrastructure as part of the beautiful epic of progress in Santos, and the sewer was one scene in that unfolding epic. In 1914, he followed up the sewer pipe painting with an airy, sunny depiction of a suspension bridge that was constructed to carry this same sewer pipe across the narrow bay to an outflow in the neighboring town of Praia Grande. The bridge is an ornately decorated steel cable structure that, when it opened, was the first of its kind in Brazil. The bridge is now a well-known local landmark that is on Brazil's national register of historic places. The sanitation project turned the problem of sewage into an infrastructural conquest. The beautiful bridge was built to carry the sewer pipe over the channel, and then the bridge itself became a work of art in the skilled hands of Calixto. The sewer pipe was beautiful in itself, then it was beautified yet again by the bridge, and then the bridge was beautified on Calixto's canvas. Sewage became aestheticized, three times over.[3]

To understand why the sewer pipe was seen as a thing of beauty, it is important to recognize how nightmarish the yellow fever outbreak had been in Santos. Throughout the late nineteenth century, as the population grew alongside foreign trade, Santos earned notoriety as the cursed port by sailors due to the prevalence of disease. The ongoing problem turned into a true disaster in 1892, when a yellow fever outbreak killed nearly 12 percent of the population in a single year (Fuertes 1894, 5). Foreign vessels refused to dock in Santos, and some ships that passed through the port were prohibited from stopping at other ports or quarantined for long periods on an offshore station until they could prove to be free of disease. Trade and immigration were the lifeblood of the economy, and they were severely disrupted by the horrific epidemic. The city was getting fabulously wealthy from the coffee trade, but it could not be a truly modern city if people lived in fear of the worst plague of the era.[4]

The government stepped in, soliciting plans from experts from around the world for a comprehensive sanitation program to solve the problem of disease. Beginning in 1870, a private company called the City of Santos Improvement Company, referred to simply as "A City," held a monopoly on municipal services such as illumination, gas, and transportation. The company was technically in charge of water, sanitation, and sewage services, but it was not overseen by the government, and sanitation was neglected. Under pressure from business interests in the city, the state of São Paulo formed a commission on sanitation in 1892. One of those invited to submit a plan was Estevan A. Fuertes, then dean of Civil Engineering at Cornell University.[5] He had designed urban sanitation plans for cities in Puerto Rico and had worked on early plans for a transoceanic canal in Central America. In 1892—at the height of the epidemic—Fuertes agreed to develop a sanitation plan for Santos, and in 1894 he delivered his report. Fuertes (1894) described a city that was utterly lacking in basic sanitary infrastructure. He wrote that the "death rate was appalling; though during six months it rivaled the plague of the 'Black Death'" (5). Santos had been totally unprepared for its rapid growth from sleepy coastal town to a center of global trade and immigration, and its infrastructure was a hodgepodge of old Portuguese colonial relics and improvised fixes.

Fuertes was astonished by the poor state of the city's infrastructure. Here is his colorful description of the Rink, an outdoor skating rink built in 1879 that was used to house recent immigrant arrivals in 1892:

> Another center of infection in the city is the building called "The Rink," a tenement for the reception of immigrants.... It is now used for this purpose, but it is totally unsuited both as to accommodations and location. The waste matters are thrown upon the ground at the lower side of the house, and allowed to putrify under the rays of the sun. At present, the condition of the ground surrounding the building is most disagreeable.... Another place which also may contribute its share to the propagation of disease is the Hospital D' Isolamento. The sewer which drains this building discharges its dangerous contents into the harbor at a place where there is no current, and where at times of low tide the sewage spreads out over a surface of putrifying black slime exposed to the winds. Large heaps of rubbish are to be found along the harbor in front of the city, consisting of decayed fruits and other refuse from stores and houses, and thrown over the harbor wall, where the water is shallow. In the course of time this matter contributes largely to transform the mud along the wall, which is uncovered at low tide, into a very dangerous locality. (1894, 53–54)

What could be more embarrassing to the city's bourgeois elite than to have a rink that they had made for theater, skating, and sporting events turn into a tenement and a source of "immigrant filth"? How embarrassing must it have been for the beautiful, modernizing city of Santos to be described this way by a distinguished foreign visitor? Fuertes emphasized the urgency of the problem in his report, pointing out that both "the savage" and "the cultured" must respond to the tragic loss of life. Introducing his report, he wrote:

> We have endeavored to put a sordid money price upon the value of losses by epidemics on human life, which the savage and the cultured man alike consider priceless. We must bear in mind that such a scourge bears most heavily upon the bread winners, and their dependents in the lower classes, whose orphaned families are thrown upon public charity and deprived of the care of natural protectors who are the best social agents to foster their comfort, education and thrift. We have not taken into account the sorrows of widows and orphans and friends; the breaking up of families; nor the miseries and sufferings entailed by the remorseless scythe of death. These losses have no price—no money can ever replace them. (8)

The comprehensive Fuertes sanitation plan, developed over two years with a team of American and Brazilian engineers, included designs for a new quarantine station on an offshore island, sanitation plans for arriving ships, an immigrant boarding house, street paving, a municipal water system, underground sewers, drainage canals, and municipal garbage disposal. The proposal was based on visits by Fuertes to a host of North American cities with modern sanitation plans, including Baltimore, New York, and Philadelphia, as well as Newport, Rhode Island, and Rochester, New York. The plan detailed everything from the kinds of detergents that should be used to disinfect the garments of immigrants to the sources of the stone that should be used to pave the roads. He even proposed the use of huge tanks of highly toxic mercuric chloride in sanitation stations, which would use large steam engines to disinfect incoming vessels and crews with poisonous vapor. The estimated total cost for the Fuertes plan was $2.5 million in 1892, equivalent to nearly $70 billion today. Despite the severity of the problem, however, the Santos government did not move ahead with the Fuertes plan. Various factions favored other plans, and they solicited more proposals over the next few years while making piecemeal changes to halt the plague. Most importantly, immigrants were rapidly transported by train to the immigrant station in São Paulo (Hospedaria dos Imigrantes) almost immediately after disembarking in Santos, and much of the energy for reform was focused on this large sanitation and boarding station where immigrants were housed until trains brought them to coffee plantations in the interior.[6]

Ultimately, in 1902, the city engaged a Brazilian engineer named Saturnino de Brito, who had worked on waterworks projects in several other Brazilian cities, to design a system of sewers and drainage canals. He was inspired by Pierre L'Enfant's design for Washington, DC, as a modern and rationally organized city.

De Brito proposed a comprehensive urbanization plan that would deal with the immediate problems of sanitation and public health while also transforming the city into a healthy, beautiful, and modern place that could adapt to future growth. The plan called for an innovative system in which stormwater and drainage traveled in pipes that were completely separate from sewage, as opposed to the combined systems that carried stormwater and wastewater through a single pipe or channel. Under De Brito's plan, sewage was carried by underground pipes to an outflow in the sea, while all the drainage and urban storm runoff flowed through six wide, open-air canals. These canals would be lined by wide, tree-lined avenues, with parks and broad sidewalks for strolling. Decorative wrought iron bridges crisscrossed the canals, where small boats could paddle. Trollies ran alongside the avenues, which were illuminated at night by electricity generated by the City of Santos Improvement Company.

As Cynthia Dos Santos (2015) describes it, the plan created a new modern vision of a bourgeois city based on European models. Santos, which in Brazil is sometimes known as the City of Avenues, also became a place of sharp class separation, where the city's coffee bourgeoisie was able to move to the newly urbanized areas, thereby separating itself from immigrants and dockworkers near the port. The sewer separated clean water from dirty, but it also separated the "clean" bourgeoisie from the unwashed masses. Work and leisure became separated as never before. The city's elite built huge mansions along the broad avenues and the beaches, which were now connected to the commercial center by a trolley system (the *bonde*). As a consequence, the port and the commercial district became spatially separate from the bourgeois residential areas that sprang up along the canals and avenues. This shifted patterns of life in the city. As Dos Santos writes: "All of the modifications proposed by [De] Brito created a new type of public space. No longer the traditional plaza, home to commercial activities and not a meeting place, but now a canal and the new avenues and parks which, beyond sanitizing and doing away with the ills of colonial times, became new spaces of sociability, sources of pride and public admiration" (2015, 73).

In 1910, the suspension bridge that Calixto painted was the last piece of the puzzle. It carried sewage away from the city and marked the end of the era of disease and filth. The curse of yellow fever was largely eradicated, and the fetid, tropical port that had scared away visitors before the project was transformed into a beautiful modern city. When Calixto sought to represent the beauty of Santos in his painting, modern infrastructure was part of, not separate from, a sublime nature.

Sacralizing the Sewer

Today, the canals and avenues that De Brito designed continue to be a source of local pride in Santos. Although they are often filled with trash and urban debris, they still empty directly into the Atlantic Ocean, and the tide washes the runoff out to sea. The nonstop streams of people that walk along the beaches cross directly over or through the canal runoff, and children swim in the deep, warm pools that form where the runoff empties into the sea. "Meet me at Canal [X]" is a common way to tell a friend where you are sitting on the beach. The city bus routes are marked with the numbers of the canals to indicate their routes (Canal 1, Canal 2, etc.). The city's most expensive real estate lines the shady canals and avenues that run perpendicular to the beaches, particularly Canals 3, 4, and 5. In sum, De Brito's plan for urbanization is remembered as a great success and has been thoroughly integrated into daily life. The presence of sewage and urban runoff is generally ignored or transformed into a point of pride, and De Brito is a local hero. Through his efforts, the shame of pollution transformed into the pride of infrastructural conquest. The canals that began as a solution to the devastating effects of yellow fever are now an iconic part of the Santos landscape. A space of pollution and filth is now a space of leisure and aesthetic appeal.

De Brito's office was built directly above the site of the former Rink theater, and the building became the headquarters of the Santos water and sewer office. De Brito died in 1929 and his office was then transformed into the Palacio Saturnino de Brito, an ornate museum that celebrates his accomplishments. At the museum's inauguration in 1937, the poet Martins Fontes wrote a tribute titled À Saturnino de Brito (To Saturnino de Brito). My translation is as follows:[7]

> My land owes you this homage
> I speak to you on behalf of my citizens
> Receive our applause in unison, the message
> That they send to you through my hands
>
> For where you walked, in the middle of a thicket
> Through forests and detours
> You performed a prodigious act of courage
> You gave a prize of love to your brothers
>
> Great engineer, the scholar Saturnino
> De Brito, high character, the shield
> That you wrapped yourself in was bronzed and diamond-studded

Your treasure scattered in bulk
You loved Auguste Comte, and his teaching
Rigidly, you were always faithful.

The palace is built atop the very spot where the infamous Rink held the immigrants described in such horrific terms by Estevan Fuertes, but there is no mention of that history in the museum, which is nothing if not a monument to Brazilian progress. In fact, the entire gruesome history of the epidemic in Santos is nowhere to be found in public history, despite the fact that the city has over a dozen museums, and monuments and historical placards on nearly every block of the historical center. On the other hand, the sewer system itself, what might be thought of as the most profane category of infrastructure, has become sacred, remembered as part of the epic march of Santos from backwardness to modernity. As I mentioned earlier, the canals are considered to be one of the most appealing parts of life in Santos. I frequently asked people if they thought the canals were beautiful, and they always answered in the affirmative, with one qualification: after storms, the canals bring the trash from the informal settlements into the city center.

From Myth to History

While the mythology of progress celebrates the sewer, the people of Santos face near-constant reminders of the inadequacy of their public works systems. The Santos beaches are usually closed to swimming due to pollution, and the "dirty waters of Santos" are a regional inside joke (like swimming in the Genesee River would be in Rochester). People rarely swim in the ocean. Instead, they cool off in dozens of public showers that line the beaches. These showers were built to wash the sand and salt off of swimmers but now substitute for bathing in the polluted ocean. The canals empty directly into the sea, and the thousands of people who stroll the beaches every day have to wade through urban detritus that eventually gets washed away by the tides. The canals have floodgates that are closed when the water levels get too high, creating deep, warm, dirty pools that children swim in. Informal urban settlements (*favelas*) creep up the hillside around the museum and along the estuaries of Santos, and these neighborhoods dispose of waste through illicit hookups into the drainage canals. These settlements, especially the Vila Gilda, which is composed of makeshift shacks on stilts over the river, suffer from fires that have destroyed hundreds of homes at a time. In 2010, a fire destroyed 150 homes, and in 2017, another fire burned 200. A *Veja* article on the decline of Santos (see chapter 3) focused on the continuing problems with water pollution. It quoted an environmental manager who explained that the vulnerable populations of the informal

FIGURE 9. Comic about illegal sewage connections. ©Mauricio de Sousa
Produções 2016

settlements on the banks of the estuary make it difficult to manage pollution in the
beaches: "They sleep in fear of water and fire. They don't even have a sewage system. It's no use dealing with formal connections if we have 270,000 people dump-
ing raw sewage. We need to solve the housing issue" (Prado and Rosario 2019).

On a visit to De Brito Palace, I was given a handout designed for school groups
about water safety and conservation. The palace is now run by SABESP, the state-
run water and sewer company of São Paulo. A publicly traded company on the
New York Stock Exchange, SABESP it engages in a host of corporate social re-
sponsibility initiatives to promote its brand. The handout was a comic book fea-
turing Monica's Gang, the Brazilian equivalent of Charlie Brown and the
Peanuts gang (fig. 9). They are perhaps the most recognizable characters in all
of Brazilian popular culture, a cartoon that has been running since the 1960s
and has spawned a whole universe of merchandise. The comic book explains how
municipal water supplies can be polluted, focusing on the role of "irregular occupations," or informal settlements. It states:

> When houses don't have services, many residents end up making ille-
> gal connections to potable water, causing leaks and running the seri-

ous risk of drinking contaminated water! Trash is thrown out all over the place, creating dirty vacant lots, and especially in the river. Sewerage runs out in the open and the inhabitants of these places, especially children, suffer from illnesses like diarrhea, verminosis, hepatitis, leptospirosis, etc. Many of these residents dump their sewage in the closest river.

I was fascinated when I received this handout at the museum, because the great achievements of the sewer system and its contemporary deficits were being presented simultaneously, with no apparent contradiction. The same pattern can be seen, modified only slightly, on the shores of Santos's most popular beach, where a giant sewage outflow pipe, called the Emissário Submarino, was constructed in the 1990s. The pipe carries sewage far out to sea, improving on De Brito's old system that discharged very close to the shore. The new outflow carries the sewage a half mile out to sea, where it is more effectively dispersed by the current. On top of the new pipe is a massive public park, with bike paths, a skate park, surfboard rentals, volleyball courts, a helicopter landing pad, and a huge abstract sculpture of waves, created by Tomie Ohtake, one of Brazil's most renowned modern artists. The sewage pipe has been completely aestheticized, with absolutely no sign or mention of what it actually is. I asked people if they thought it was odd to build a beautiful park on top of a sewage outflow pipe, but I never heard anyone say they felt that something was out of place. I expected a structural contradiction between sacred and profane, clean and dirty, pure and impure, nature and culture, but I found none. Like De Brito Palace, the huge park encases the sewer in a modern, outward-facing veneer. It is an almost compulsive response to the inadequacies of Brazilian public works to layer upon them the most excessive and costly examples of leisure and entertainment, always oriented toward elite consumption. The same thing happened a century ago, when the Rink was contaminated by waste from the immigrant tenement and disease. De Brito's solution was to create beautiful canals that turned sewage infrastructure into a space of leisure and entertainment.

How does this connect to the *bandeirantes*? Atop the abandoned Rink theater sits a marble palace emblazoned with their story, in honor of De Brito. When entering the palace, the first thing a visitor encounters in the marble hall of this grand Italianate structure is a twenty-foot-high stained-glass mural called *The Bandeirantes* (fig. 10). The mural, created in 1936, shows six bearded *bandeirantes* scaling the Serra do Mar. The *bandeirantes* are leading two Indian slaves in loincloths and headdresses, who are carrying large sacks of riches through the jungle. Just under the sacks of plundered riches is the seal of the São Paulo state government's sanitation bureau. Why were the *bandeirantes* used to celebrate the sewer?

FIGURE 10.   *Bandeirantes* in the sewer palace (Photo by author, 2016)

When the building was created, the Brazilian minister of culture, poet Cassiano Ricardo, referred to the *bandeirantes'* movement into the interior as nothing less than "the rhythm of Brazilian civilization" (Morse 1965, 211.) Ricardo wrote about the *bandeirantes* in grandiose terms, saying that each stage of civilization leads to its own frontier, each cultural horizon has its *bandeira* on the march, and parallel *bandeiras* will extend the moving frontiers, until they one day combine in a single geographic, economic, spiritual, and sentimental frontier, like three waves along a single stretch of beach.

At the time of the palace's construction, the *bandeirantes* symbolized a new historical phase based on economic nationalism. Under Getúlio Vargas, the new *bandeirantes* would modernize Brazil through state-led initiatives that brought foreign capital under national control. Recall that, "The oil is ours!" was the slogan when the national oil company, Petrobras, was formed by Vargas. The sewer palace turned the outward movement of the *bandeirantes* in space into the forward movement of the Brazilian nation in time.[8] And infrastructure was the fulcrum that allowed for the progress. The same pattern endures in the present wave of development. The sewer is no longer celebrated with a grand marble palace and a stained-glass mural, but with a helicopter pad and a skate park. At both moments, what was once a failure and national embarrassment was transformed into a triumph, creating social spaces for well-to-do people to enjoy. The basic template for progress through infrastructure is unchanged. The difference lies in the aesthetics and tastes of the modern bourgeoisie.

From Valley of Death to Green City

The small city of Cubatão sits directly adjacent to Santos, creeping up the hillsides of the Serra do Mar from the coastal mangroves and rising into the lush cloud forests that Lévi-Strauss rhapsodized about when he first arrived in Santos. Cubatão begins at the sea and ends in the mountains, only a few miles from the urban fringes of the São Paulo megalopolis. If Santos was the city shaped by the agricultural vision of progress of the nineteenth century, defined by coffee, then its neighbor, Cubatão, epitomizes twentieth-century industrial developmentalism, which was defined by heavy industry, oil, chemicals, plastics, and steel production.[9] Whereas Santos was a mercantile and agricultural hub, Cubatão is a hub of factory labor and industrial production, known throughout Brazil as the country's first hub, or *polo*, for the petrochemical industry. Cubatão is the site of the first Petrobras oil refinery, built in 1950. Shortly thereafter, it became the first place in Brazil to be designated as a federally controlled "industrial zone." Cut off from local democratic control, with absolutely no political space for resistance, it became home to one of the country's largest steel plants (operated by Cosipa, the São Paulo Steel Company). Huge petrochemical factories owned by Dow Chemical, Union Carbide, and other large multinationals popped up all along the mangrove-lined estuary. By the 1980s, more than twenty industrial factories lined the small strip of swampy land between the port of Santos and Cubatão, producing everything from jet fuel to ammonia gas to fertilizers and plastics. At that time, the reigning ideology of the military dictatorship was "development at any cost," and the country attracted foreign investment by touting the fact that it had extremely lax environmental and labor regulations. "Brazil can still afford to import pollution," a Brazilian planning minister is quoted as saying in Ulrich Beck's landmark work *Risk Society* (2013, 43), a statement that reflected a philosophy in which economic growth was prioritized above all else.

In the center of downtown Cubatão lies the Children's City, a large, shady, and pleasant park that was built in the mid-1980s. Chickens roam freely through the park under shady palms and a somewhat incongruous ski chairlift that circles overhead. Coati and other small animals roam alongside the park's spurting fountains, colorful playgrounds, sports fields, indoor basketball courts, ropes course, and skateboard park. The park, which is officially called the Anilinas Park, is built on the site of one of Brazil's first major chemical factories (established in 1916), and one of the factory's buildings is preserved as part of the park. The Anilinas Chemical Company functioned until 1964, after which the site was abandoned, torn down in the early 1970s, and then reinaugurated as a park in 1979. In 2011, it was again inaugurated after a large-scale expansion and renovation. The park epitomizes the city of Cubatão's transformation from a notoriously polluted industrial wasteland to a space of leisure and green industry. Like the sewer pipes, the scars of the past have been overlain with a veneer of progress, transforming a space of work into a space of play. Work and play or clean and dirty are not held apart here. They overlay one another like a palimpsest. As in Santos, industrial blight in Cubatão became aestheticized and sacralized on the path to twenty-first-century modernity.

The Children's City is only one example—the pattern repeats throughout Cubatão. Forests that had been burned or denuded by chemical pollution in the 1980s have been rechristened as state forests, with miles of marked trails sprawling out from the oil refineries and steel mills, which are still active. A park designed by Burle Marx, arguably the world's most famous modern landscape architect, sits between a highway, the oil refinery, and rows of Petrobras storage tanks. The migrant workers, once a source of embarrassment and prejudice, have been embraced as a part of Cubatão's rich cultural life, and each year the city celebrates a festival of northeastern Brazilian food, dance, and expressive culture called, fittingly, *danado de bom*—"damn good."[10] All around Cubatão are attempts to resignify history by transforming sites of shame into sites of honor, turning culture into nature, work into play, and blight into beauty.

The parallels with the yellow fever epidemic in Santos a century earlier are striking, with the petrochemical boom of the twentieth century replacing the coffee boom of the nineteenth. In both cases, the population swelled with immigrants living in precarious conditions, and the region's government was totally unprepared for the social, environmental, and health effects of rapid growth. As when the yellow fever outbreak occurred before, the economic boom in Cubatão would be halted by a public health scandal that achieved international infamy. In February 1984, a pipeline that carried gasoline from the Petrobras refinery in Cubatão to the Port of Santos developed a leak that would have tragic consequences for the informal settlement of Vila Socó. This neighborhood of makeshift shacks housed many of the poor families who had come from the northeast to work in Cubatão, mainly on road construction. In fact, the edge of the neighborhood directly abutted the highway (the Anchieta) that connects Santos to São Paulo. The shacks were built in a mangrove swamp alongside the highway, right next to or directly over the pipeline. In some cases, the shacks used the pipes as structural supports. As the leaking gas began to seep into the swampy ground, people used the leak to fill household gas cans for free. But the leak continued for hours without anyone realizing it, and the ground became totally saturated. Late at night, the gas exploded in a massive fireball that consumed the whole neighborhood. The government estimated about one hundred deaths in the Vila Socó disaster, but international groups concluded that as many as five hundred people were burned to death in the fire.

Less than a year later, another accident struck the *favela* of Vila Parisi, located on the other side of Cubatão, only a mile or so from Vila Socó. Vila Parisi was the neighborhood closest to many of the chemical plants, and for years, residents there had suffered from some of the highest levels of chemical exposure in the world. In fact, the state's own public health agency had already issued reports about the dangers in Vila Parisi by the time the accident occurred. When a chemical pipeline finally sprang a leak in January 1985, releasing fifteen tons of ammonia gas into the air, it forced the immediate evacuation of five thousand residents. Newspapers around the world used the two stories to weave a tale of complete governmental and corporate negligence, leading to Cubatão's reputation as "the dirtiest town on earth" and "the valley of death." These disasters were a major reckoning for the military dictatorship and are now remembered as the end of Brazil's "development at any cost" philosophy.

Sociologist Lúcia da Costa Ferreira studied the political aftermath of the two accidents. Her book, which I translate as *Ghosts of the Valley*, tells the story of the groups that victims formed to exert pressure on the military government and oil companies for restitution and improvements after the accidents. This kind of activism was unheard of during the military period, and scholars consider the Vila Socó disaster to be a turning point that steered the country toward democracy and ended the era of development at any cost, coalescing civil society groups to oppose the military government. The activism that sprang up in 1984 and 1985 involved a cluster of political groups, including the Workers' Party, Catholic groups associated with liberation theology and workers' rights, and progressive evangelical churches. It also involved academics and journalists, all of

whom sought to publicize the devastation caused not only by the chemical ac-
cidents but also by the long-term exposure to pollution that had taken place in
Cubatão over two decades. Without a doubt, the aftermath of Vila Socó and Vila
Parisi changed the ways that businesses operated in Cubatão.

Cubatão's bad reputation even made it into popular culture. In 1985, the popular São Paulo rock band Premeditando o Breque put out a single called "Honey-
moon in Cubatão," which satirized the city's odd juxtaposition between natural
beauty and environmental destruction. One verse reads:

> Clouds of sulfur
> View from the mangrove at dusk
> And on the pipeline
> Our love will burn
> Clouds of ash
> Smell of gas
> Honeymoon

There were two levels to the problems in Cubatão. One level was the actual devastation caused by rapid, unregulated industrial growth—death and environmental destruction. The other level was symbolic—the stigma and international
shame that the problems caused for a military government that was hell-bent
on modernizing the country at any cost. As Nei Serra, an environmentally con-
scious steel executive who became Cubatão's longtime mayor, put it in 1986,
"Smoke coming out of a smokestack was considered a sign of progress. . . . Our
society, on the part of its elites, didn't worry about pollution; it didn't even have
conscience of the problem. The main preoccupation was to implant basic industry, fundamentally to generate profit. One thing that characterized this is the
symbol of the presence of industry—smoke coming out of a smokestack" (Ferreira 1993, 96). If stevedores loading ships with an endless supply of coffee was
the image of nineteenth-century progress in Santos, then the belching smokestack of a Cubatão factory was the symbol of the twentieth century.

The negative public perception of Cubatão ran deep in popular culture. News
articles from around the globe solidified the "hell on earth" and "valley of death"
images, which was not pleasing to a government that still needed to partner with
foreign multinationals to build factories. Ferreira shows that the public outcry
over pollution in Cubatão created a change in mindset in the military government. No longer able to control public opinion, the government began to think
about public relations to strategically improve the image of Brazilian industry
at home and abroad. The smokestack could no longer be the symbol of progress,
and the government engaged the public relations firm Ogilvy and Mather to im-

prove the image of Cubatão through campaigns called "Cubatão Heart" (Cubatão Coração) and "Cubatão Looks for Solutions" (Cubatão Busca Soluções). A public relations executive put it this way:

> A person from Cubatão today is shown as a sick child with a distended belly and this is only 5% of the population, the other 90% are normal people. The city is beautiful, there is a lot of green. Cubatão has an excellent renaissance orchestra, a music band of the highest quality, choral groups, and these things need to be shown. . . . We know that emotional phrases like Valley of Death will be difficult to do away with. But we think that a day will come when Premeditando o Breque, with its "Honeymoon in Cubatão" will find other themes, not the pollution of Cubatão, to make fun of. (Ferreira 1993, 98)

The public relations strategy seemed to pay off. In 1991, the *New York Times* published a story called "Signs of Life in Brazil's Valley of Death," lauding the city as a "striking example of a turnaround in industrial pollution in Latin America."

"Today," the article states, "a verdant mantle of trees and bushes cover mountainsides that surround the steel, fertilizer and petrochemical plants of Cubatão Valley. Less than a decade ago, clouds of ammonia and fluorides rendered the

FIGURE 11.   Newspaper advertisement for Vila Bandeirantes housing development, *A Tribuna*, June 29, 1952

FIGURE 12. General Motors advertisement, *O Estado de São Paulo*, April 22, 1947

mountain ridges a lifeless skyline of dead tree trunks" (Brooke 1991). The change was far more than a matter of perception. Cubatão's business and governmental leadership had indeed developed strategies to mitigate pollution and improve the health of people and the environment. The changes were no less dramatic than those that had occurred a century earlier under De Brito's sanitation plan. With support from the World Bank, factories installed the latest environmental

technology to cut toxic emissions to the air and the water. The government re-
planted deforested hillsides. The state of São Paulo's environmental agency,
CETESB, took on an active and meaningful role in monitoring pollution and
enforcing environmental regulations. The municipal government started a cam-
paign called "Cubatão—City of Ecology," which involved environmental education in schools and reforestation. The Serra do Mar State Park set aside more
than three hundred thousand hectares of forest, reaching from the outskirts of
São Paulo all the way to Cubatão, and has developed ecotourism throughout the
region. The region has adopted the image of the scarlet ibis (*guara vermelho*) as
a symbol of its environmental recuperation. Thanks to the success of Cubatão's
environmental cleanup, this protected bird once again nests in the area.

Throughout this chapter, I have shown how various attempts to overcome crisis through engineering were incorporated into the *bandeirantes* narrative. Cubatão has a deep historical association with the *bandeirantes*. In addition to being
the location of the *calcada lorena*, the mule trail that the early *bandeirantes* used
to access the interior from the coast, the city was strongly associated with the
bandeirsmo of the miracle years. The workers who migrated to Cubatão to build
the Anchieta highway were called *bandeirantes*. A General Motors bus advertisement called the highway "the mark of *bandeirantes* dynamism" (fig. 12). The
oil workers for Exxon were called *bandeirantes* (Holston 1989, 212). There is even
a housing development called Vila Bandeirantes, on a spit of land sandwiched
between the shores of the Casqueiro River and the highway that connects Santos to Cubatão. Built in the 1950s, the lots were described as "picturesque and
futuristic," and the newspaper ad (fig. 11) showed a neatly organized grid of
streets with a highway and a train in the foreground and mountains in the
background.

CITIZEN OF THE WORLD, KING OF ALL NATIONS

Globalization and the FIFA Class at the Pelé Museum

> **"Pelé is one of the only people that contradicted my theory. Instead of fifteen minutes of fame, he will have fifteen centuries."**
>
> —Andy Warhol, as quoted in the Pelé Museum

> **"A second trend was a shift away from the consumption of goods and into the consumption of services—not only personal, business, educational, and health services, but also into entertainments, spectacles, happenings, and distractions. The 'lifetime' of such services (a visit to a museum, going to a rock concert or movie, attending lectures or health clubs), though hard to estimate, is far shorter than that of an automobile or washing machine."**
>
> —David Harvey, in *The Condition of Postmodernity*, 1989

The structure of this chapter deviates from the others. It presents a clash of timescapes between myth and reality, but in this case the mythology is not directly depicted through the *bandeirantes* story. Instead, I argue that the next stage in the *bandeirantes* chronotope, in which Brazil would become a "First World power" (to use a phrase favored by the Workers' Party), was going to be spawned by the spectacles of the 2014 World Cup and 2016 Rio Olympics. This stage of the developmentalist plot rested on the assumption that Brazil would become an economy of mass consumption rather than production, a full participant in globalized consumer capitalism. I argue that soccer superstar Pelé, and the mythology around him, was mobilized in Santos as a symbol of this new globalized, consumerist Brazil.

Let me offer a preemptive apology. I am not really a soccer fan, so writing anything about Pelé, the most famous player of the world's most popular sport, is likely to get me in trouble. What more is there to say about him? Until his death in December of 2022, he was arguably the most famous living human, and hundreds of talented and passionate writers have covered his life exhaustively across genres. In addition to all the popular texts about his life story and his significance to the world of sports, the anthropology of Brazilian soccer contains a rich literature on the relationship between *futebol* and society in which Pelé figures prominently.[1] Thankfully, this chapter is not about Pelé or soccer per se—it is about how Pelé's life story was represented and mythologized in the short-lived Santos Pelé Museum, and how the museum materialized a new chronotope of progress in which Valongo would become a place of leisure and consumption. My analysis integrates two different aspects of the museum: its material role in the transformation of Valongo, and its symbolic role in narrating a particular story of Brazil's development. As a material object, the museum was an expensive construction project and a centerpiece of the redevelopment of Valongo. As a text, the museum told the story of a triumphant Brazil in the run-up to the World Cup, using Pelé's biography as allegory. The most fascinating aspect of the museum is that it traced the same historical plot—the chronotope that I have developed throughout this book—at three levels: the history of the building itself, the narrative of Pelé's life, and the story of Brazil's development over time. Across all three dimensions of the narrative, the museum—as material object and cultural text—traced the transformation of Brazil from rural backwardness to national modernization to full participation in global consumer capitalism.

The Story of the Pelé Museum

Every postindustrial downtown needs its museum. In his classic diagnosis of postmodern cities, *The Condition of Postmodernity*, David Harvey (1989) wrote that museums play a key role in the "ideological labor of inventing tradition" by representing the past through a formalistic ordering of objects (272). He notes that bursts in museum culture tend to take place when the flattening of cultural differences through the growth of global capital "implied a loss of identity with place and repeated radical breaks with any sense of historical continuity" (ibid.). In the nineteenth century, as colonialism and world trade created the first iteration of globalization, it was necessary to have an archeological heritage museum to have a modern nation. Like Benedict Anderson (1997), Harvey draws out the similarities between maps and museums: the former is a concrete formalization of space, the latter of time.[2] In the present, to have a museum is to particularize an otherwise homogeneous urban space. Chain stores and consumer products may all be the same everywhere, but the museum appears unique, creating uniqueness and character in spaces that have been standardized by consumer capitalism. The museum form gets adapted and replicated, while the content may adapt to local conditions. In this sense, even the uniqueness is standardized. Harvey argues that museums are one kind of spectacle of consumption—along with malls and entertainment districts—that marks postmodern urbanity. While particular museums may narrate local stories, having a museum is now part of any downtown redevelopment as a way to assert some kind of particularity.

The Pelé Museum was a big part of the plan to make Valongo into a historical tourist district. The official planning for the museum began in 2007, and it opened in 2014. The museum is housed in the Mansion of Valongo, a large building that is directly across from the train station and "widely regarded as the city's most prominent work of civil engineering during the 19th Century—and a reflection of the wealth generated by the booming coffee industry of the time . . . an important physical symbol of the 'coffee architecture' representing the beginning of the economic cycle that transformed the city of Santos" (Medeiros 2014, 14). The mansion, built between 1867 and 1872, was the former home of Manoel Joaquim Ferreira Netto, a merchant from a Portuguese colonial family who earned a fortune in sugar, coffee, shipping, and land speculation. Designed in a neoclassical style, the grand building would not be out of place in the French Quarter of New Orleans. Over the years, the mansion was used in many different ways. After Netto's death, it housed two German-owned import/export businesses: Theodor Wille, which, as described in chapter 2, was the world's largest coffee merchant; and later, Zerrenner and Bülow, a German firm that owned the Antarctica beer company, which, along with Brahma, was one of the two most popular domestic beer brands in Brazil. (Ironically, Antarctica and Brahma merged to form Ambev in 2000, one of the world's largest brewers, a corporate sponsor of the museum, and a company that attracted a great deal of criticism during the 2014 World Cup as symbol of global capitalist greed.)

In 1895, the mansion became the home of the Santos City Council, which was located there until 1939, when the Getúlio Vargas government constructed a complex of new, modern municipal offices. The building then fell into a period of decline, used at times as a tavern, hotel, tire repair shop, and car garage. The mansion's decay matched that of the neighborhood of Valongo after the Great Depression, which had precipitated a massive crash in the Brazilian coffee industry. The hub of Brazil's banking and coffee trade shifted from Santos to São Paulo. After the military coup of 1964, Santos lost its political autonomy. Its municipal government was essentially inactive until 1983, when local control was restored. By 1980, much of Valongo had become a ruin of abandoned buildings. The state of São Paulo granted the mansion historic landmark status in 1983, taking control of its preservation. However, two fires led to the almost complete destruction of the building by the 1990s. After a 1992 fire (when the mansion was used as a tire shop), all that was left standing was a crumbling facade and piles of rubble surrounding a courtyard of weeds and garbage.

Plans for a Santos museum dedicated to Pelé began in the late 1990s, when the municipal government solicited proposals for redevelopment of the beachfront park that sits on sewage outflow pipes (see chapter 4). Originally, Pelé himself partnered with a large developer in the Santos region to build his museum there. The plan was approved, and the city allocated funds for the project. However, construction was blocked by the federal government in 2003 because no one had conducted an environmental impact study and the federal government was concerned about the municipality of Santos handing over a well-used public recreational space to a private developer.

In 2007, the plans for the museum were rekindled. The Alegra Centro program, begun in 2003, had already launched an ambitious plan to restore the historic center of Santos, including the Valongo neighborhood. The government created a variety of tax breaks to stimulate the restoration of cultural heritage sites, and urban redevelopment linked to tourism was prioritized, especially in the port of Valongo. All along, the redevelopment of the neighborhood by creating a more attractive image of the city was supposed to be a catalyst for future investment to "transform the abandoned and deteriorated state of the urban landscape" (Medeiros 2014, 68). In 2006, the pre-salt discovery was announced, and the goals of the Alegra Centro program became even more ambitious. Now the new business and tourism district would be anchored by the new Petrobras office towers, which would bring white-collar professionals to join the tourists downtown. The Pelé Museum would be the centerpiece of the new Valongo. The museum was funded through a combination of federal, state, and municipal contributions, as well as private contributions from large corporations such as Petrobras, Vale, Santander Bank, Odebrecht, Mitsubishi, and Ambev. The construction and development process was managed by an NGO called Ama Brazil, under a 1999 law that gave certain NGOs the authority to act as quasi-public institutions.[3]

After more than a decade of construction, at a cost of $10 million, the museum opened in June 2014, coinciding with the start of the World Cup. The city of Santos made a very public (but ultimately unsuccessful) attempt to position itself as a host city for the Cup. Santos was ultimately chosen as a training site for the Mexican national team, but this was a bitter disappointment to the local government, which dreamed of the tourism revenues and international fame that would come with being a host city—not to mention, the bonanza of funds that are directed toward construction and development to redevelop cities to meet the requirements of FIFA. While the bid to be a host city was unsuccessful, Santos did get some international publicity during the World Cup. Because the opening ceremony of the museum was timed to occur at the very beginning of the Cup, the ceremony was attended by Pelé and Michel Temer, who was then vice president, and covered by ESPN and other international TV networks that were already in Brazil for the start of the tournament. After a brief burst of interest, however, the museum began to fail. It fell into dire financial straits due to low visitorship and the cumulative effects of Brazil's economic crisis. By early 2015, just months after it had officially opened, the museum was operating at an unsustainable monthly deficit. It was taken over by the Santos municipal government in 2016 and was only open to the public on a greatly reduced schedule. In 2017, the museum was set to be managed by an Argentinian company before the deal fell apart. It had become, in the words of the conservative news magazine *Veja*, an example of "decay by the sea," attracting only forty-five thousand visitors in all of 2018. (For comparison, the children's museum in Rochester, New York, attracts about ten times as many visitors per year.) Plagued by construction problems, the building was severely damaged in a storm in 2018. By 2021, it was condemned, and the museum closed.

Notice that over the course of the building's history, it transformed from a colonial mansion (Netto's home) to the offices of a foreign coffee exporter (Theodore Wille), to an industrial company (Zerrenner and Bülow) mass-producing a product (beer) for the Brazilian market and to a public agency (municipal government), followed by a long period of decline during the Vargas dictatorship. The building was then revitalized as a postindustrial tourist attraction through heavy public investment and corporate sponsorship, becoming a museum for a short period of time before it closed. This trajectory follows the basic episodic sequence of Brazilian developmentalism that I have traced over the course of this book—a transformation from colonialism to agriculturist to industrialism to consumer globalization and renewal.

Santos and Soccer

To understand why the Pelé Museum was so important, it is necessary to know that Santos is sacred ground for international soccer. The Santos Football Club is one of the world's most legendary teams, and it is the club where Pelé rose to fame. The team's tiny hundred-year-old stadium is hidden in Vila Belmiro, a squat middle-class neighborhood in central Santos, equidistant from the beach area and downtown. The stadium itself is a tourist attraction, even though it is smaller and more bare bones than many college stadiums in the United States, with a capacity of only about eighteen thousand people, who sit on poured concrete bleachers in a simple, white-tiled structure. A visit to the stadium, particularly a behind-the-scenes tour that includes a visit to the locker rooms, the playing field, and the Memorial of the Conquest museum, is a must for loyal Santos fans. When I took the tour, I saw a young man break into tears in the locker room while standing in front of the locker of his favorite player, Gabriel Barbosa, known as "Gabigol."

Pelé played in Santos from 1956 to 1974, and the images of his achievements wearing the black-and-white uniform of the Santos Football Club are iconic in the history of the sport. It was often said that Pelé was the world's most famous person—and this was not too much of an exaggeration. There was a famous joke in Brazil: Who is more popular, Pelé or Jesus? The answer, of course, is Pelé, because there are far more soccer fans in the world than Christians. In the museum's exhibits, he is called the "King of All Nations" without a hint of self-consciousness. The museum exhibits intentionally follow the narrative of a hero's journey in which Pelé overcomes obstacles to achieve his destiny, becoming the greatest soccer player who ever lived and redeeming Brazil's 1950 World Cup defeat by leading the national team to two Cup victories.

The introductory text to the main exhibit gallery makes the dramatic structure of the exhibit clear: "The story of Pelé's participation in four World Cups could have been written by the most creative screenwriters. It contains all the elements of the journey of a great hero. In truth, it goes beyond, for, after the supreme goal is achieved, new obstacles arise and, with them, an even greater challenge. Witness the courage, the joy, the sadness, the doubts, the fears, the resolve, and, finally, the incomparable glory of the greatest hero of our time!" Entering the main exhibit hall, visitors encounter a bright, open central area with a large cafeteria and gift shop. The gift shop sells replica Pelé jerseys and soccer balls, and one can buy coffee from Cafe Pelé (Pelé's coffee company) along with drinks and snacks. Signs advertise the role played by corporate sponsors, and a bronze plaque celebrates the support of the government of Dilma Rousseff and Michel Temer. A large panel of screens, about fifteen feet high, plays a short video presentation in a loop, with music and sound that echoes through the space. The video shows highlights of Pelé's career, starting with old black-and-white clips and then moving to color images. The film is accompanied by the following song, written specifically for the museum. The song begins with fanfare, and it is then sung by a group of children in sing-along style.

> Once upon a time there was a boy who never dreamed he would be
>   king
> But it was his destiny. He was born to shine.
> And today the King has so many stories to tell
> For such talent it was easy to be happy
> A ball between his feet

Rehearsing his goals and *olés*
And the imaginary fans shouted for him to hear
Go, boy, go! Play ball to make our country happy!
And so it was. He gave us such emotion
And he united with a strong gesture so many hearts
Citizen of the world
King of all nations
Spreading so much peace, inspiring generations
Noble knight, so many glories he achieved
With his strength and his faith, he showed us how beautiful are
The green-yellow jersey and indigo blue shorts [the national team
    uniform]
Today the king has his castle
And one more goal among the thousand
Far more than a thousand
One more goal for my Brazil!

Once the song has ended, a full-body holographic image of Pelé (at about seventy years of age) appears. He is dressed in white from top to bottom and is standing against a black background. He welcomes the visitor to his "castle" with open arms.

Once visitors leave the main hall, they enter a gallery that displays artifacts and memorabilia from Pelé's life, from childhood to the present. The gallery is organized in a rectangle, presenting a chronology from Pelé's birth to the present as we follow along the perimeter of the gallery, which begins and ends at the same point in the room. The very first image we see is a black-and-white photograph of Pelé as an adult with his mother, seated across from each other. This is the only image of a woman in the entire museum (except for female celebrities such as England's Queen Elizabeth). This image is followed by black-and-white photographs of Pelé as a child, his baptismal certificate, and a shoeshine box that he used to earn money as a child in the interior agricultural city of Baurú, where his father was a minor league soccer player. Here are all the signs of rural traditionalism—Pelé's baptismal certificate, his shoeshine box, a piggy bank, and stories of a boy playing barefoot soccer out in the country. The first stage in Pelé's life is as a poor country boy in the agricultural interior.

Then a radio is featured in the exhibit, a model from 1945 that was owned by Pelé's father. It was through this radio that the young Pelé, who was named Edson after Thomas Edison, listened to the Brazilian national team's dramatic defeat by Uruguay in the final of the 1950 World Cup, a national tragedy called the "Maracanãzo" (because it took place in the Maracanã Stadium in Rio).

Through this radio, the country boy learns of his place in a national media landscape—the radio connects country and city. After listening to the Maracanãzo on the radio, Pelé promises his parents that he will lead the team to a world championship. So begins "the birth of a myth," according to the museum narration Pelé is discovered by a scout, Waldemar de Brito, who takes him via train to Luz Station in São Paulo and then on to Santos. In this stage of the developmentalist plot, Pelé takes over soccer at the national level, leading Santos to Brazilian league titles. In the process, he moves from the county to the city, leaving the farmland behind to become a part of urban, industrial, and modern Brazil. The symbolism in the exhibit shifts from traditional to modern, from rural to urban. (Even the traditional iconography on the trophies—winged victory, angels, and golden balls—changes over time. For instance, Pelé's trophies for being named Brazil's player of the year in 1963 and 1964 depict silver, art deco skyscrapers.)

The hero's redemption is complete when Pelé leads the national team to victory in the 1958 World Cup at the age of seventeen. Encased in plexiglass is one of the only prizes awarded to the team, a General Electric television painted in bright green and yellow (fig. 13). Here, we begin to see a change as Pelé's heroic

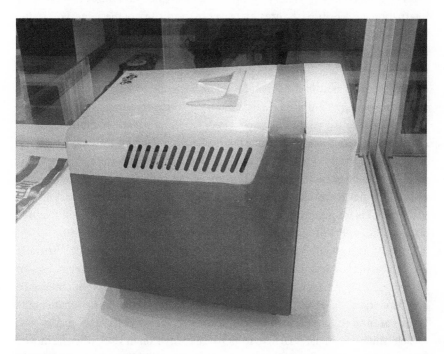

FIGURE 13.   General Electric television given to 1958 World Cup winning team (Photo by the author, 2016)

journey becomes modern and is perpetuated in mass media. As journalist David Goldblatt (2014) writes:

> From the early 1930s until the mid-1960s, radio had been the main way in which Brazilians had consumed football. Indeed, outside of the small circle of newspaper readers, radio was for most of the country the key source of news, drama and entertainment. The years of the dictatorship, by contrast, were synonymous with the rise of television. In 1960 there were just 600,000 sets in the whole country. By 1986, as the generals withdrew to their barracks, there were 26.5 million, a phenomenal forty-four-fold increase that had been underwritten by government-subsidized installment plans for buying sets. (133)

The museum tracks the arrival of television as a new stage in Pelé's story. The Brazilian national imagery becomes linked to international symbols—Pelé with the Beatles, Pelé winning an award from the BBC, and so on. The gallery shifts to a new theme, "Live and In Color," and a large color TV test pattern announces that the 1970 World Cup was the first to be broadcast live and in color around the world. This Cup was the scene of Pelé's greatest and last performance in the World Cup, a dominant victory for Brazil that launched him into a new phase of international celebrity as the greatest player in the history of the game. Politically, Pelé was an ally to the military dictatorship, who used success in world soccer to mobilize nationalistic support. Their ambitions to create "O Grande Brasil" involved investing huge sums of money to build giant soccer stadiums around the country, most famously the construction of Mineirão in Belo Horizonte, which could seat over one hundred thousand people. These stadiums were infrastructural icons of Brazil's modernization. Goldblatt describes the stadium in Mineirão as "a deep-angled concrete bowl, set off with a flat roof through which the giant angular cantilevers and buttresses of the stadium walls were set. It was unambiguously large, industrial and brutish—a machine for staging football, the players tiny figures on the vast green swathe, the whole set against a vast flat car park, full to brimming with the Volkswagens and Mercedes coming off the production lines of Brazil's new and explosively growing car industry" (140).

In 1972, Pelé publicly supported the military government, saying, "There is no dictatorship in Brazil. Brazil is a liberal country, a land of happiness. We are a free people. Our leaders know what is best for us and govern us with tolerance and patriotism" (Goldblatt 2014, 139). His image was used on nationalist billboards around the country to communicate messages of patriotism and loyalty.

Pelé' shifted from national hero to global celebrity icon in 1973, when he moved to New York to join the fledgling Cosmos team. There, he became something of a commodity himself, appearing in advertisements for companies such as American

Express, Mastercard, Visa, and Subway. In 1978, he was painted by Andy Warhol in his *Athletes* series, along with Muhammad Ali, Kareem Abdul Jabbar, O. J. Simpson, and other sports celebrities. The museum traces this transformation from national hero to icon of global capitalism in its final exhibit, called *Pelé: Citizen of the World*. Here, Pelé is transformed into a person whose identity hovers above national origins or citizenship. Gone are the patriotic symbols, such as the green, yellow, and blue of the national team. There are no images of his teammates and no more mention of his accomplishments on the soccer field Instead, we see pictures of Pelé with Richard Nixon, Gerald Ford, Ronald Reagan, Muhammad Ali, four popes (Paul, Benedict, John Paul, and John), and Queen Elizabeth, as well as a smiling group photo with Mikael Gorbachev and model Brooke Shields. The photographs have no accompanying text or captions. The people are supposed to be famous enough not to require explanation. Here, the chronology ends, and Pelé's journey from country boy to national hero to citizen of the world is complete.

At this point, a visitor can look out the window of the old mansion and see another iteration of this developmentalist plot. Right there is the Santo Antonio Church, built in 1640. Just down the block, and also visible from the window, lies the old Valongo wharf where Brazil's coffee boom was born. The terminal of the Santos-Jundiaí railroad is right across the street. High-tech shipping cranes load container ships, and the brand-new Petrobras headquarters and Ibis Hotel rise above the tree line, just beyond the train station. Here, we see the story of Brazilian capitalism shifting from the colonial period to the coffee era to the new age of oil wealth right before our eyes. Pelé's journey from country boy to citizen of the world parallels Brazil's development.

A museum is many things: a building, a narrative text, a work of art, an educational medium, an aesthetic experience, an instrument of economic development, a political statement, a symbol of a city or a nation. To understand the full meaning of any museum, we have to consider all of these different interrelated functions. A museum says something, but it also does something. In the case of the Pelé Museum, what it says and what it does are completely intertwined. In theoretical terms, its function as a narrative is inseparable from its role in the material re-creation of Valongo as a postmodern "historic center." The museum's narrative turns Pelé into an icon of Brazilian modernization and globalization. In telling Pelé's life story, from poor country boy to global icon, the museum is also telling a mythic tale of national progress. Add to this the fact that the museum itself was intended to launch Santos forward as an international tourism and business destination, and the narrative is one of transformation and modernization at every level, from the building itself to the exhibits within. The narrative sequence within the museum is exactly the same as the biography of the building, and the next stage in the plot would be the creation of global consumer citizens—full integration into consumer capitalism. The agents of this transformation took on the name "FIFA class."

Pelé and the FIFA Class

Soccer—and, particularly, soccer as a spectacle for tourists—was at the center of the nationwide protests that broke out in June 2013 during the FIFA Confederations Cup, widely seen as a dress rehearsal for the World Cup. During the tournament, one of the main rallying cries among opponents of the Workers' Party government was "We want schools and hospitals of FIFA class!" This demand was a reference to the government's massive and wasteful spending on soccer stadiums, airports, and hotels to prepare for the 2014 World Cup. In addition, FIFA, which oversees the World Cup, required that sports facilities and tourism amenities be brought up to international standards. The host cities of Rio de Janeiro, Brasília, São Paulo, Salvador, Manaus, Porto Alegre, Natal, Fortaleza, Curitiba, Recife, Cuiabá, and Belo Horizonte received the lion's share of investment, but the World Cup provoked a nationwide conversation about the state of the country's infrastructure—a debate that reached far beyond the host cities. Anthropologist José Leite Lopes and others (2017) write:

> Remember the shock that put the complaints about FIFA's conditions in gear. The construction of infrastructure revealed the distance between international norms and standards and Brazilian reality. At first, the press judged that these conditions would lead Brazil to modernize itself. Nevertheless, progressively the other side of the coin revealed itself. FIFA had, before everything else, demands that were contrary to local practices, like the forced reintroduction of bottled beer in the stadiums and the prohibition of small businesses on the outskirts of the enclosures. In addition, FIFA was the only judge of what to build and how it ought to have been built. Across the country, a sentiment grew that national sovereignty had rotted away.
>
> It was a great paradox that the popular forces, once in power, turned the "national passion" to the benefit of the most privileged classes, following the impositions of FIFA with support of the multinational sponsors and the interests of a press who was completely dependent on the large economic and financial groups. (182)

The outcry over public spending on the sporting events was a subgenre of an even broader political debate about whose interests should be served by the programs of the Workers' Party. After all, it had risen to power with a mandate to fight severe poverty, and the resources that the governments of both Lula Da Silva and Dilma Rousseff devoted to the World Cup and the Olympics signaled either a shift in priorities or an abandonment of principles, depending on whom one asked. The main narrative that emerged in the run-up to the Cup was that the Workers' Party had become too focused on two overarching strategies: expensive social welfare programs such as Minha Casa Minha Vida, which would benefit the very poor; and grandiose international spectacles such as the 2016 Olympics and the 2014 World Cup, which would materially benefit the very rich while also appealing to nationalistic pride. The two-pronged strategy led to rising discontent among members of the middle classes, who felt left behind.

The historic 2013 protests were sparked by a protest against a small increase in the (already expensive) public bus fare in São Paulo. Brazil's economy had boomed, and the revenues from the pre-salt oil reserves were only adding to a sense of a growing bonanza of wealth. Yet, Brazil's cost of living rose steadily amid the boom. Incomes were increasing, but quality of life for the middle classes was not improving. A July 22, 2013, *New York Times* headline read, "Prices Fuel Outrage in Brazil, Home of the $30 Cheese Pizza"—and this was not hyperbole. During my fieldwork, nearly every consumer good in urban Brazil was priced well above what it would cost abroad. For example, a simple spiral notebook, which might cost $2 or less in the United States, was $8 in Brazil in 2013. Adjusted for average income, life in Brazil was incredibly expensive, and it was becoming even worse as the economy boomed. In this economic context, middle- and working-class people felt squeezed by a government that was spending untold amounts of money on outward-facing events while ignoring inward-facing investments in public services such as schools and hospitals. The increase in the bus fare added insult to injury because Brazil's municipal buses were well below "FIFA-class" standards, and they were already expensive, equal in cost to bus fares in most US cities and more expensive than fares in my hometown of Rochester, despite the fact that average incomes in Brazil were far lower than in the United States.

The tourists who would visit for the World Cup would be traveling on private coaches or shuttles, not municipal buses, so it was the locals who would absorb the proposed cost increase. The government promised that the other infrastructural investments would last well after the spectacle events ended. The public would be able to utilize the new infrastructure far into the future. The São Paulo metro subway and rail system, for example, underwent a massive expansion and renovation, making it one of the best systems in the Americas. However, much of the spending was focused on sports facilities, airports, and downtown hotel and leisure districts that would not impact the daily quality of life for most Brazilians.

The term "FIFA class" therefore took on a double meaning. When applied to hotels, airports, or other facilities to be used by foreign visitors, it meant a "global standard" of quality, as in first class and on par with the most modern facilities in Europe and North America. It also meant the "FIFA class" in the Marxist sense of the word—a group with a particular relationship to the means of production and a political interest in preserving that relationship. Roughly speaking, the FIFA class was the transnational financial elite, the group whose interests were in line with transnational capital and the private investment firms that benefited from the construction projects and the tourists from all over the world who would travel to Brazil to experience these new amenities. In short, bringing hotels and infrastructure up to FIFA-class standards would make Brazil more appealing to the FIFA class. In Santos, attracting the FIFA class to the Santos downtown was the major objective of urban redevelopment. As discussed in previous chapters, it meant transforming Valongo into a tourist and white-collar area with Petrobras jobs, chain hotels, condos, and a nightlife district.

In preparation for the Cup, there was near-constant anxiety about whether Brazilian facilities would be adequate to handle the arriving throngs without embarrassing the country. This anxiety about being viewed as inferior by Europeans and North Americans has a long historical trajectory in Brazil, going back to *para ingles ver*. In 2013, I met a group of foreign travel agents in Santos who were on a junket paid for by Brazil to assess the state of the tourist infrastructure. They were from South Africa, which had hosted the 2010 Cup, and felt that Brazil lagged behind the FIFA class standards. They had no compunctions about describing all the things that needed to change, emphasizing that Brazil was "even behind South Africa," a comment made to wound Brazil's aspirations to First World status. In the final desperate months before the start of the World Cup, a series of accidents and scandals led to public protests against the Cup. A construction accident in Belo Horizonte killed two people and injured twenty-two, and a monorail collapse in São Paulo killed another. Throughout 2013 and 2014, protestors marched outside stadiums, chanting, "Nao vai ter copa!" ("There will not be a World Cup!"). What was supposed to be a triumph for the Workers' Party turned into an embarrassment, which was compounded by the Brazilian national team's humiliating semifinal loss to eventual champion Germany by a shocking 7–1 score.

By ironically invoking the "FIFA class," the Brazilian public was identifying a major shift in the politics of progress. The Workers' Party was working within a new timescape defined by participation in a transnational system of capitalist consumption. Where the older models of progress were largely based on growing Brazil's power as a producing nation—whether through agriculture or industry—the new model was devoted to national uplift through consumerism. This claim does not require a big interpretive leap. When the Pelé Museum opened, the museum designers published their own account of its development and raison d'être, a coffee-table book called *The Pelé Museum: History and Legacy*. The text describes the role of the museum in a new form of economic development, touting the benefits of gentrification. Drawing on the work of Marxist philosopher and architectural historian Otilia Arantes, the book says of Santos, "The region is no longer a center of production. It has become instead an object of consumption. Culture has come to be treated as a business in the coalition of classes and the interests of capital, responsible for urban development, and has itself come to be managed and consumed as a commodity" (Medeiros 2014, 58). This Marxist critique of postindustrial urban development, derived from the ideas of David Harvey, is not presented in the museum book as a critical analysis. Instead of a critique of the commodification of culture, it becomes a template for a new model of capitalist development in which the museum plays an important part. The book states that the museum, "coupled with the establishment of the headquarters of Petrobras," would fuel the revitalization of the region (Medeiros 2014, 63).

In her 2018 book, which I translate as *The Brazilian Waltz: From Boom to Economic Chaos*, Brazilian economist Laura Carvalho argues that the protests of 2013 to 2015 were based on class politics, with the highest-income bracket of Brazilians (the FIFA class) and the lower income brackets gaining ground relative to the position of the middle classes, whose discontent fueled the protests against the Workers' Party. While incomes rose for all income brackets from 2000 to 2013, they grew at a much faster pace for the very rich and the poor. The middle classes saw their *relative* position in Brazilian society decline, as rising wages for service providers (drivers, cleaners, food and beverage workers, personal care providers) created inflation in this sector that hit the middle classes hard, a process called the "squeezed middle." Sean Mitchell (2021, 87) argues that "a time of economic decline and the reversal of substantial social-democratic gains fostered a hopelessness about the possibility of collective social projects" for Brazil's middle classes, which he calls "cruel pessimism." The unending series of corruption scandals intensified this sense of pessimism about the future. This pessimism followed a period of giddy optimism, in which "Brazil was taken as demonstrating a reduction of economic inequalities on a global scale" and "people's euphoria about their improving life conditions remained palpable" (83). This swing (or waltz) from euphoric optimism to cruel pessimism, with the 2014 World Cup as a pivot point, materialized with almost exquisite timing in the rise and fall of the Pelé Museum.

Coda

Even though the museum had only been open for less than two years when I was conducting research for this book, it was clear to me that it would probably close soon. I visited the museum dozens of times, and it was eerily empty. I was saddened to learn, via a newspaper story, that the building was condemned after such an extensive and beautiful restoration. I hoped others would have had the chance to see it. As an anthropologist, I never thought I would be writing an analysis of the failure of a museum, but now that it has closed, I am glad to have captured the moment when I did. It was clear to me from the first time I set foot in that space that I was seeing the dramatization and formalization of a particular moment in Brazilian history, when dreams that coalesced around soccer, capitalism, and nationalism came to an abrupt halt.

The 2014 World Cup was a spectacle that combined breathless optimism, feverish developmentalism, dreams of reinvention, and nationalist pride. It quickly turned to impassioned pessimism, scandalous corruption, frustrated aspiration, and fierce anger. The Pelé Museum miniaturized that experience: a monument to Brazil's transformation into a "global citizen" and perhaps a king among nations turned into a short-lived story of corruption, mismanagement, and infrastructural decay. The museum's beautiful facade and aesthetics certainly attracted my attention, but the reality beneath the surface was shoddily built and unstable.

Conclusion

THE SHAPES OF PROGRESS: CONFIGURING SOCIAL CHANGE IN THEORY

In the preceding chapters, I have described clashes of timescapes, demonstrating how certain narratives get demarcated as progress through museums, monuments, and rituals while others get left aside. In Santos, the timescape of progress—epitomized by the *bandeirantes*—shapes how particular events are swept up into a mythic chronotope that defines different historical events, some of which carry completely opposite political meanings, as "progress." From colonial encounters to coffee plantations to factories to oil wells to sewers to call centers, wildly different events, objects, and experiences have been encompassed by a single narrative plot.

How and why do certain kinds of social change get demarcated as progress while others are just thought of as change? Anthropologist Michael Herzfeld (1997) uses the term "social poetics" to describe certain types of activity in which the form of the behavior carries more meaning than the practical result of the activity. Just as a poem calls attention to the form of language to produce an effect on the reader, "poetic" social activity separates itself from everyday interaction by calling attention to form. For example, think of the difference between having a drink at your kitchen table versus having a drink at a formal banquet with toasts and other associated rituals. The activity, drinking, is the same, but the banquet has a specific set of poetic rules attached. That's why we call these events "formal" occasions. Knowing the formal code and being able to perform in a certain way indicate all sorts of things about social class and status.

I believe progress is a form of temporal poetics, in which certain events attain special meaning and are woven into mythic transformations. In a world where everything everywhere is changing, certain kinds of change need to be set apart, to invoke Émile Durkheim's famous definition of the sacred. Progress is change, but it is change that follows a particular form and requires a kind of poetics to be set apart from events and activity in the normal (profane) temporalities of life. In Brazil, I argue, the content of progress has shifted radically in the recent past, while the form of progress has remained remarkably stable.[1]

The idea of progress as a form has implications for how we think about the future. Let me return to the anecdote that I began this book with, when, in a discussion with an NGO employee, I tried to argue that low carbon emissions were a sign of progress while my colleague insisted that low emissions were a sign of poverty. This brief conversation exemplified how the moral polarity of a particular social trait can be flip-flopped, viewed positively or negatively depending on particular value judgments. As Max Weber (1949) insisted, perhaps it is impossible to define progress in a value-neutral way. This claim should be obvious to anyone with a passing familiarity with cultural relativism. Any student who made it through introductory anthropology would likely say, "Of course, concepts of progress are relative to particular value systems. It's no surprise that the same social trait could hold opposite meanings for different people." True enough, but my assertion is that pure relativism is not enough—progress always has a formal, aesthetic dimension. While the content of specific visions of progress might change, the forms and shapes that people use to imagine progress might enable us to make connections across cultures. These patterns will always, to a certain degree, format how social groups delineate plain old change from meaningful progress, a special genre of change that occupies a higher—more socially meaningful—temporal level. The content of progress may indeed be culturally relative, but its formal dimensions replicate themselves across cultures and historical periods. These formal patterns give a shape and form to historical events, determining the kinds of social change that we define as progress.

Shapes of Progress and Anthropological Theory

At this point, I would like to turn the lens of my analysis back onto anthropology, exploring the implications of my argument for an anthropology of progress. Social theories of progress are no more or less affected by formalism than any other kind of thought. Formal patterns are how progress becomes "thinkable" (Helmreich 2020), and we therefore cannot imagine progress without a recognizable

form that lifts particular events out of the normal stream of history and config-
ures them into recognizable patterns. What do these patterns look like, and how
have they changed over time? Progress is often thought of as a quintessentially
modernist concept, a process of social change through which a nation (or any
other social group) advances along an empty homogenous timescape that is ultimately filled up by historical events. Bruno Latour (1999) defines progress as the
continual thrusting forward of the "arrow of time" (200). While anthropologists
have indeed configured progress through linear shapes at certain historical con-
junctures (e.g., unilineal evolution in the nineteenth century or modernization
theory in the twentieth), progress has not always been imagined as a forward-
moving arrow or a vertical line. It can also be a repetitive, rhythmic wave, a ripple
of vibratory energy, or a spiral that moves upward or downward.

In the nineteenth century, progress was configured as a straight line moving
upward or downward. The very first sentence of chapter 1 of Lewis Henry Morgan's (1877) *Ancient Society* reads, "The latest investigations respecting the early
condition of the human race are tending to the conclusion that mankind com-
menced their career at the bottom of the scale and worked their way up from
savagery to civilization through the slow accumulations of knowledge" (7). Morgan's revolutionary idea was that humanity was a single species created in a "low"
or "rude" state that evolved over long periods of time along a single upward path,
"[working] their way up" from the "bottom of the scale" to reach the summit of
"civilization."

In the early twentieth century, unilineal evolution came under fire from anthropology. Boasian anthropology rejected universal schemes in favor of historical particularism, which defined civilization as a "planless hodgepodge . . . a
thing of shreds and patches" lacking a fundamental trajectory or pattern (Lowie
1920, 441). From this point of view, human progress was not completely amor-
phous, but if it had a shape, it was complex, chaotic, "patchy." Later on, wavy
chronotopes of cultural diffusion began to emerge. Helmreich (2013) has sug-
gested that waves of electricity were at the core of the episteme of the late nineteenth century, after discoveries in electromagnetism and optics produced an
understanding of "the body electric." From this perspective, the world vibrated
with unseen forces of electric energy. In the social sciences, Gabriel Tarde developed his laws of imitation based on "undulations" that begin as ripples in a pond
and reverberate outward to produce consequential social changes. Tarde's writings are replete with references to waves, vibrations, undulations, and pulses.[2] He
argued that the ceaseless imitation and transformation of ideas through commu-
nication and interaction, or "vibration" in his terms, was the only scientific way
to study social change. Social changes radiated "or flashed out spontaneously"
around the globe. Inventions, ideas, or beliefs "tended to propagate themselves

through imitation in a geometrical progression, like waves of light or sound, or like animal or vegetal species" (Tarde 1963, 22).

Later, Tarde's vibratory model of social change became rhythmic and predictable. Through a famous analysis of European women's dress, Alfred Kroeber (1919) believed he had discovered a formal pattern of historical change that he called "the principle of order in civilization." His 1944 opus *Configurations of Culture Growth* modeled rhythmic, wavelike rises and falls over history as cultures followed repeating patterns of expansion and decline. This work came at the end of a period in which wave models of progress were influential across the intellectual landscape. Kroeber's *Configurations* is a lengthy critique of Oswald Spengler's (1929) *Decline of the West*, which proposed a cycle of civilizational rise and fall following the seasons (spring, summer, fall, and winter). Whereas Spengler proposed an "irreversible" tendency for civilizations to grow and decay (Kroeber 1963, 98), Kroeber proposed a rhythmic model of rises and falls over time.

During the height of the Cold War, W. W. Rostow (1960) used linear, upward aviation metaphors to define the "takeoff" that occurs when countries reach a state of self-sustaining capitalist growth. At the same time, Gunnar Myrdal's (1969) principle of "circular causation" spawned the chronotope of the "upward or downward spiral" based on the idea that a change in one aspect of a social system would create a pattern in which changes intensify over time, moving in the same direction as the original change with ever-greater force, like a whirlpool. Particular changes would magnify with force over generations unless the government (or some other entity) acted to reverse the movement of the spiral. He used the history of American antiblack racism as his main example, arguing that historical patterns of racism and poverty would not change over generations without strong governmental intervention.

Within anthropology, Clifford Geertz's (1963) *Agricultural Involution*, arguably the most influential book ever in the anthropology of international development, provides the most extreme example of a formalist account of progress. In contrast to Rostow, his contemporary (and former MIT colleague), Geertz describes describes a society in which agricultural modernization leads to "involution" rather than a takeoff. In contrast to Rostow's aviation theory, Geertz presents a "grounded" theory of progress. In Indonesia, for example, the Dutch created large plantations for sugar and coffee on lands seized by the government. As export agriculture expanded, the landless population increased dramatically. Yet, relatively few displaced peasants migrated to cities and towns, and subsistence rice farming remained their main source of food production. The land pressure created by plantation agriculture did not lead to a revolution in small farm agricultural techniques, but instead created a process of "involution" in which the same traditional rice farming system was practiced on smaller and smaller plots of land, without any change to the underlying relations of production. Geertz calls this "change without progress," a situation where agricultural development does not lead to structural transformation.

Geertz took the "involution" concept from the Boasian anthropologist Alexander Goldenweiser (1936), who wrote, "The primary effect of pattern is . . . to check development or at least to limit it. As soon as the pattern form is reached, further change is inhibited by the tenacity of the pattern" (81). Goldenweiser was describing formal complexity in Maori and Gothic art, in which innovations are restrained by formal constraints, and virtuosity becomes a process of baroque detail within a predetermined form—"technical hairsplitting" (103). Goldenweiser used a Bach fugue as a Western example of involution because it contained a "deliberate limitation of invention" in melody matched by inventive "playing with . . . elements, repeating, combining, and recombining" (104). Geertz (1963) also applies this musical metaphor to his own theory of culture, writing that "logico-meaningful integration, characteristic of culture, is the sort of integration one finds in a Bach fugue" (34). Geertz uses the example of a musical form to explain how agricultural development created change but not progress.[3]

In both theory and practice, the persistence of a formal cultural pattern shaped real-life activity for Geertz. It is quite telling, then, that the cover and frontispiece of the first edition of *Agricultural Involution* have a repeating complex pattern of interlocking circles. In the illustrations, the same formal pattern expands and contracts in size with no change to the underlying shape. On the one hand, this image is an illustration of the "baroque" structure of the rice paddies; on the other hand, it illustrates the persistence of a cultural pattern within a process of "involuted" change—progress as a cultural system.

Pattern Thinking and New Chronotopes of Progress

Pattern thinking and, in general, anthropological formalism have largely been rejected in contemporary anthropology, but they remain important to the anthropology of Brazil. Recall the importance of the debate over *bovarismo*, dualism, and Brazilian social logics that I described in the introduction of this book, or the mini-debate between Anthony Leeds and Maxine Margolis over the existence of a cyclical pattern of thinking among Brazilian farmers. The oft-repeated criticism of pattern thinking, from Kroeber on, has been that it is overly idealist, placing too much emphasis on essentialized attitudes or cultural beliefs which determine how people act. Where do these patterns come from? Are people unable to adapt their mindsets to suit a changing world?

The concept of the chronotope enables us to understand why these formal patterns of progress are more than mere attitudes: they dialectically shape practical activity. In his analysis of creation myths in Central Brazil, Terence Turner (Turner et al. 2017, 29) argues that myths serve as narrative templates, or schemas, of the total process of social production, a concept that integrates the social, material, and symbolic dimensions of activity into an extremely broad understanding of *production*. Groups of people collectively create and re-create their social world through their everyday activity, while also producing a symbolic narrative or story about that process. Therefore, myths are narratives that reflect the act of creation itself—stories that are about the production of self and society and that emerge from practical activity.

I would argue that whenever groups identify progress as something to work toward, they are, in effect, creating a myth that imagines a future that they will bring into being. At a deeper level, by creating and articulating this myth, they are depicting their power to re-create society as they wish, according to a particular vision of a better world.

Turner was a Marxist, and probably the best way to understand his ideas is to begin with this famous segment from chapter 1 of Marx's *Capital*:

> We presuppose labor in a form that stamps it as exclusively human. A spider conducts operations that resemble those of a weaver, and a bee puts to shame many an architect in the construction of her cells. But what distinguishes the worst architect from the best of bees is this, that the architect raises his structure in imagination before he erects it in reality. At the end of every labor-process, we get a result that already existed in the imagination of the laborer at its commencement. He not only effects a change of form in the material on which he works, but he also realizes a purpose of his own that gives the law to his modus operandi, and to which he must subordinate his will. (Tucker 1978, 344)

This paragraph could be summarized as, "Only humans work to achieve ends that they imagine before they set out to do something."[4] What people usually call "labor" or "work" is different from all other activity because human labor follows an idealized form that people intellectualize before, during, and after they act. Unlike spiders and bees, who also create things, humans imagine and objectify the end result of their actions. Therefore, human activity has both objective and subjective aspects—it changes both the material world and the world of ideas. It leaves behind material traces and memories, both of which should be considered equally valuable "products" of labor. Creation is therefore always both material and immaterial, physical and intellectual. Humans create tangible effects in the world *and* narratives about them, and the ways in which people imagine the goals of their activity are what give labor meaning and value. Labor creates value, but value (a symbolic creation) also determines what we do or do not define as labor.

For Turner, narrative genres such as myths are based on repetitive activities in society that people imagine as standardized patterns and narrative plots, which he called schemas, drawing on the work of developmental psychologist Jean Piaget. Whereas Piaget focused on the development of the cognitive function of individuals as they grew up, Turner applied Piaget's concepts to the development of social groups, including individuals, families, villages, and even nation-states. For example, among the Kayapó, an indigenous group in Central Brazil with whom Turner worked for nearly fifty years, many of the most important myths are ultimately stories about the socialization of people through the life cycle: birth, the transformation of children into adults, the formation of families and other kin groups, their transformation through marriage, birth, dissolution, and death. The myths are stories about creating full social people out of raw biological material. The "social production of the person" was the guiding paradigm for how the Kayapó imagined their world. For Turner, these myths were not abstract mental concepts. They were narratives that symbolized and reproduced actual behaviors in the world. Human activity creates stories, and then the stories become the guides to future activities. These stories (narratives) could also produce distorted pictures that reproduce patterns of social inequality across generations, such as the political dominance of older men over younger men and women in the case of the Kayapó. If myths were symbolic mirrors of social life, they were funhouse mirrors.

It might seem like a strange intellectual leap of faith to apply a theory of Amazonian myth to the myths of progress in modern nation-states, but bear with me. Turning back to Marx, imagine a society where one kind of activity called "work" is pulled out from everything else we do and marked as special. The value of this special genre of activity called work is measured by the quantity of a powerful symbolic medium called money. Work creates this symbolic medium: money seems to give work its value. In this society, this special category of activity (work) would guide how children are educated and what kinds of labor matter more than others (in factories, offices, homes, etc.). In turn, these relative distinctions (rankings or value judgments) about what kinds of activity are special would shape gender relationships, age groupings, marriage, kinship, and almost every other aspect of life. Those value judgments would determine whose labor in society matters and whose does not. In turn, those distinctions over value would lead to vast inequalities in society. People would divide "work" from "life" and speak of balances, pressures, and tensions between differently valued genres of activity.

This is an oversimplification of Turner's theory but the basic point holds: if capitalist value is the dominant schema or pattern that organizes the social world, it will largely (though not exclusively) structure how people define the ultimate ends of their lives. In such a society, you will have myths that emphasize the ability of people to make money (rags-to-riches stories, heroic entrepreneurs, *The Apprentice*, *Shark Tank*, *bandeirantes*, etc.), and the progress of a community or a country would probably be measured by the ability of its population to create quantities of money through work. In short, you would have a capitalist society in which progress is measured by GDP per capita, which is ultimately a quantification of a specific quality: the capacity to produce value in capitalist terms.

Late in his career, Turner (2003) applied his theory to modern nation-states and the notion of progress specifically. He has argued that modern notions of progress are based on a chronotope he calls "diachronic assimilation." Within this chronotope, different social groups are assimilated into some unitary category called "the nation" over time, creating a more inclusive social whole that encompasses divisions of class, race, ethnicity, language, and so on. In this chronotope, the modern state acting in the name of the people is the agent that brings about progress. As inequality widens in the context of globalization, the modern homogeneous definition of progress, diachronic assimilationism, is replaced by what Turner calls "synchronic pluralism," a chronotope that emphasizes the coordination of different social and political groups who are all joined together in the capitalist market without a future-oriented temporal horizon (that is, beyond full integration into global capitalism). The global market, rather than the nation-state, becomes the agent that brings about progress in this chronotope, and equal participation in the world market becomes the marker of modernity and progress, rather than assimilation into some form of integrative nationalism.

Unlike Turner's highly abstract and relatively monolithic view of progress, other new chronotopes of progress in anthropology embrace indeterminacy and multiplicity. Anna Tsing's (2015) *Mushroom at the End of the World* serves as a paradigm. With a title that playfully refers to the ultimate Cold War doomsday image, the mushroom cloud, Tsing situates her work against modernist visions of progress, writing, "the problem is that progress stopped making sense. More and more of us looked up one day and realized that the emperor had no clothes" (21). Her vision of progress is more attuned to salvage than salvation. In Tsing's work, the matsutake mushroom symbolizes a process of renewal after disaster— it is a delicacy (and valuable commodity) that only springs up in landscapes that have been "blasted" by capitalist modernity. Then new assemblages of labor, new communities, and new aesthetics of taste and pleasure form around the mushroom. These lively, "polyphonic" systems of life serve as a metaphor for the future of life in the aftermath of modernist notions of progress, which Tsing defines as a "time-making project" under which multiple temporalities and ways of life are subsumed into a single pulsing beat (23).

Tsing writes, "Progress is a forward march, drawing other kinds of time into its rhythms. Without that driving beat, we might notice other temporal patterns" (21). One of her goals in the book is to replace the "unified rhythms" of modern understandings of progress (which she compares to rock and roll) with a polyphony that allows for "multiple melodies" to be heard simultaneously.

In a fitting complement to Geertz's *Agricultural Involution*, Tsing (2015) conjoins musical metaphors to an analysis of Indonesian agriculture. In Borneo, plantations have replaced systems of shifting cultivation (swidden plots) in which "many crops grew together in the same field," each with its own natural rhythm of planting and harvest times (24). Tsing sees the "polyphonic assemblage" of the swiddens as an illustration of an "open ended gathering" with "indeterminate and multidirectional" possibilities (23). The incredible biodiversity of swidden agriculture represents a hopeful alternative to the "segregation" of commercial agriculture, with plantation monocrops serving as the epitome of hegemonic modernization. Where Geertz saw inefficiency, Tsing sees promise.

It is revealing to dwell on the musical metaphors used by Geertz and Tsing to describe the same socioeconomic system separated by fifty years. The exact same agricultural system was viewed positively or negatively in the span of two generations. As mentioned previously Geertz used the Bach fugue to describe what he meant by cultural integration—multiple melodies integrated into a single formal pattern. Tsing also uses the example of the fugue, but in the opposite way—to emphasize a lively, open-ended assemblage without a predetermined structure.[5] Where Geertz saw (or heard) structure, Tsing sees (hears) anti-structure. The common thread in both of their perspectives is the formalism. Even anti-structuralists such as Geertz and Tsing refer back to shapes and rhythms. Patchiness and involution are both chronotopes of progress.

Anti-Plantationism or Green *Bandeirantes*?

Returning to Brazil, it is important to note that Tsing (2015) uses Brazilian plantations as the paradigm of capitalist ruin. She writes, "In their sixteenth- and seventeenth-century sugarcane plantations in Brazil, for example, Portuguese planters stumbled on a formula for smooth expansion. They crafted self-contained, interchangeable project elements, as follows: exterminate local people and plants; prepare now empty, unclaimed land; and bring in exotic and isolated labor and crops for production. This landscape model of scalability became an inspiration for later industrialization and modernization" (38–39). Tsing continues:

> Interchangeability in relation to the project frame, for both human work and plant commodities, emerged in these historical experiments. It was a success: Great profits were made in Europe, and most Europeans were too far away to see the effects. The project was, for the first time, scalable— or, more accurately, seemingly scalable. Sugarcane plantations expanded and spread across the warm regions of the world. Their contingent components—cloned planting stock, coerced labor, conquered and thus open land—showed how alienation, interchangeability, and expansion could lead to unprecedented profits. This formula shaped the dreams we have come to call progress and modernity. (39–40)

Anti-plantation politics are certainly present in Brazil, in both theory and practice. As I have described at various points in this book, there is a strong movement against the *bandeirantes* attitude, which manifests itself not only in the destruction of *bandeirantes* monuments, described in chapter 1, but also in the broader politics of resistance against the *ruralistas* and capitalist productivism and extractivism. The anti-*bandeirantes* attitude is best expressed by Déborah Dankowski and Eduardo Viveiros de Castro (2016) in their book *The Ends of the World*, which articulates a politics of environmental repair using some of the same concepts that I mentioned above: "In almost all the dominant forms of 'our' historico-futurological imagination today, there is only one thinkable and desirable direction, the one that goes from 'negative' to 'positive': from less to more, from the possession of little to the property of much, from 'technologies of subsistence' to 'cutting-edge technology,' from Paleolithic nomad to the modern cosmopolitan citizen, from the savage Indian to the civilized worker" (121). The authors ultimately argue for a reversal of the values of modernization—saving the future of earth by embracing Amerindian concepts of sufficiency, ecological harmony, and resistance to commodity culture. This resistance is often linked with radical demands to decolonize progress and reject consumer capitalism altogether, but that is not the only form the resistance has taken. A variety of more mainstream forms of Brazilian environmentalism are infected with the ethics of sustainability, often drawing on indigenous ontologies that do not presuppose a division between humanity and the rest of the "natural" world.

While I do not intend to minimize the importance of anti-*bandeirantes* politics, another trend is beginning to emerge in Brazil, in which climate activism and sustainable development get drawn into the *bandeirantes* narrative. "Solving" the climate problem through technology has the potential to become a new iteration of the *bandeirantes* attitude. Anthropologist Renzo Taddei (2014) describes how the field of geoengineering is developing large-scale technological fixes for global warming, such as "manipulation of the cloud cover of the planet, the changing of the chemical composition of the oceans, or the covering of the planet with a layer of particles that reflect part of the solar radiation back into space" (2). Nicole Labruto (2018) has shown how green energy initiatives in Brazil convert sugarcane into biofuels, taking the violent colonial legacy of the plantation and turning it into a future-oriented project of climate repair. In this paradigm of progress, huge sugar plantations become signs of a hopeful future rather than a destructive past. Brazil's effort to become energy independent through ethanol (and other biofuels) production and hydropower are certainly part of this narrative. More recently, multinational companies have begun to use massive amounts of Brazilian sugarcane to fuel microbial fermentation, which produces synthetic molecular compounds for the chemical industry without utilizing fossil fuels. These products are labeled as "clean" alternatives to products derived from petrochemicals, and frequently use sustainable and fair-trade sugar to fuel the production process. As Brazilian agro-capitalism conquers nature through new technologies like these, it is likely that "fixing" the climate crisis through grand-scale engineering will be woven into narratives of progress, just as it was in at the peak of the Miracle years.

It would be tempting to dismiss the emerging "green *bandeirantes*" as an ideological defense of the status quo, but I think there is a deeper issue than power politics at stake here. From another vantage point (familiar to old-school Marxists and techno-utopians alike), the twenty-first-century plantation could be viewed as a model of sustainable capitalism if we define "sustainability" as efficiency in productivity relative to land use. From this perspective, superproductive farming allows the world to feed a growing population with fewer natural resources than would be required under less efficient conditions.[6] This vision, which I would call "productivism," celebrates the technologies that allow farmers to produce large volumes of food relative to land use and energy consumption. Under this way of thinking, the farms in the Cerrado with record-setting yields would be avatars of progress.[7] This version of sustainability is completely compatible with plantation agriculture as long as there are systems to accurately account for the human and environmental costs of resource use by providing accurate measurements of water use, chemical inputs, impact on regional ecosystems, public health, air quality, and so on, so that public harms are not minimized in the pursuit of private gains. This is the model that has been embraced by philanthropic organizations such as the Gates Foundation in partnership with large biotechnology companies. In his bestseller *Enlightenment Now*, Steven Pinker (2018) names yield increases through Green Revolution agriculture as an example of how technology "outsmarted evolution" to end hunger and bring about progress (75). Even more celebratory is James Davidson's (2012) *Brazil Is the New America* (endorsed by Donald Trump on the back cover), which describes Brazil as nothing less than the future of food production in the twenty-first century. My point here is not to affirm this model of sustainability as better or worse than any other in an a priori sense; I am simply trying to point out that the exact same sociocultural formations can be defined as positive or negative depending on value judgments. Anti-plantation politics and pro-plantation politics can be—and have been—encompassed within the *bandeirantes* chronotope. What matters is which version becomes formalized, sacralized, and cemented in popular consciousness.

Center of American Progress

Over more than three decades of study in Latin America, I have come to notice how many towns throughout the region are named after progress. From Mexico to Central America to the Andes to Brazil to the Southern Cone, every country is dotted with communities and neighborhoods named something like Progreso. In the Spanish-speaking countries, it is El Progreso or Nuevo Progreso. In Brazil, it is O Progresso, Novo Progresso, and the like. Mexico alone has more than twenty communities named with some variation on the term. In the two countries I know best, Honduras and Brazil, communities with some variation of "progress" in their name are all over the map. Yet, in the United States—the country that served as the model of American material "progress" for two centuries—it would be almost unheard of for a town to call itself "Progress." There are indeed a few small rural towns with progress-oriented names in Indiana, Pennsylvania, and Texas, but none contain more than a few thousand people and their names are viewed as small-town oddities—one of those places where you would take a picture of the road sign as you passed it by: Progress, Texas. Population 340. In America, no sane person would name a town Progress. But once we move south of the Rio Grande, towns named after progress are quite common, frequently in very poor regions. It is as if there were an inverse relationship between actual socioeconomic progress—defined narrowly as material prosperity—and aspirations to progress. If your actual material condition fits your definition of progress, you do not need to name your town after it. You are already where you want to be.

One explanation for this difference is to be found in regional histories. Most Latin American countries achieved independence from Spain and Portugal between 1810 and 1840. In the early decades of the new republics (Mexico, Venezuela, Argentina, and many others), the philosophy of positivism, originally developed in France but modified by Latin American thinkers, was highly influential. Positivism, as formulated by philosophers Auguste Comte and Herbert Spencer, viewed governments as the rational, scientific agents of progress that were set against the traditionalism and backwardness of the Iberian monarchies and the Catholic clergy. Independence from Europe came a generation or two later in Latin America than it did in the United States, so the philosophical underpinnings of the new nations were also somewhat different. Under positivism, the job of the government was to bring about progress by doing away with a stodgy, conservative colonial system and replacing it with the latest and greatest modern ideas, no matter where they were to be found. Progress became a mantra for these newly independent nations, an objective goal to be achieved by an activist government.

Most famously, "Order and Progress" became the national motto for Brazil when it proclaimed itself an independent republic, and the phrase has been emblazoned on the country's flag since 1889. While positivism had some influence in the United States, its government did not seize on "progress" as an objective goal to the degree that the newly independent Latin American states did. While the progressive movement thrived for a brief period under President Theodore Roosevelt, the federal government's ability to actively shape social conditions was balanced by other cultural attitudes that sought to constrain the power of the federal government in the name of deep-rooted American values such as individual liberty and limited government. While various US movements have of course called themselves progressive, positivist visions of progress never attained the all-encompassing influence in the United States that they held in Latin America, and Brazil is case in point.

The fixation on progress in Latin America also had a neocolonialist aspect to it, because the leaders of the new Latin American republics often felt that they were "backward" and needed to catch up to the leading lights of London, Paris, and New York. Although these nations had gained formal independence from Spain and Portugal, the long history of colonialism seemed to limit the new republics' capacity to determine their own national identity, to plot their own course, so to speak. At times, this led to a feverish sense of inferiority that manifested itself across many different areas of life, from art and literature to architecture to education to business to understandings of race and ethnicity. In Brazil, for example, the newly independent nation embarked on an official policy of *branqueamento*, or whitening, "as Brazil's ticket into the community of 'civilized' nations" (Guzmán 2013, 90) by attracting European immigrants after the abolition of slavery. Along with whiteness, infrastructure (particularly railroads) was a major obsession of the positivists, who saw modern industry as the sine qua non of civilization. This was part of a much deeper obsession with the technological achievements of European modernity, particularly of France, that lasted well into the twentieth century. After World War II, North American models of development began to surpass European ones, but the basic paradigm remained. Under the banner of "development" (instead of "civilization"), the endpoint of positivism changed. Dams, factories, tractors, and airports replaced railroads.[8] What remained was a general, somewhat utopian gaze toward a better future.

This history is important, but it can only partly explain the fetish for progress. History alone does not do justice to the multiple meanings of progress that ripple through Latin American culture and continue to exert force in the present. In 2021, the founding residents of a new neighborhood on the periphery of San Pedro Sula or São Paulo are not thinking about Auguste Comte or *branqueamento* when they put up a homemade sign by the side of the road, naming their new community Nuevo Progreso or Novo Progresso. They are using progress as a close synonym for hope—an abstraction that refers to a more positive future. This is why towns named Progress tend to be located on rural frontiers or urban peripheries: they are formed by migrants with dreams of a brighter future—either people moving from the country to the city or founding a new settlement on the edge of an established territory. For people putting up a shack on a muddy Honduran hillside overlooking a highway or in a patch of jungle on the edge of the Brazilian rainforest that they recently cleared for farming, *progreso* or *progresso* are simply terms for a better life. The stories that people use to express these hopes for the future will ultimately determine whether they are realized, in one form or another.

Notes

INTRODUCTION

1. This claim has been made by Da Matta throughout his career and was the central point of the 2014 documentary film *A Day at the Beach with Roberto Da Matta*. It has been disputed by Julia O'Donnell (2013) and others who focus on patterns of race and class exclusion.

2. The proximate cause of these protests began in 2013 with an increase in the cost of a bus pass in the city of São Paulo, which provoked a nationwide reaction against a government that was investing massive amounts of money in social programs to combat poverty and in international spectacles such as the Confederations Cup (2013), World Cup (2014), and Rio Olympic Games (2016) while seemingly ignoring the everyday needs of the middle classes. This cycle of protests was followed in 2016 by nationwide protests against systematic corruption in the government, revealed in a sprawling anti-corruption investigation (the "car wash," or *lava jato*, scandal). This led to the impeachment of President Rousseff in 2016 and the imprisonment of former President Lula in 2017. Our understanding of the causes and consequences of this upheaval continues to unfold as of this writing, and I am therefore hesitant to offer any kind of definitive statement on its significance for anthropology. I leave it to other Brazilian specialists to offer detailed accounts of the contemporary political situation. See Junge et al. 2021 for a comprehensive ethnographic account of this saga and its effects on differently situated populations across Brazil.

3. I am, of course, aware that this is a broad generalization. There are anthropologists of all political stripes, including many anthropologists who would call themselves "progressive" but who reject contemporary left-liberalism in favor of more radical philosophies of social change, particularly decolonial politics that challenge the legitimacy of the liberal nation-state. This viewpoint has become increasingly common in the past decade as mainstream liberalism has been associated with white supremacy (Shange 2019) and settler colonialism (Simpson 2011).

4. Certainly there have been moments in the history of the discipline when things were different. Anthropologists of the nineteenth century viewed human social evolution as an uphill climb that led toward the heights of the Euro-American civilization that embodied human progress. While these early anthropologists had a deep appreciation for human cultural diversity, they viewed non-European peoples as lagging behind the West on a single path toward progress, a theory called unilineal social evolution. In the twentieth century, unilineal social evolutionism was partially readapted by Marxist scholars such as Leslie White, who emphasized technological forces (especially a society's capacity to harness energy) as determining factors of a society's position on the evolutionary continuum, which was now stripped of Eurocentric chauvinism and given a veneer of hard science. After World War II, many anthropologists (particularly those working in rural Latin America) championed modernization as development in what was then called the Third World. These scholars had a clear vision of progress, which they defined through measurable social outcomes such as poverty, literacy, health, nutrition, and political participation. It was the job of anthropologists to help make progress real. To see how optimistic these anthropologists could be, consider the book *A Village That Chose Progress* by Robert Redfield, one of the most important ethnographies

of Latin America in the post-war period. Describing the reception of American experts in the small village of Chan Kom in Yucatán, Mexico, he wrote, "The wave of enthusiasm for progress was reaching its crest; the Americans were progressive; they had skills and knowledge which Chan Kom could use. So each American visitor . . . was welcomed with cordiality and respectful formality, and some were invited to make improving speeches on technical and scientific subjects" (1950, 16).

5. The optimism toward twentieth-century blueprints for progress has all but disappeared in the anthropology of the twenty-first century. A representative example of contemporary anthropological progressivism could be found in the July 2021 edition of *Anthropology News*, the official newsletter of the American Anthropological Association, our field's largest professional association. In it, five anthropologists responded to the question, "What can anthropology do in the world to address humanity's many problems?" Their responses included "confronting the radical challenge of unveiling and undoing the destructive machinations of global capitalism"; "advancing progressive social change"; "using anthropological and other knowledge to propose solutions to problems and alternatives to a status quo that is so brutally harmful to so many"; "sit apart from and, thereby, challenge the prevailing value systems, power structures, and the political economy they justify"; and "dismantling the ivory tower and decolonizing anthropology, engaging specific movements—from Black Lives Matter to Extinction Rebellion and the Dreamers—who hail a deliberately inclusive, contingent humanity. Truly, this is humanity's last stand" (Vine et al. 2021). This is a good example of the pessimistic progressivism of contemporary anthropology, in that all of the responses focus on dismantling or challenging the mainstream status quo.

6. There are many differing interpretations of class relationships under the Workers' Party and the origins of the 2013–2016 crisis. As of 2022, the debate over what happened politically, economically, and socially in the first decades of the millennium is at the core of Brazil's intensely polarized political climate, which seemingly changes by the minute. That is why I am hesitant to offer a definitive statement on the legacy of the Workers' Party. The crux of the debate is whether the protests that began in 2013 were the product of a media-fueled attempt to remove the Workers' Party from power using anti-corruption as a pretense that would ultimately lead to the imprisonment of former president Lula and bring the far right to power. Some of the most important analyses of the rise and fall of the Workers' Party include Boito (2021), Carvalho (2018), Saad Filho and Morais (2019), Singer (2018), and Junge et al. (2021). Boito (2021, xvii) describes the Workers' Party as "neodevelopmentalists, given that they sought to stimulate economic growth and reduce poverty through state intervention in the economy, moving away from the neoliberal program and ideology of the so-called minimal state." Singer (2018, 42) refers to this neodevelopmentalism as a "Rooseveltian dream" that would integrate the rich and poor through state intervention, overcoming a legacy of social exclusion that had roots in the colonial era. Carvalho (2018) astutely shows how the policies of the Workers' Party led to an unprecedented period of economic growth until 2013, but those policies fragmented the Brazilian middle classes, who experienced a decline in their quality of life relative to the upper and lower classes.

7. A *quilombo* is a community formed by the descendants of Afro-Brazilian maroons, or escaped slaves.

8. I recognize that there many important nonlinear or nonteleological chronotopes of progress that exist in Brazil and elsewhere. Terence Turner (Turner et al. 2017) argues that the Kayapó people imagine space based on their own ideal model of a village, which consists of a series of residences organized in concentric circles with a ceremonial men's house at the center. The ideal village is defined by a sharp boundary between the socialized human world of the village and the antisocial natural world outside of it. For the

Kayapó, progress would mean the realization of this ideal form expressed through the word *mêtch,* for "beauty" or "completion." In a somewhat different vein, Danowski and Viveiros de Castro (2016, 117) reject the Western "accelerationist" notion of progress as "the epic conquest of nature," replacing it with an indigenous vision of the earth as a living entity. They argue that the Western world must reimagine its relationship to nature by "rebecoming indigenous" (122). As with Amitav Ghosh (2022), their challenge to modernist understandings of progress is based on the Gaia hypothesis, which posits that the earth is a living entity with something like a soul that must be cared for to maintain the conditions of life on the planet. Sahlins and Henry (2022) make a related point by arguing for the reenchantment of the natural sciences by collapsing the differences between the material and spiritual worlds. *The Falling Sky* (2013) by Davi Kopenawa and Bruce Albert is the most influential example of how anthropology can challenge Western teleologies of progress through an analysis that foregrounds indigenous ways of knowing, critiquing capitalism through non-Western intellectual categories.

9. Da Matta's critique of Western linear thinking is, in some respects, similar to influential writings on decoloniality such as Mignolo (2011, 164), which argues that the terms "progress" and "development" "cannot be conceived without a linear concept of time defining a point of arrival." Like Mignolo, Da Matta has attempted to "crack the code" of Western thought by bringing the Enlightenment tradition into dialogue with Latin American cultural history. I would not consider Da Matta a decolonial theorist, however, because he places non-Western ways of knowing within the Enlightenment intellectual tradition, attempting to expand the purview of the Western canon without rejecting it. His defense of Brazilian national culture is completely different from a decolonial perspective, in that he celebrates the unique aspects of Brazilian culture that formed through centuries of Portuguese colonialism—from food to language to literature, art, and sport—and does not obsessively focus on an "original sin" of colonialism that casts a shadow over history. Da Matta's popularity and influence as a public intellectual in Brazil is largely due to the pride that his work instills through the interpretation of distinctively Brazilian cultural traits.

10. Da Matta's argument calls to mind the more recent work of Dutch anthropologist Peter van der Veer (2016), who compares prevailing attitudes toward inequality in Western Europe, China, and India. Van der Veer asks why contemporary Indian society seems more indifferent toward the plight of the urban poor than Europe and China, and he draws on historical and religious attitudes toward hierarchy to make a culturalist case. He writes, "In my view, there is no escaping the fact that a continuing hierarchical mentality prevails in India that prevents care arrangements from being extended to the urban poor. We do not thereby return to a holistic view of an Indian caste system, as in Dumont's *Homo Hierarchicus,* because that would be a wrong perspective on modern India. However, it does imply that turning our back on the significance of hierarchical values in Indian society by focusing on youth culture and media and other manifestations of an Indian cosmopolitanism does not make hierarchy go away" (139). It is not a coincidence that both Da Matta and Van der Veer invoke the work of Louis Dumont, a French anthropologist whose work on the all-encompassing hierarchical worldview produced by the Indian caste system has been largely discredited but who remains influential as a social theorist who challenged Enlightenment assumptions about the individual as the basic unit of social interaction. Van der Veer and Da Matta both deploy a kind of "soft Dumontianism," arguing for the persistence of hierarchical attitudes in two of the world's largest and most highly unequal societies, India and Brazil, while rejecting the more deterministic aspects of Dumont's theories.

11. To be more precise, in the chapter "The Meaning of 'Ethical Neutrality' in Sociology and Economics" (1949, 1–47) Weber considers "the applicability of the concept of

'progress' (in the evaluative sense) in the sphere of art," arguing that "there is naturally no 'progress' in art with respect to the aesthetic evaluation of works of art" (29). He ultimately argues, "If any aspect of human conduct (of any sort whatsoever) is oriented in a technically more correct manner than it was previously, *technical progress* exists" (35). His claim is that "progress" cannot be used to describe the meaning or ends of any activity, but only the technical means by which these ends can be achieved.

1. SPECTACLES OF COLONIALISM

1. More recently, Roberto Da Matta (1991) reaffirmed this aspect of Moog's thesis, defining the *bandeirantes* myth as the "dream of getting rich, mainly through predatory activity" (206).

2. Translated by author from https://umaincertaantropologia.org/2014/01/07/eduardo-viveiros-de-castro-o-capitalismo-sustentavel-e-uma-contradicao-em-seus-termos-ihu-on-lineenvolverde/.

3. "Mercado Aberto," *Folha de São Paulo*, June 16, 2016. At first I thought it was funny that a sandwich chain was compared to a sixteenth-century slave raider, but then I thought, "If a paper in the United States called Subway a 'pioneer' in the sandwich business, that wouldn't be so strange—so maybe this isn't so strange."

4. In his 1965 book on the place of the *bandeirantes* in Brazilian history, American historian Richard Morse wrote that "Paulistas [separatists] invoked the bandeirante spirit as a cry for autonomy" while the Vargas government invoked the *bandeirantes* in "an appeal to national unity" (33).

5. "Luann Vive Ajuda Indios Em São Vicente," *A Tribuna*, April 10, 2016.

6. Recently, Brazilian anthropologist Daniel Pierri has studied the Guaraní communities in São Paulo state.

7. Both the date of arrival and the location of the site that can claim to be the birthplace of Brazil are fraught with controversy. There are at least four different positions about the date of discovery, ranging from the generally accepted date of April 21, 1500, to sometime in 1498. Two other historians have mentioned April 22 and April 23, 1500, as the "real" date of discovery. Canonically, the story is that Cabral landed in Porto Seguro, in what is now Bahia, in April 1500. However, Cabral did not stay in Brazil, and it is São Vicente, founded directly next to Santos in 1530, that is considered the oldest Portuguese settlement in Brazil and thus the country's "real" birthplace.

8. As of August 2021, the version of the reenactment described here could be viewed on YouTube, at https://www.youtube.com/watch?v=-F4luM8vj-4.

9. The aesthetics of the ritual sacrifice drew heavily from the account of Hans Staden in 1600, a foundational source for accounts of indigenous captivity and cannibalism in Brazil.

10. The esteemed scholar of nationalism, Benedict Anderson, once told me that the best place to begin to understand the position of indigenous people in Brazilian nationalism is with *O Guarani*, an 1857 novel by José de Alencar that was made into a famous opera by Carlos Gomes. *O Guarani* (*The Guarani*) is a romance between Peri, an Indian, and Cecilia ("Ceci"), a young white (by Brazilian standards) woman who lives on a ranch in the interior of the country. Peri is a loyal guard of the white family. He lives on the property and protects them against a band of dangerous cannibalistic Indians called the Aimore. Peri and Ceci develop a close friendship, in some ways similar to the friendship between Mark Twain's Huckleberry Finn and Jim, which *O Guarani* predated by thirty years. In the climax of the novel, Peri saves Ceci from drowning in a storm, and the book ends with the two floating down a river together on a palm frond. Alcida Ramos (1998, 67) argues that *O Guarani* exemplifies "the ambivalence of nascent Brazilian society towards the Indians." On the one hand, Brazil was a country whose population developed out of racial mixture, so the Indian had to be incorporated

into the national narrative. On the other hand, the narrative placed the Indian in the position of "noble savage" whose way of life had been surmounted by modernity and civilization. Ramos writes, "Peri is almost as strong as the natural elements and the epitome of abnegation [self-denial], altruism, and strength of character. A true noble savage who knew his place, that is, a social outcast, he was never allowed to enter white society as an equal" (67). A mural depicting the story of O Guarani is painted on the ceiling of the restored Guarany Theater in downtown Santos.

11. Lest one be shocked by this account of cruelty, recall that Native Americans in the United States were given smallpox-infested blankets by the US Army in the mid-eighteenth century and that bounty hunting for native people was carried out in the state of California in the mid-nineteenth century.

12. Later that week, I was sitting with a group of people on the beach, in a tent sponsored by retired municipal employees who were holding a fundraiser. A radio report about the Day of the Indian came on, and I asked an acquaintance what he thought of the Indians' protests. "Ah," he told me, "they were here last year marching along the beach. Hundreds of them. Some of the women were good looking, but some of the groups were really ugly. There was one *india brava* that had her hair shaved to the middle of her head and a really ugly painted face." He went back to drinking his beer.

13. "Papo De Domingo—'Os Índios São Senhores Dessa Mata,'" Diario do Litoral, October 4, 2015, https://www.diariodolitoral.com.br/cotidiano/papo-de-domingo-os -indios-sao-senhores-dessa-mata/65743/.

2. COFFEE OF THE PAST, COFFEE OF THE FUTURE

1. Anthropologists have debated whether a pattern of "cyclical thinking" is a hallmark of Brazilian attitudes toward capitalism and entrepreneurialism. In the 1970s, there was a mini-debate between anthropologists Anthony Leeds and Maxine Margolis over this very issue. Leeds, who became a prolific and influential figure in economic anthropology, titled his 1957 doctoral dissertation "Economic Cycles in Brazil: Persistence of a Total Culture Pattern." His manuscript was based on fieldwork in a cacao-producing town in Bahia, which he analyzed within long-term historical cycles of Brazilian commodity production in the world system. Inspired by Kroeber's formalist model of "configurations" of civilization development (which I discuss in depth in the conclusion of this book), Leeds argues that the cyclical boom-bust pattern of Brazilian capitalism was shaped by a system of values that emerged as a historical product of the plantation system. "He argues that the two-class system, in which a handful of people own the strategic resources and control a vast number of impoverished workers, has led the owners to resist change, particularly any arising from technological innovation . . . which has led to a 'strike-it-rich' mentality" (Margolis 1973, 4). Through a detailed ethnography of a frontier coffee-growing region in the state of Parana in the late 1960s, Margolis shows that the boom-bust cycle in coffee was a logical adaptive strategy that was "the result of clearly identifiable ecologic and economic conditions" (5). The availability of cheap, fertile lands in the expanding Brazilian frontier made it more profitable for coffee farmers to seek out new land than to invest in improving old, unproductive land, which they could easily convert into pastures for cattle. The ever-present agricultural frontier promotes a cyclical way of thinking: as long as land is available, it will always make sense for farmers to move on to greener pastures, so to speak, rather than make capital investments in existing crops. Though Margolis here is describing the move from established coffee regions such as São Paulo state into Paraná, a similar process can be seen today as farmers move into the Cerrado, the Amazon, or Paraguay, where, as Kregg Hetherington (2011) describes, Brazilian plantation owners have made huge investments, often displacing local people.

Margolis uses her study of coffee to make a broader case in support of a cultural materialist argument. She believes that cultural attitudes—such as cyclical thinking or a "strike it rich" mentality—are ultimately rooted in ecological and economic conditions. Those attitudes may indeed have dialectically shaped the patterns of behavior as history unfolded, but, following Marx, ideas or cultural patterns are "in the last instance" created by material prerequisites—infrastructure determines superstructure. While I think that Margolis's 1973 work is probably the best ethnography of a coffee-producing town ever written, I also find it necessary to recuperate some of the formalism or "idealism" of Leeds. The debate between Leeds and Margolis can also be thought of as a clash of timescapes. Coffee farmers certainly make shrewd decisions based on the material conditions in which they find themselves, but these decisions are cumulatively represented back to them through narratives of cycles, declines, and *bandeirantes* expansionism. This higher-level narrative connects their behavior to a national story of progress, which in turn shapes policy decisions. As Stefan Helmreich has argued, we only experience abstractions through the formalisms that inscribe them or make them materially real. This argument is often associated with STS scholarship—the basic idea that technologies of measurement and observation play a constitutive role in how we experience reality. However, the exact same logic was used by Benedict Anderson (1997), for example, to show how the rise of nationalism depended on technologies—newspapers, census, maps, and museums—that allowed far-flung populations to connect with one another and take part in the shared ideological project of the nation-state.

2. For many urban Brazilians, coffee production is either invisible or associated with the old agrarian world of slavery, hardscrabble immigrant farmers, grand plantation houses, and steam locomotives. There is a historic trolley tour of the Santos downtown that takes visitors through the old port infrastructure while completely ignoring the ongoing business in the port that it travels through. When I told people in Santos that I was studying coffee, they assumed that I was interested in the history of coffee. The agricultural past is nostalgized in popular television shows (*novelas*) that depict the romance of the plantation society. Brazilian city dwellers might learn about coffee farming on field trips to historic *fazendas* (plantations) on the outskirts of São Paulo or Rio, but coffee is not a part of the imagined narrative of the new, thriving, modern Brazil. For American readers, the best comparison for coffee's place in modern Brazil would be cotton in the US South. The United States remains the dominant producer of cotton in the world, yet the industry is invisible to most Americans, and it is symbolically associated with the antebellum past. The old historic coffee plantations around São Paulo are somewhat like historic cotton plantations in the American South. They have become part of the region's aesthetic memory and historical identity, and are therefore set apart from its present way of life. The United States is still among the world's largest producers of cotton, but it is a mechanized, international agribusiness that is largely invisible to urbanites. This is quite similar to Brazilian coffee.

3. There is an old saying among farmers in Honduras: "El café siempre da." ("Coffee always gives.") For small-scale farmers, coffee is the "old reliable" of crops—something that can be counted on to produce and generate income year after year. The market swings wildly from year to year and can be quite risky if someone is in it for only a short time, but over a lifetime (or across multiple generations) coffee can be a steady provider. In Brazil, on the other hand, coffee has a different history—it is a plantation crop. Whereas it was totally normal for an anthropologist studying in Central America to focus on coffee, Brazilian anthropologists seemed a bit puzzled by my interest.

4. Obviously, futures trading plays a vital part in the coffee economy, and the neighborhood around the museum is filled with professionals who take part in this kind of trading; but futures trading, I would argue, is still oriented toward making profits in the present and is therefore part of the ongoing historical timescape.

5. Readers can find excellent details about this ceiling at http://www.novomilenio.inf .br/santos/calixt78b.htm.

6. This quote comes from Calixto's own description of the stained glass ceiling, published in a booklet that commemorated the grand opening of the coffee exchange's central salon. It is available online at https://www.novomilenio.inf.br/santos/calixt78b.htm.

7. https://umaincertaantropologia.org/2014/01/07/eduardo-viveiros-de-castro-o-capital ismo-sustentavel-e-uma-contradicao-em-seus-termos-ihu-on-lineenvolverde/.

8. From this perspective, Brazilian coffee epitomized the evils of the plantation system—the plantation as (literally) the breeding ground for systems of violence, alienation, and ecological ruin that would define capitalist modernity. Within anthropology, this view has been most eloquently expressed by Anna Tsing, who uses Brazilian plantations as the paradigmatic example of capitalist destruction (2015, 38–39). See this book's conclusion for details.

9. It is important to note that Santos was the center of the Brazilian abolitionist movement. The *quilombo* of Jabaquara, the largest settlement of escaped slaves in the country, was located in what is now a neighborhood in Santos. Leaders of the abolition movement, such as Jose Bonifacio and Qunitino de Lacerda, lived in Santos, but this history is notably absent from public culture, especially when compared with the ubiquitous presence of *bandeirantes* symbolism.

10. In fact, the former CEO of Goldman Sachs, Lloyd Blankfein, began his career as a trader at J. Aron before it was absorbed by Goldman Sachs, and I have been told by contacts in the industry that the alumni of J. Aron are still a distinct group within the company. Goldman Sachs, one of the world's largest and most powerful investment banks, has roots in Santos coffee, but this history is completely invisible. The building that housed the original offices of Leon Israel lies just a few steps from the Santos Coffee Museum. The only indicators of its past are a series of decorative stone lions (a symbol for *Leon*) that form a motif on the building's aging facade.

11. Maxine Margolis's 1973 ethnography *The Moving Frontier* provides a detailed account of this process as it occurred in the town of Ouro Verde in Paraná. Margolis shows how the land grab in Paraná was a direct outcome of a colonization and settlement plan by British investors who had "worked for the British government in the Anglo-Egyptian Sudan" (21).

12. The employment of *boias frias* is still commonplace in some parts of Brazil. A 2019 investigation by Reuters called "Picked by Slaves: Coffee Crisis Brews in Brazil" documented the widespread abuses of migrant day laborers, who were sometimes paid as little as forty-nine cents per hour. Despite these abuses, the use of *boias frias* labor has declined dramatically since the 1970s, largely as a result of mechanization.

13. http://www.worldfoodprize.org/en/laureates/20002009˙laureates/2006˙lobato˙mccl ung˙paolinelli/cerrado/.

3. PORT OF THE PAST, PORT OF THE FUTURE

1. Road naming is a way that the Brazilian government publicly reproduces the mythology of progress. The highway names Anchieta, Immigrants, Bandeirantes, and Anhanguera all reference major figures in the historical epic of São Paulo.

2. See https://www.reuters.com/article/us-brazil-transport-grains/the-long-brutal -haul-from-farm-to-port-in-brazil-idINBRE8A014020121101.

3. In a sense, the conflict here illustrates the role of the port in bringing together the two chronotopes of progress—horizontal and vertical—that were laid out by Gilberto Freyre almost a century ago. The horizontal dimension (symbolized by the *bandeirantes*) is based on agricultural expansion, clearing and "settling" new lands for extractive

gain. The vertical dimension is based on a kind of urbanization that reinforces social hierarchies (especially class and racial differences) that were rooted in agrarian patriarchal society. The relationship between the "big house" and "slave quarters" in colonial society epitomizes the vertical tendency.

4. As of August 2021, this commercial can be viewed on YouTube at https://www .youtube.com/watch?v=sAva65Wnaug.

5. Extensive details on the stevedores monument can be found at http://www .novomilenio.inf.br/santos/h0360m046.htm.

6. Almost immediately, Freyre's thesis was challenged by São Paulo–based historians who argued that he downplayed the importance of the *bandeirantes*' "horizontalism" and the degree to which the colonial system was transformed by the explosion of the coffee economy in the nineteenth century, leading up to the abolition of slavery in 1888. In the mid-nineteenth century, the coffee region around São Paulo became the country's political, cultural, and economic focal point. This region was peripheral to the colonial slave economy, and its society developed along somewhat different lines. The debate over verticalism versus horizontalism was also a debate about the relative importance of sugar versus coffee and North versus South in the history of Brazil. It raged on for decades among scholars, but as Brazil modernized, there is no doubt that the horizontalism of the *bandeirantes* became the dominant metaphor for social development. During the rule of Getúlio Vargas, poet Cassiano Ricardo referred to the *bandeirantes*' movement into the interior as nothing less than "the rhythm of Brazilian civilization" (Morse 1965, 211).

4. SACRALIZING THE SEWER

1. The sewer pipe painting is called *A Praia de São Vicente*. It can be found online at http://www.novomilenio.inf.br/santos/calixt127.htm. I believe it was painted around 1910 because the space that is depicted became the site of another famous landmark, the Pencil Bridge, or *ponte pensil*, which was built between 1911 and 1914. The canvas was probably done just before construction on the bridge began, because the bridge carries the pipe across the channel. The Pencil Bridge was another favorite subject of Calixto.

2. I often compare Calixto's painting to *The Lackawanna Valley* by American artist George Inness, which is in the collection of the National Gallery of Art in Washington, DC. Inness's work shows a steam locomotive rumbling through a bucolic landscape in western New York, and it is often thought of as a critical commentary on industrialization. It is on the cover of Leo Marx's (1964) *The Machine in the Garden: Technology and the Pastoral Ideal in America*, one of the foundational texts in American environmental history. The difference, I believe, is that Calixto did not paint the sewer as a criticism of rapid modernization.

3. The question of how mundane objects such as sewers become sacralized in certain contexts is part of the politics of infrastructure, analyzed by anthropologists Susan Leigh Star (1999), Julie Chu (2014), Brenda Chalfin (2014), and Mónica Salas Landa (2016).

4. Sidney Piochi Bernardini's 2006 book, which I translate as *The Plans of the City: The Politics of Urban Intervention in Santos from Estevan Fuertes to Saturnino de Brito*, provides extensive detail about the origins of the Fuertes plan, the politics of the project at the municipal, state, and national levels, and the technical differences between the Fuertes proposal and the plan that was ultimately implemented.

5. Bernardini (2006) describes a close connection between Cornell University and the Brazilian government that reaches back to the 1860s (85–90). Charles Frederick Hart, a Cornell geologist, traveled to Brazil as part of the Thayer Expedition with Louis Agassiz in 1865. Hart led another expedition to Brazil in 1870 with Orville Derby, his Cornell student, who created the first systematic geological surveys of Brazil and led the Geo-

graphic Commission of São Paulo. A large contingent of elite Brazilian students enrolled in Cornell in the 1870s, even creating a Portuguese periodical, *Aurora Brasileira*, that covered news and literature and was published on campus in 1873.

6. This complex is now the Immigration Museum of the State of São Paulo, which provides a wonderful introduction to the history of Brazilian immigration.

7. This poem is fairly well known and reproduced in several different sources. See, for example, http://memoriasantista.com.br/?p=695.

8. The stained glass was placed in 1936, during the dictatorship of Vargas, who launched an ambitious strategy to develop cultural and historical knowledge about Brazilian history and identity designed to break down the hegemony of regions such as São Paulo and Rio de Janeiro and to develop a national identity. The *bandeirantes* had been a symbol of São Paulo's explosive economic growth and prosperity, as the ceiling in the Coffee Museum shows. According to Tracy Devine Guzmán, Vargas turned the *bandeirantes* into icons of national, rather than regional, expansion. Under him, the modern *bandeirantes* would colonize the interior and modernize the cities through the development of heavy industry.

9. One of the centerpieces of Vargas's plan was the nationalization of Brazil's oil industry, which barred foreign corporations from access to Brazil's petroleum under the slogan "The oil is ours!" This rallying cry has become synonymous with the Vargas years, exemplifying the philosophy of state-led industrialization and economic nationalism. Brazil's first oil refinery was constructed in Cubatão (which was then a part of Santos) in 1950 and opened in 1955.

A brief digression is necessary here. Oil was not discovered in Brazil until the late 1930s. Up until the 1950s, the country was entirely dependent on oil imported by multinational companies such as Shell and Standard Oil, and the reliance on imported oil (purchased with profits from agricultural exports) was seen as a major barrier to Brazil's progress. How could a country become a global power if it had no access to oil, the lifeblood of industrialization? The discovery of domestic oil set off a furious race to develop the sector, which pitted a political faction that was allied with the interests of the multinational companies against Vargas and others on the left who sought to nationalize the oil and protect Brazil from dependency on foreign capital. The slogan "The oil is ours!" began with left-wing groups, such as the communists and labor unions in Santos, who were the sworn enemies of Vargas, but it was adopted (some would say co-opted) by the Vargas regime and used to galvanize nationalist support. When Vargas committed suicide, he believed that a military cabal, aided by the United States and the oil companies, was plotting a coup against him to ensure foreign access to Brazil's oil. Vargas, however, managed to pass a law creating the national oil monopoly Petrobras in 1954, shortly before his death. The oil refinery in Cubatão was originally planned as a foreign-owned enterprise under President Eurico Dutra, who preceded Vargas's second term as president, but it opened as a state-run enterprise in 1955, after Petrobras had been established. Santos thereby became a major piece in the puzzle of Brazil's state-led modernization.

10. It is also important to note that the area just north of Cubatão is home to Brazil's first hydroelectric dam (the Henry Borden Dam) and reservoir (the Billings Reservoir), which provide energy and drinking water for much of São Paulo. It is worth noting that both facilities carry the names of the foreign engineers who designed them. Henry Borden was a Canadian, and Asa Billings was an American.

5. CITIZEN OF THE WORLD, KING OF ALL NATIONS

1. This is a vast literature, but some of the best examples are Roberta Da Matta's *O Universo do Futebol* and the work of José Sérgio Leite Lopes.

2. Anderson (1997) argues that museums take sacred sites and make them profane objects of the secular state, eventually leading to a commoditization of tradition. Once a sacred past becomes part of a secular museum, "it is only a step into the market" (182).

3. Ama Brasil is also responsible for the redevelopment of Fordlandia, the Ford Company's utopian experiment in the Amazon documented by historian Greg Grandin (2009).

CONCLUSION

1. A Marxist would be likely to challenge my own Durkheimian position by asking where these chronotopes come from and arguing that they are always the products of class relationships. That argument makes a lot of sense in Santos. As Brazil transformed historically from a colonial economy to an exporter of coffee to an industrial hub and, finally, to a global "consumerist" nation, the *bandeirantes* exemplified the class that was supposed to be leading the march towards progress at each historical moment. Different classes may have been in control, but each one used the *bandeirantes* to symbolize its ideological project. As I see it, the problem with this approach is that it begs the question: What is a class? If we think of class as an ethnographic object (like progress, society, structure, or other abstractions), then how do we know a class when we see it, especially in a country of over 200 million people with an extremely complex modern economy that is riven by political and cultural divisions that cut across class lines? If there is any definition of class struggle that seemed to fit modern Brazil, it would be James O'Connor's (1973) model of "the fiscal crisis of the state," in which government payments (such as social programs, direct cash payments, tax breaks, or subsidies) become the focal point in class struggle.

Class, like progress, requires some formalizations to make it thinkable. In the past century, theorists have moved from metaphors like "blocs" to "chains" to "networks" in how they imagine and discuss class in social theory. In a field like anthropology, which largely rejects statistical analysis in favor of interpretive methods, how do we know a class when we see it? Is class defined solely by access to the means of production? By income level and lifestyle? By the forms of social and cultural capital?

2. Tarde was embraced by diffusionists in the Boasian school, especially Robert Lowie and Elsie Clews Parsons, the latter of whom translated Tarde into English. As Herbert Lewis (2001) writes, "Boas drew upon *Les lois de l'imitation* by Gabriel Tarde, which stresses the importance of individual initiative in change and the tendency of others to adopt, or imitate, these innovations. . . . course notes taken by Ruth Benedict show Boas's interest in Tarde, innovation, and imitation in cultural change" (391).

3. There is an interesting (and perhaps intentional) double meaning here. In his elusive style, Geertz argues that the "tenacity" of a cultural pattern shaped the economic decisions of Javanese peasants; at the same time, he critiques the dominant formalism—Rostow's takeoff—that was supposed to explain the behavior of those very same peasants. The submerged point may be that Rostow's progress is just as constrained by formal patterning as any other cultural system.

4. It is fascinating that Karl Marx, Max Weber, and Clifford Geertz (for whom culture is "webs of significance that man himself has spun") all use spider webs as a metaphor for human meaning-making.

5. She writes, "In Western music, the madrigal and the fugue are examples of polyphony. These forms seem archaic to many modern listeners because they were superseded by music in which a unified rhythm and melody holds the composition together" (Tsing 2015, 23). Contrast this with Geertz, who uses the fugue's polyphony to describe diversity within a fixed cultural structure. Neither Tsing nor Geertz remark on the fact that Weber (1949, 31–32) also used the example of the transformation of harmonic music from polyphony in the West to analyze the meaning of progress.

6. Dankowski and Viveiros de Castro (2016) see this perspective as a technological utopianism, the supreme expression of which is the "singularity thesis," an idea that there is a technical, engineered solution to any human problem (47–49).

7. It is worth noting that this viewpoint has an analog in urban planning, where experts associate "sustainable urbanism" with population densification and the efficient use of land, water, and energy.

8. One of the most influential postwar ethnographies about rural Latin America is *A Village That Chose Progress: Chan Kom Revisted* by Robert Redfield (1950). In it, Redfield unambiguously associates progress with the end of rural traditionalism, embodied by "the road to the light," a paved road that connects a remote village in the Mexican state of Yucatán with the city of Mérida. This quintessentially modernist book uses schools, roads, electricity, education, health, and civic participation as indicators of progress.

References

Alencar, José de. 2017/1857. *O Guarani*. São Paulo: Paulus Editora.

Anderson, Benedict. 1997. *Imagined Communities: Reflections on the Origin and Spread of Nationalism*. London: Verso.

Ansell, Aaron. 2014. *Zero Hunger: Political Culture and Antipoverty Policy in Northeast Brazil*. Chapel Hill: University of North Carolina Press.

Bacha, Edmar Lisboa, and Robert Greenhill. 1993. *Marcellino Martins & E. Johnston: 150 Anos De Café*. Rio de Janeiro: Salamandra Consultoria Editorial.

Bakhtin, Mikhail M. 1981. *The Dialogic Imagination: Four Essays*. Translated by Michael Holquist. Austin: University of Texas Press.

Barbosa, Américo, and Dirce Alves. 2012. *Agenda 21 De Cubatão: Uma História feita por Muitas Mãos*. Cubatão, SP, Brazil: Centro de Integração e Desenvolvimento Empresarial da Baixada Santista.

Beck, Ulrich. 2013. *Risk Society: Towards a New Modernity*. Washington, DC: Sage.

Bernardini, Sidney Piochi. 2006. *Os Planos Da Cidade: As políticas De intervenção Urbana Em Santos: De Estevan Fuertes a Saturnino De Brito (1892–1910)*. São Paulo: Rima Editora.

Besky, Sarah. 2014. *The Darjeeling Distinction: Labor and Justice on Fair Trade Tea Plantations in India*. Berkeley: University of California Press.

Besky, Sarah. 2021. "Teawords: Experiments with Quality in Indian Tea Production." *American Anthropologist*, 123: 96–107. https://doi.org/10.1111/aman.13508.

Biehl, João. 2005. *Vita: Life in a Zone of Social Abandonment*. Berkeley: University of California Press.

Biehl, João. 2013. "The Judicialization of Biopolitics: Claiming the Right to Pharmaceuticals in Brazilian Courts." *American Ethnologist* 40 (3): 419–36. https://doi.org/10.1111/amet.12030.

Biehl, João. 2016. "The Postneoliberal Fabulation of Power: On Statecraft, Precarious Infrastructures, and Public Mobilization in Brazil." *American Ethnologist* 43 (3): 437–450. https://doi.org/10.1111/amet.12337.

Blanc, Jacob. 2019. *Before the Flood: The Itaipu Dam and the Visibility of Rural Brazil*. Durham: Duke University Press.

Blanc, Jacob. 2021. "The Bandeirantes of Freedom: The Prestes Column and the Myth of Brazil's Interior." *The Hispanic American Historical Review* 101 (1): 101–32. https://doi.org/10.1215/00182168-8796484.

Blaser, Mario, Harvey A. Feit, and Glenn McRae. 2004. *In the Way of Development: Indigenous Peoples, Life Projects and Globalization*. London: Zed Books.

Bliska, Flávia, Celso Luís Rodrigues Vegro, Paulo César Afonso Júnior, Elessandra Aparecida Bento Mourão, and Cleide Helena Santos Cardoso. 2009. "Custos De Produção De Café Nas Principais Regiões Produtoras Do Brasil." *Informações Econômicas* 39(9): 5–20.

Boito, Armando. *Reform and Political Crisis in Brazil*. Leiden, Netherlands: Brill, December 13, 2021. https://doi.org/10.1163/9789004467743.

Breglia, Lisa. 2013. *Living with Oil: Promises, Peaks, and Declines on Mexico's Gulf Coast*. Austin: University of Texas Press.

Brookes, James. 1991. "Signs of Life in Brazil's Industrial Valley of Death." *New York Times,* June 15, 1991.

Burdick, John. 1993. *Looking for God in Brazil: The Progressive Catholic Church in Urban Brazil's Religious Arena.* Berkeley: University of California Press.

Caldeira, Teresa. 2000. *City of Walls: Crime, Segregation, and Citizenship in São Paulo.* Berkeley: University of California Press.

Carneiro da Cunha, Manuela, Ruben Caixeta, Jeremy M. Campbell, Carlos Fausto, Antonio Kelly José, Claudio Lomnitz, Carlos D. Londoño Sulkin, Caio Pompeia, and Aparecida Vilaça. 2017. "Indigenous Peoples Boxed in by Brazil's Political Crisis." *HAU: Journal of Ethnographic Theory* 7 (2): 403–426. https://doi.org/10.14318/hau7.2.033.

Carvalho, Laura. 2018. *Valsa Brasileira: Do Boom Ao Caos Econômico.* São Paulo: Todavia.

Chalfin, Brenda. 2014. "Public Things, Excremental Politics, and the Infrastructure of Bare Life in Ghana's City of Tema." *American Ethnologist* 41(1): 92–109. https://doi.org/10.1111/amet.12062.

Chu, Julie Y. 2014. "When Infrastructures Attack: The Workings of Disrepair in China." *American Ethnologist* 41 (2) (05/01; 2021/08): 351–67. https://doi.org/10.1111/amet.12080.

Clarence-Smith, W., and Steven Topik. 2003. *The Global Coffee Economy in Africa, Asia and Latin America, 1500–1989.* Cambridge: Cambridge University Press.

Clastres, Hélène. 1995. *The Land without Evil: Tupí-Guaraní Prophetism.* Urbana: University of Illinois Press.

Collins, John F. 2015. *Revolt of the Saints: Memory and Redemption in the Twilight of Brazilian Racial Democracy.* Durham, NC: Duke University Press.

Coronil, Fernando. 1997. *The Magical State: Nature, Money, and Modernity in Venezuela.* Chicago: University of Chicago Press.

Da Matta, Roberto. 1982. *A Divided World: Apinayé Social Structure.* Cambridge, MA: Harvard University Press.

Da Matta, Roberto. 1991 *Carnivals, Rogues, and Heroes: An Interpretation of the Brazilian Dilemma.* Trans. by John Drury. South Bend, IN.: University of Notre Dame Press.

Da Matta, Roberto. 2016. "Progress, Democracy, and Hope." *O Estado De São Paulo,* May 11, 2016.

Da Matta, Roberto, and Elena Soárez. 2006. *Eagles, Donkeys and Butterflies: An Anthropological Study of Brazil's Animal Game.* South Bend, IN: University of Notre Dame Press.

Daniel, Calazans Pierri. 2013. "Como Acabará Essa Terra? Reflexões Sobre a Cataclismologia Guarani-Mbya, à Luz Da Obra De Nimuendajú." *Tellus* 13 (24): 159.

Danowski, Déborah, and Eduardo Viveiros de Castro. 2016. *The Ends of the World.* Oxford, UK: Polity Press.

Davidson, James Dale. 2012. *Brazil Is the New America: How Brazil Offers Upward Mobility in a Collapsing World.* Hoboken, NJ: Wiley.

Davis, Shelton H. 1977. *Victims of the Miracle: Development and the Indians of Brazil.* Cambridge: Cambridge University Press.

Dean, Warren. 1976. *Rio Claro: A Brazilian Plantation System, 1820–1920.* Palo Alto, CA: Stanford University Press.

Dean, Warren. 1997. *With Broadax and Firebrand: The Destruction of the Brazilian Atlantic Forest.* Berkeley: University of California Press.

Dent, Alexander Sebastian. 2009. *River of Tears: Country Music, Memory, and Modernity in Brazil.* Durham, NC: Duke University Press.

Doctor, Marukh. 2018. *Business-State Relations in Brazil: Challenges of the Port Reform Lobby.* London: Routledge.

Dozier, Craig L. 1956. "Northern Paraná, Brazil." *Tropical Housing & Planning Monthly Bulletin* 2 (1): 13–19.

Dinius, Oliver J., and Angela Vergara, eds. 2011. *Company Towns in the Americas: Landscape, Power, and Working-Class Communities.* Athens: University of Georgia Press.

Dos Santos, Cynthia Regina de Araújo Evangelista. 2015. "Santos Das Avenidas: A Moradia Burguesa no Início do Século XX." Novas Edições Acadêmicas. Brazil.

Dumont, Louis. 1980. *Homo Hierarchicus: The Caste System and its Implications.* Chicago: University of Chicago Press.

Dumont, Louis. 1986. *Essays on Individualism: Modern Ideology in Anthropological Perspective.* Chicago: University of Chicago Press.

Eakin, Marshall C. 1989. *British Enterprise in Brazil: The St. John d'El Rey Mining Company and the Morro Velho Gold Mine, 1830–1960.* Durham, NC: Duke University Press.

Eakin, Marshall C. 1997. *Brazil: The Once and Future Country.* New York: St. Martin's Press.

Eakin, Marshall C. 2017. *Becoming Brazilians: Race and National Identity in Twentieth-Century Brazil.* Cambridge: Cambridge University Press.

Easterbrook, Gregg. 1997. "Forgotten Benefactor of Humanity." *Atlantic Monthly* 279 (1): 74–82.

Edelman, Marc, and Angelique Haugerud. 2004. *The Anthropology of Development and Globalization: A Reader.* Malden, MA: Blackwell.

Ewing, Reese. 2015. "Brazil Ditches Standard Jute Coffee Bags, Leading Move Toward Bulk." Reuters, December 20, 2015.

Ferrante, Lucas, and Philip M Fearnside. 2019. "Brazil's New President and 'Ruralists' Threaten Amazonia's Environment, Traditional Peoples and the Global Climate." *Environmental Conservation* 46 (4): 261–63. doi:10.1017/S0376892919000213.

Ferreira, Antonio Celso. 2002. *A epopéia Bandeirante: Letrados, instituições, invenção histórica (1870–1940).* São Paulo: UNESP.

Ferreira, Lúcia Da Costa. 1993. *Os Fantasmas do Vale: Qualidade Ambiental e Cidadania.* Campinas, Brazil: Editora da Unicamp.

Fischer, Edward F., and Peter Benson. 2005. "Something Better: Hegemony, Development, and Desire in Guatemalan Export Agriculture." *Social Analysis: The International Journal of Social and Cultural Practice* 49 (1): 3–20. http://www.jstor.org/stable/23175292.

Fischer, Edward F., and Jonathan A. Shayne. 2013. *Cash on the Table: Markets, Values, and Moral Economies.* Santa Fe, NM: School for Advanced Research Press.

Fischer, Edward F., and Bart Victor. 2014. "High-End Coffee and Smallholding Growers in Guatemala." *Latin American Research Review* 49 (1): 155–177. https://doi.org/10.1353/lar.2014.0001.

Font, Maurício A. 1990. *Coffee, Contention, and Change.* Oxford, UK: Blackwell.

Font, Maurício A. 2010. *Coffee and Transformation in São Paulo, Brazil.* Lanham, MD: Lexington Books.

Fortun, Kim. 2001. *Advocacy after Bhopal Environmentalism, Disaster, New Global Orders.* Chicago: University of Chicago Press.

Freyre, Gilberto. 1945. *Brazil, an Interpretation.* New York: Knopf.

Freyre, Gilberto. 1946. *The Masters and the Slaves: A Study in the Development of Brazilian Civilization.* Trans. by Samuel Putnam. New York: Knopf.

Freyre, Gilberto. 1959. *New World in the Tropics: The Culture of Modern Brazil.* New York: Knopf.

Freyre, Gilberto. 1963. *The Mansions and the Shanties (Sobrados e Mucambos): The Making of Modern Brazil*. New York: Knopf.

Freyre, Gilberto. 1970. *Order and Progress: Brazil from Monarchy to Republic*. New York: Knopf.

Fuertes, Estevan Antonio. 1894. *Sanitary Improvements for the City and Port of Santos, Brazil*. Ithaca, NY: Cornell University Department of Civil Engineering.

Furtado, Celso. 2007. *O Capitalismo Global*. São Paulo: Paz e Terra.

Geertz, Clifford. 1963. *Agricultural Involution: The Process of Ecological Change in Indonesia*. Berkeley: University of California Press.

Ghosh, Amitav. 2022. *Nutmeg's Curse: Parables for a Planet in Crisis*. Chicago: University of Chicago Press.

Gitahy, Maria Lucia Caira. 1991. "The Port Workers of Santos, 1889–1914: Labor Movement and Urban Culture in an Early 20th Century City." PhD diss., University of Colorado.

Gitahy, Maria Lucia Caira. 1992. *Ventos do Mar: Trabalhadores do Porto, Movimento operário e Cultura Urbana Em Santos, 1889–1914*. São Paulo: UNESP.

Goldblatt, David. 2014. *Futebol Nation: The Story of Brazil through Soccer*. Boulder, CO: Nation Books.

Goldenweiser, Alexander. 1936. "Loose Ends of Theory of the Individual, Pattern, and Involution in Primitive Society," in *Essays in Anthropology Presented to A. L. Kroeber*, ed. by Robert Lowie, 99–104. Berkeley: University of California Press.

Gonçalves, Alcindo, and Luiz Antonio de Paula Nunes. 2008. *O Grande Porto Modernização no Porto De Santos*. Santos, Brazil: Realejo.

Graham, Richard. 1968. *Britain and the Onset of Modernization in Brazil 1850–1914*. London: Cambridge University Press.

Gramsci, Antonio. 1971. *Selections from the Prison Notebooks*. Ed. by Quintin Hoare and Geoffrey Nowell-Smith. New York: International Publishers.

Grandin, Greg. 2009. *Fordlandia: The Rise and Fall of Henry Ford's Forgotten Jungle City*. New York: Picador.

Green, James Naylor, Victoria Langland, and Lilia Moritz Schwarcz. 2018. *The Brazil Reader: History, Culture, Politics*. Durham, NC: Duke University Press.

Guimarães, Carlos Gabriel, and Robert Greenhill. 2021. "Trading in an Emerging Market: E. Johnston & Co and the Brazilian Coffee Trade 1840–1880." *Revista De Historia Económica/Journal of Iberian and Latin American Economic History* 39 (1): 157–90. doi:10.1017/S0212610919000120.

Gusterson, Hugh. 1997. "Studying Up Revisited." *Political and Legal Anthropology Review* 20 (1) (2021/08): 114–19. https://doi.org/10.1525/pol.1997.20.1.114.

Guzmán, Tracy Devine. 2013. *Native and National in Brazil: Indigeneity after Independence*. Chapel Hill: University of North Carolina Press.

Harvey, David. 1989. *The Condition of Postmodernity: An Enquiry into the Origins of Cultural Change*. Oxford, UK: Blackwell.

Harvey, David. 1989. *The Urban Experience*. Baltimore, MD: Johns Hopkins University Press.

Harvey, David. 2009. *Social Justice and the City*. Athens: University of Georgia Press.

Harvey, David. 2010. *The Enigma of Capital: And the Crises of Capitalism*. New York: Oxford University Press.

Harvey, David. 2016. *The Ways of the World*. New York: Oxford University Press.

Helmreich, Stefan. 2011. "Nature/Culture/Seawater." *American Anthropologist* 113, no. 1: 132–44. http://www.jstor.org/stable/41407381.

Helmreich, Stefan. 2011. "What Was Life? Answers from Three Limit Biologies." *Critical Inquiry* 37 (4): 671–696. https://doi.org/10.1086/660987.

Helmreich, Stefan. 2013. "Potential Energy and the Body Electric: Cardiac Waves, Brain Waves, and the Making of Quantities into Qualities." *Current Anthropology* 54: 139–48. https://doi.org/10.1086/670968.

Helmreich, Stefan. 2014. "Waves: An Anthropology of Scientific Things." *HAU Journal of Ethnographic Theory* 4 (3): 265–284. https://doi.org/10.14318/hau4.3.016.

Helmreich, Stefan. 2020. "Wave Theory ~ Social Theory." *Public Culture* 32 (2): 287–326. https://doi.org/10.1215/08992363-8090094.

Herzfeld, Michael. 1991. *A Place in History: Social and Monumental Time in a Cretan Town*. Princeton: Princeton University Press.

Herzfeld, Michael. 1997. *Cultural Intimacy: Social Poetics in the Nation-State*. New York: Routledge.

Herzfeld, Michael. 2009. *Evicted from Eternity: The Restructuring of Modern Rome*. Chicago: University of Chicago Press.

Hess, David J., and Roberto Da Matta, eds. 1995. *The Brazilian Puzzle: Culture on the Borderlands of the Western World*. New York: Columbia University Press.

Hetherington, Kregg. 2011. *Guerrilla Auditors: The Politics of Transparency in Neoliberal Paraguay*. Durham, NC: Duke University Press.

Holloway, Thomas H. 1980. *Immigrants on the Land: Coffee and Society in São Paulo, 1886–1934*. Chapel Hill: University of North Carolina Press.

Holston, James. 1989. *The Modernist City: An Anthropological Critique of Brasília*. Chicago: University of Chicago Press.

Holston, James. 1999. *Cities and Citizenship*. Durham, NC: Duke University Press.

Holston, James. 2008. *Insurgent Citizenship: Disjunctions of Democracy and Modernity in Brazil*. Princeton: Princeton University Press.

Innerarity, Daniel. 2012. "Chronopolitics: A Theory of Social Rhythm," in *The Future and Its Enemies: In Defense of Political Hope*, 77–89. Redwood City, CA: Stanford University Press. https://doi.org/10.1515/9780804782210-007.

Irvine, Judith T. 2004. "Say When: Temporalities in Language Ideology." *Journal of Linguistic Anthropology* 14 (1): 99–109. https://www.jstor.org/stable/43104023.

Junge, Benjamin, Sean T. Mitchell, Alvaro Jarrín, and Lucia Cantero, eds. 2021. *Precarious Democracy: Ethnographies of Hope, Despair, and Resistance in Brazil*. New Brunswick, NJ: Rutgers University Press.

Kane, Stephanie C. 2012. *Where Rivers Meet the Sea: The Political Ecology of Water*. Philadelphia: Temple University Press.

Kopenawa, Davi, and Bruce Albert. 2013. *The Falling Sky: Words of a Yanomami Shaman*. Cambridge, MA: Harvard University Press.

Kroeber, A. L. 1919. "On the Principle of Order in Civilization as Exemplified by Changes of Fashion." *American Anthropologist* 21 (3): 235–63.

Kroeber, A. L. 1944. *Configurations of Culture Growth*. Berkeley: University of California Press.

Kroeber, A.L. 1963. *Style and Civilizations*. Berkeley: University of California Press.

Labruto, Nicole. 2018. "The Plantation Network: Brazilian Bioenergy Science and Sustainability in the Global South." PhD diss., Massachusetts Institute of Technology Program in Science, Technology and Society.

Landa, Mónica Salas. 2016. "Crude Residues: The Workings of Failing Oil Infrastructure in Poza Rica, Veracruz, Mexico." *Environment and Planning A: Economy and Space* 48: 718–735. https://doi.org/10.1177/0308518X15594618.

Lanna, Ana L. D. 1996. *Uma Cidade Na Transição:Santos, 1870–1913*. Santos, Brazil: Editora Hucitec.

Latour, Bruno. 1999. *Pandora's Hope: Essays on the Reality of Science Studies*. Cambridge, Mass.: Harvard University Press.

Lea, Vanessa R. 2017. "Ontological Conflicts Concerning Indigenous Peoples in Contemporary Brazil." *ab-Original* 1 (2): 151–175. doi: https://doi.org/10.5325/aboriginal .1.2.0151.

Leite Lopes, José Sérgio. 2000. "Class, Ethnicity, and Color in the Making of Brazilian Football." *Daedalus* 129 (2) (2021/07): 239–270. https://www.jstor.org/stable /i20027624.

Leite Lopes, José Sérgio, Afrânio Garcia Jr, and María Virginia Garcia. 2017. "Derrotas Lacerantes y Victorias Deslumbrantes El Imaginario Nacional En Brasil a través De Las Copas Mundiales." *RMA Revista Del Museo De Antropología* 10 (2): 177.

Lemon, Alaina. 2009. "Sympathy for the Weary State? Cold War Chronotopes and Moscow Others." *Comparative Studies in Society and History* 51 (4): 832–64. doi:10.1017/ S0010417509990156.

Levine, Robert M., and John J. Crocitti. 1999. *The Brazil Reader: History, Culture, Politics*. Durham, NC: Duke University Press.

Lévi-Strauss, Claude. 1968. *Structural Anthropology*. London: Allen Lane.

Lévi-Strauss, Claude. 1971. *Tristes Tropiques*. New York: Atheneum.

Lévi-Strauss, Claude, and Sylvia Modelski. 1995. *Saudades do Brasil: A Photographic Memoir*. Seattle: University of Washington Press.

Lewis, Herbert S. 2001. Boas, Darwin, Science, and Anthropology. *Current Anthropology* 42 (3): 381–405. https://doi.org/10.1086/320474.

Li, Tania Murray. 2014. "Involution's Dynamic Others." *Journal of the Royal Anthropological Institute* 20 (2): 276–92. https://doi.org/10.1111/1467-9655.12104.

Lomnitz-Adler, Claudio. 2001. *Deep Mexico, Silent Mexico: An Anthropology of Nationalism*. Minneapolis: University of Minnesota Press.

Lomnitz-Adler, Claudio. 2005. *Death and the Idea of Mexico*. Brooklyn, NY: Zone Books.

Lowie, Robert. 1920. *Primitive Society*. New York: Boni and Liveright.

Lyons, John and Paul Kiernan. 2015. "How Brazil's China-Driven Commodities Boom Went Bust; Developing Nation's Big Bet on China Turns Sour as China's Appetite for Exports Dims; 'Looking at a Lost Decade.'" *Wall Street Journal, Eastern Edition*, August 27, 2015.

Mankekar, Purnima, and Akhil Gupta. 2016. "Intimate Encounters: Affective Labor in Call Centers." *Positions: East Asia Cultures Critique* 24 (1): 17–43. https://doi.org /10.1215/10679847-3320029.

Mankekar, Purnima, and Akhil Gupta. 2017. "Future Tense Capital, Labor, and Technology in a Service Industry." *HAU Journal of Ethnographic Theory* 7 (3): 67–87. https://doi.org/10.14318/hau7.3.004.

Mankekar, Purnima, and Akhil Gupta. 2019. "The Missed Period: Disjunctive Temporalities and the Work of Capital in an Indian BPO." *American Ethnologist* 46 (4): 417–28. https://doi.org/10.1111/amet.12837.

Margolis, Maxine L. 1973. *The Moving Frontier: Social and Economic Change in a Southern Brazilian Community*. Gainesville: University of Florida Press.

Matory, James Lorand. 2005. *Black Atlantic Religion Tradition, Transnationalism, and Matriarchy in the Afro-Brazilian Candomblé*. Princeton: Princeton University Press.

Maybury-Lewis, David. 1990. "Brazil's Significant Minority." *Wilson Quarterly* 14 (3): 33–42. https://www.jstor.org/stable/i40010026.

Medeiros, Marjorie De Carvalho, Ney Caldatto Barbosa, and Gino Caldatto Barbosa. 2014. *Museu Pelé: Restauração e Legado*. São Paulo: Magma Cultural e Editora.

Mignolo, Walter. 2011. *The Darker Side of Western Modernity: Global Futures, Decolonial Options*. Durham, NC: Duke University Press.

Mitchell, Sean T. 2017. *Constellations of Inequality: Space, Race, and Utopia in Brazil*. Chicago: University of Chicago Press.

Mitchell, Sean T. 2021. "Cruel Pessimism: The Affect of Anticorruption and the End of the New Brazilian Middle Class," in *Precarious Democracy: Ethnographies of Hope, Despair, and Resistance in Brazil.* Ed. by Benjamin Junge, Sean T. Mitchell, Alvaro Jarrín, and Lucia Cantero. New Brunswick, NJ: Rutgers University Press. 79–90.

Monteiro, John M. 1985. "São Paulo in the Seventeenth Century: Economy and Society." PhD diss., University of Chicago.

Monteiro, John M., Barbara Weinstein, and James P. Woodard. 2018. *Blacks of the Land: Indian Slavery, Settler Society, and the Portuguese Colonial Enterprise in South America.* Cambridge: Cambridge University Press.

Moog, Clodomir Vianna. 1964. *Bandeirantes and Pioneers.* New York: G. Braziller.

Morgan, Lewis Henry. 1877. *Ancient Society, Or Researches in the Line of Human Progress from Savagery through Barbarism to Civilization.* Chicago: C. H. Kerr.

Morse, Richard M. 1965. *The Bandeirantes: The Historical Role of the Brazilian Pathfinders.* New York: Knopf.

Morton, Gregory Duff. 2015. "Managing Transience: Bolsa Família and Its Subjects in an MST Landless Settlement." *Journal of Peasant Studies* 42 (6) 1283–1305. https://doi.org/10.1080/03066150.2014.978298.

Myrdal, Gunnar. 1969. *Economic Theory and Underdeveloped Regions.* London: Methuen.

Nader, Laura. 2018. *Contrarian Anthropology: The Unwritten Rules of Academia.* New York: Berghahn Books.

Needell, Jeffrey D. 2015. *Emergent Brazil: Key Perspectives on a New Global Power.* Gainesville: University Press of Florida.

O'Connor, James.1973. *The Fiscal Crisis of the State.* New York: St. Martin's Press.

O'Donnell, Julia. 2013. *A invenção De Copacabana: Culturas Urbanas e Estilos De Vida no Rio De Janeiro (1890–1940).* Rio de Janeiro: Zahar.

Ortega, Antonio C., and Clésio Marcelino Jesus. 2011. "Território, Certificação De Procedência e a Busca Da Singularidade: O Caso do Café do Cerrado." *Políticas and Sociedade* 10 (19): 305–30.

Ortner, Sherry B. 2016. "Dark Anthropology and Its Others: Theory since the Eighties." *HAU Journal of Ethnographic Theory* 6 (1): 47–73. https://doi.org/10.14318/hau6.1.004.

Pedro, Carina Marcondes Ferreira. 2015. *Casas Importadoras De Santos e Seus Agentes: Comércio e Cultura Material (1870–1900).* São Paulo: Ateliê.

Perry, Keisha-Khan Y. 2013. *Black Women against the Land Grab: The Fight for Racial Justice in Brazil.* Minneapolis: University of Minnesota Press.

Pinker, Steven. 2018. *Enlightenment Now.* New York: Viking.

Pompeu de Toledo, Roberto. 2010. "Conheça a História De João Ramalho e Tibiriçá." *Veja São Paulo*, October 22, 2010.

Ramos, Alcida Rita. 1998. *Indigenism: Ethnic Politics in Brazil.* Madison: University of Wisconsin Press.

Ramos, Alcida Rita. 2008. "Neither Here nor There: On the Ambiguity of Being Indian in Brazil." *Vibrant—Virtual Brazilian Anthropology,* 5 (1). http://www.vibrant.org.br/issues/v5n1/alcida-rita-ramos-neither-here-nor-there/.

Ramos, Alcida Rita. 2012. "The Politics of Perspectivism." *Annual Review of Anthropology* 41 (1): 481–94. https://doi.org/10.1146/annurev-anthro-092611-145950.

Read, Ian. 2012. *The Hierarchies of Slavery in Santos, Brazil, 1822–1888.* Palo Alto, CA: Stanford University Press.

Redfield, Robert. 1950. *A Village That Chose Progress: Chan Kom Revisited.* Chicago: University of Chicago Press.

Reichman, Daniel R. 2011. *The Broken Village: Coffee, Migration, and Globalization in Honduras.* Ithaca, NY: Cornell University Press.

Rock, David. 1994. *Latin America in the 1940's: War and Postwar Transitions*. Berkeley: University of California Press.

Rodrigues, Sabrina. 2019. "'Esse governo é de vocês,' diz Bolsonaro a Ruralistas." *Oeco*, July 4, 2019. https://www.oeco.org.br/noticias/esse-governo-e-de-voces-diz-bolso naro-a-ruralistas/.

Roseberry, William. 1996. "The Rise of Yuppie Coffees and the Reimagination of Class in the United States." *American Anthropologist*, 98: 762–75. https://doi.org/10.1525 /aa.1996.98.4.02a00070.

Roseberry, William, Lowell Gudmundson, and Mario Samper K. 1995. *Coffee, Society, and Power in Latin America*. Baltimore, MD: Johns Hopkins University Press.

Rostow, W. W. 1960. *The Stages of Economic Growth, a Non-Communist Manifesto*. Cambridge: Cambridge University Press.

Saad Filho, Alfredo, and Lecio Morais. 2019. *Brasil: Neoliberalismo Versus Democracia*. São Paulo, Brazil: Boitempo Editorial.

Sahlins, Marshall. 1999. "Two or Three Things That I Know about Culture." *Journal of the Royal Anthropological Institute* 5 (3): 399–421. https://doi.org/10.2307/2661275.

Sahlins, Marshall, and Frederick B. Henry. 2022. *The New Science of the Enchanted Universe: An Anthropology of Most of Humanity*. Princeton: Princeton University Press.

Schwarcz, Lilia Moritz, and Heloisa Maria Murgel Starling. 2018. *Brazil: A Biography*. New York: Farrar, Straus and Giroux.

Scott, James C. 1998. *Seeing Like a State: How Certain Schemes to Improve the Human Condition Have Failed*. New Haven, CT: Yale University Press.

Seigel, Micol. 2009. *Uneven Encounters: Making Race and Nation in Brazil and the United States*. Durham, NC: Duke University Press.

Shange, Savannah. 2019. *Progressive Dystopia: Abolition, Antiblackness, + Schooling in San Francisco*. Durham, NC: Duke University Press.

Shapiro, Judith. 1987. "From Tupã to the Land without Evil: The Christianization of Tupi-Guarani Cosmology." *American Ethnologist* 14 (1): 126–39. https://doi.org/10 .1525/ae.1987.14.1.02a00080.

Simpson, Audra. 2011. "Settlement's Secret." *Cultural Anthropology* 26: 205–17. https:// doi.org/10.1111/j.1548-1360.2011.01095.x.

Singer, André. 2018. "Do sonho rooseveltiano ao pesadelo golpista." *Revista Piauí* 142: 42–48.

Spengler, Oswald. 1929. *The Decline of the West*. New York: A.A. Knopf.

Star, Susan Leigh. 1999. "The Ethnography of Infrastructure." *American Behavioral Scientist* 43 (3): 377–91. https://doi.org/10.1177/00027649921955326.

Starr, Kevin. 1985. *Inventing the Dream: California through the Progressive Era*. New York: Oxford University Press.

Stein, Stanley J. 1985. *Vassouras, a Brazilian Coffee County, 1850–1900: The Roles of Planter and Slave in a Plantation Society*. Princeton: Princeton University Press.

Stolcke, Verena. 1988. *Coffee Planters, Workers, and Wives: Class Conflict and Gender Relations on São Paulo Plantations, 1850–1980*. New York: St. Martin's Press.

Taddei, Renzo. 2014. "Alter Geoengineering." Paper presented at the Thousand Names of Gaia international colloquium, Rio de Janeiro, September 16, 2014.

Tarde, Gabriel. 1963. *The Laws of Imitation*. Gloucester, Mass: P. Smith.

Taunay, Afonso de E. (Afonso de Escragnolle). 1945. *Pequena história do Café no Brasil (1727–1937)*. Rio de Janeiro: Departamento nacional do café.

Taussig, Michael T. 1997. *The Magic of the State*. New York: Routledge.

Teixera da Silva, Fernando. 2011. "The Port and the City of Santos: A Century-Long Duality" in *Company Towns in the Americas: Landscape, Power, and Working-Class*

Communities. Ed. by Oliver J. Dinius and Angela Vergara, 68–90. Athens: University of Georgia Press.

Tsing, Anna Lowenhaupt. 2015. *The Mushroom at the End of the World: On the Possibility of Life in Capitalist Ruins.* Princeton: Princeton University Press.

Tucker, Catherine M. 2011. *Coffee Culture: Local Experiences, Global Connections.* New York: Routledge.

Tucker, Robert C., ed. 1978. *The Marx-Engels Reader.* 2nd ed. New York: Norton.

Turner, Terence. 1973. "Piaget's Structuralism. Genetic Epistemology." *American Anthropologist* 75 (2): 351–73. https://doi.org/10.1525/aa.1973.75.2.02a00010.

Turner, Terence. 1990. "On Structure and Entropy: Theoretical Pastiche and the Contradictions of 'Structuralism'." *Current Anthropology* 31 (5): 563–68. https://www.jstor.org/stable/2743962.

Turner, Terence. 2002. "Shifting the Frame from Nation-State to Global Market: Class and Social Consciousness in the Advanced Capitalist Countries." *Social Analysis* 46 (2): 56–80. https://www.jstor.org/stable/23170151.

Turner, Terence. 2008. "Marxian Value Theory: An Anthropological Perspective." *Anthropological Theory* 8 (1): 43–56. https://doi.org/10.1177/1463499607087494.

Turner, Terence S. 1977. "Narrative Structure and Mythopoesis: A Critique and Reformulation of Structuralist Concepts of Myth, Narrative and Poetics." *Arethusa* 10 (1): 103–63. https://www.jstor.org/stable/26307828.

Turner, Terence, Jane Fajans, and David Graeber. 2017. *The Fire of the Jaguar.* Chicago: Hau Books.

Veer, Peter van der. 2016. *The Value of Comparison.* Durham, NC: Duke University Press.

Vine, David, David N. Gellner, Mark Schuller, Alpa Shah, Chandra L. Middleton, Gwen Burnyeat, and Melissa Maceyko. 2021. "Collaborative Manifesto for Political Anthropology in an Age of Crises." *Anthropology News,* July 16, 2021. https://www.anthropology-news.org/articles/collaborative-manifesto-for-political-anthropology-in-an-age-of-crises/.

Viscidi, Lisa, and Nate Graham. 2019. "Brazil Was a Global Leader on Climate Change. Now It's a Threat." *Foreign Policy,* January 4, 2010.

Viveiros de Castro, Eduardo, and Roy Wagner. 2015. *The Relative Native: Essays on Indigenous Conceptual Worlds.* Chicago: Hau Books.

Wagley, Charles. 1963. *An Introduction to Brazil.* New York: Columbia University Press.

Wagley, Charles, Maxine L. Margolis, and William E. Carter. 1979. *Brazil, Anthropological Perspectives: Essays in Honor of Charles Wagley.* New York: Columbia University Press.

Weber, Max. 1949. *Max Weber on the Methodology of the Social Sciences.* 1st ed. Glencoe, IL: Free Press.

West, Paige. 2012. *From Modern Production to Imagined Primitive: The Social World of Coffee from Papua New Guinea.* Durham, NC: Duke University Press.

Index

Figures are indicated by "f" following the page numbers.

Venezuela: government as "magician" in, 7; as oil-dependent petrostate, 101

verticalism vs. horizontalism, 104, 106, 161–62n3, 162n6

Vespucci, Americo, 38

Vietnam, coffee production in, 73

Vila Bandeirantes housing development, 123*f*, 125

Vila de São Vicente, 35

Vila Gilda (*favela*), 115

Vila Parisi, chemical pipeline leak creating toxic air pollution in (1985), 121–22

Vila Socó disaster from gas pipeline leak (1984), 121–22

violence: *bandeirantes* mythology and, 28, 42–43, 55; Constitutionalist Rebellion (1930s), 29–30; high violent crime rate in Brazil, 32; between indigenous people and newcomers, 27; murder and urban crime, 31–33; in pre-colonial period, 37; during soy boom, 26

Viveiros de Castro, Eduardo, 29, 48, 56, 157n8, 165n6; *The Ends of the World* (with Dankowski), 150

Warhol, Andy: Pelé portrait, 135

Washington, DC, as model urban plan, 112

water pollution: beaches and, 3–4, 4*f*, 45, 115; De Brito urbanization plan (1902) and, 113; industrial measures to mitigate, 124–25; Santos and, 17, 115–17

Weber, Max, 22, 142, 157–58n11, 164nn4–5

White, Leslie, 155n4

Wilson, Bradley, 75

Workers' Party: agribusiness and, 105; on Brazil as "First World power," 126; Brazilian Miracle and, 8; class relationships and, 156n6; environmental disasters catalyzing activism by, 121; on indigenous peoples and lands, 29; mission of, 6; as neodevelopmentalists, 156n6; oil industry revenues and, 80, 101; protests against, 136–39; World Cup (2014) and, 136–38

World Bank, 124

World Cup: 1950–"Maracanãzo" (Brazil's defeat by Uruguay), 132–33; 1958–Brazil as victor, 133, 133*f*; 1970–broadcast live and in color, 134; Pelé's victories, 131

World Cup (2014): building boom to meet FIFA requirements, 19, 48, 83, 129, 136–39; from euphoric optimism to cruel pessimism, 139, 140; nationalist pride related to, 126, 137, 140; protests related to, 128, 138, 155n2; semifinal loss of Brazil to Germany, 138; South African travel agents assessing Brazilian readiness for, 138

Yanomami: anthropological works on treatment of, 35; massacre (1988), 27; territory of, 41

yellow fever, 107, 108, 110, 112–15, 120. *See also* epidemics

youth incarceration programs, 32

Zapatistas (Mexico), 105

Zerrenner and Bülow (German import/export business), 128

Printed in the USA
CPSIA information can be obtained
at www.ICGtesting.com
LVHW040321060823
754366LV00005B/279